The Image
and Its Public
in the Middle Ages

**Form and Function
of Early Paintings of the Passion**

The Image
and Its Public
in the Middle Ages

Form and Function
of Early Paintings of the Passion

Hans Belting

Translated by
Mark Bartusis and Raymond Meyer

Aristide D. Caratzas, Publisher
New Rochelle, New York

This translation was prepared with the assistance of the J. Paul Getty Trust

Aristide D. Caratzas, Publisher
30 Church Street, P.O. Box 210
New Rochelle, N.Y. 10802

ISBN: 0-89241-403-0

Belting, Hans.
  The Image and its public.

  Translation of: Das Bild und sein Publikum im Mittelalter.
  Bibliography: p.
  Includes index.
  1. Jesus Christ—Passion—Art. 2. Mary, Blessed Virgin, Saint—Art. 3. Pietà.
4. Icons, Byzantine.
I. Title.
N8189.3.J47B413 1989 704.9'4853'0902 89-7363

Book Design: Dennis Hermanson
Halftones: Dot Generation of Ct. Inc.
Printed in the United States of America by Jan Press, Inc., Bronx, N.Y.

Wie mit einem riesigen Schwamm zog
Gott alles Mitleid auf sich. Die Leiden-
den fanden Trost im Erbarmen, das sie
einem Gott spenden durften

—M. Sperber, *Der verbrannte Dornbusch*

Contents

Acknowledgements

The author would like to acknowledge the diverse support and assistance he received without which this book would not have been possible. Above all I wish to thank the Dumbarton Oaks Harvard University's Center for Byzantine Studies (Washington, D.C.) and its former director, Professor Giles Constable. The text acquired its essential form in the years 1977–80 during numerous extended stays at Dumbarton Oaks, and also, at the Bibliotheca Hertziana in Rome. Dumbarton Oaks has supported the project "The Icon in the West" through grants for travel, photographs and the production of a catalogue of works under the direction of Mrs. Susanna Partsch (Heidelberg). The German Research Association provided a travel grant for a trip to Italy during an early stage in the collection of material. For advice and help in the procurement of photographs I am indebted to friends, colleagues and students, above all to Mrs. A. Bank (Leningrad), D. Blume (Heidelberg), G. Cavallo (Rome), M. Chatzidakis (Athens), A. Emiliani (Bologna), M. Fanti (Bologna), C. Gnudi (Bologna), R. Hamann-MacLean (Mainz), Mrs. I. Hueck (Florence), Mrs. G. Kopp (Heidelberg), H. van Os (Groningen), V. Pace (Rome), Mrs. S. Papadaki-Okland (Heraklion), Mrs. S. Partsch (Heidelberg), M. Sediel (Göttingen), I. Sevcenko (Harvard), Cavall. Sorlini (Venice), K. Weitzmann (Princeton) and J. Wollesen (Munich). I would also like to thank the institutions which allowed the publication of photographs in their possession, especially Foto Hirmer (Munich), the Courtauld Institute (London), Dumbarton Oaks (Harvard University), the museums in Berlin (Staatliche Museen), Budapest, Cambridge, Mass. (Fogg Art Museum), Cleveland, Karlsruhe (Kunsthalle), Leningrad (Hermitage), London (National Gallery), Milan (Brera and Bibl. Ambrosiana), New York (Metropolitan Museum), Washington (National Gallery) and Vienna (Albertina). I am obliged to Mrs. A. Kartsonis (Athens) for her many suggestions concerning Chapter V.

Photo Credits

The author and publisher wish to thank the religious authorities and private owners, the museums, libraries and institutes for their kind help in assembling the photographic reproductions. If no other indication is given, the source was a museum photograph. The following illustrations were made available to us:

Alinari, Florence: 10, 15, 35, 87; D. Blume, Heidelberg: 98; Böhm: 11, 79; Brisighelli, Udine: 91; Brogi, Milan: 5; Bront: 95; Carli: 37; Cavall. Sorlini: 90; Chatzidakis: 49, 50; Fotofast: 18; F. Gandolfo: 109; Garrison: 13, 103; Hamann-MacLean: 77; Hirmer, Munich: 4, 70; Van Os: 12, 94; Pineider: 19, 20, 38, 84, 105; Powell: 54, 64; Tasic: 61; Author: 74.

The following illustrations were reproduced from the books of

Bank: 71; Carli: 92, 93; Meiss: 34, 43, 46; Onasch: 63, 68, 69; Pallucchini: 97; *Riv. Arch. Crist.* (1968): 6; Toesca: 99; Velmans: 53; Wentzel: 56; Willoughby: 57, 58.

Introduction

The general theme of this book is dealt with in the form of a case study of the Passion portrait of Jesus (the Imago Pietatis). Indeed, the material presented here is only one applied case in the attempt to develop further the possibilities of interpreting images. A certain amount of overlap with iconography and iconology was unavoidable, although the motives and purposes of this study—and also, one hopes, the results—do not lie along those lines.

Images are the real object of this investigation. Not images in general, no matter how much investigations of this type, in the last analysis, must remain receptive to all images, but particular images for which our terminology is still underdeveloped. Historically they are situated between the Middle Ages and the Renaissance. They still did not possess autonomy as art, but they did have a status of their own, which was even secured through external conditions. These images neither "illustrate" a theme nor decorate a larger unit; rather, they have a well-defined object form. For the most part they are portable and either openly "displayed," for example, on the altar, or they are privately accessible in such ways as to be predestined to carry on a dialogue with a viewer in a group or individually. Moreover, they give presence to the persons portrayed. The traditional concepts of cult image, miraculous image, and devotional image designate some of their functions; the genre of panel painting designates strictly their material form.

The history of such images begins with icon painting, and for this reason the present study is part of a long-range project dealing with "the icon in the West." This encompasses both the history of particular Byzantine icons transported to the West as well as the history of the early European panel painting that adopted the functions and concepts of the icon and developed them further. The idea of the icon therefore does not apply to the historical product of eastern art, but to a principle that determined the form and function of images. Only when this is understood can the project be given a broad historical framework. The pioneering works in this area are the relevant studies by H. Hager and S.

Ringbom. The Passion portrait, with its associations and affiliations to the pictorial staging of the Passion, is well suited to be a case study for illustrating the goal of the project. Hence, our study is related to a similarly conceived treatment of the Virgin of Mercy.[1] Even the impartial historian will soon encounter the fact that the very proliferation of the panel painting was historically conditioned in much the same way that certain themes characteristic of these panels had proven to be effective. But if such conditions can be detected then it is also justifiable to investigate the form of the pictorial product, that is, in the context of its cultural functions.

At the same time it is important to present the example selected in such a way that the context in which it emerged and in which it could exert its overwhelming effect also becomes a topic for discussion. It is certainly one of the most remarkable pictorial creations produced by Christian culture, and the significance of the degree to which it touches the "nerve" of the Christian Weltanschauung cannot be overestimated. Even in its extraordinary success throughout many centuries one can see that it was conceived of as a paradigm of Christian belief in a visual medium. Therefore it is necessary to consider comprehensively the complexity of its meaning.

The kind of image we are speaking about is a male nude in half length, a portrait in the conventions of the Middle Ages, depicting a dead man (fig. 8). The visible paradoxes in the person depicted express one of the greatest paradoxes of the Christian faith: the God who died as a man. Christian teaching restricts His death to that of His human nature and explains it as an episode lasting only until Easter morning. The one paradox, the joining of life and death, results from the other, greater paradox, the joining of God and man in a single person. Naturally, to the faithful these paradoxes appear as a cognitively inaccessible "mystery" because they were produced by (divine) grace within restricted (human) nature and can only be accepted by this nature in faith.

Theologically, the concept of the dead God occupies such a comprehensive position in all areas of Christian thought that its interpretation cannot be limited to one particular "meaning" but, rather, gives rise to many arguments and symbols. This also applies to the image we are dealing with. It could be objectively determined (that is, intelligible to or binding on everyone), for example, on the altar where the sacrificed Jesus could serve as an eidetic image of the sacrament along with the liturgical repetition of his expiatory death, or on a tomb in such a way that it established a relationship between Jesus' redeeming death and the death of the person there interred. Yet it was allowed subjective use permitting individual associations to be projected into the image; for example, it could present the divine figure as a partner upon whom one could convey sorrow in the form of compassion and exchange solace. The intersubjective relation between Jesus and the contemplating believer presupposes what has been called devotion (*devotio*),[2] that is, a religious dialogue that an individual or community conducts with a partner imagined in a particular way. When it was supported by an image that made the partner in the image present as a living participant in the dialogue, one can describe this as image devotion.

The concept of *pietas*, to which the description of the image was connected ex post facto, naturally furnishes no historical explanation of the image itself. How is this image to be evaluated "in itself" as a paradigm and in its individual manifestations on a long historical course?[3] Even if inferences between form, function, and content are not always possible, it was nevertheless precisely these factors that shaped the image and its history. Its metamorphoses range from the icon in Byzantium through the so-called devotional image in the West; the cultic and psychological reception of the latter gradually, in turn, gave way to an aesthetic conception of the image in the Renaissance. The history of the image cannot be understood if one merely traces the internal changes of its form or pays attention only to external influences. The image as much referred to other images by its form as it adapted to cultural or religious patterns of behavior in its function. Written speeches of the figure it represents enhanced the "speaking" image's power[4] until through its own, that is, visual, means the image could "speak." During the Renaissance religious power of expression was tied to the artistic capacity for expression controlled by the artist (cf. Belting, *Bellini*).

It is important to keep the investigation open to questions about the choice and means of using the religious image. In this way we can gain a perspective on the structural changes that shaped the image between the Middle Ages and the Renaissance. The investigation will therefore not remain limited to the example selected. Practical considerations recommend the study be limited geographically to Byzantium and Italy, where the history of the image was uninterrupted. Chronological bounds are determined by the material itself. The image first appears around 1200, after the opening of new contacts with the Greek East. In the sixteenth century the image becomes either so rigid or so transformed that the questions we are asking no longer appertain. Thus the three centuries between ca. 1200 and 1500, together with its Byzantine prehistory, form a suitable field of inquiry. Unfortunately our study can only be presented in a first volume. This limits the cogency of the argumentation, the diachronic analysis of which should hold good for the entire period from the middle Byzantine era through the High Renaissance. For this period the structural change that the independent painted image underwent in official and private use is to be investigated through a suitable example.

Nevertheless, due to external reasons, because more could not be undertaken at the moment, and internal reasons, because a certain uniformity in the line of questioning was possible, the author has restricted himself to the present volume for the time being. In the chapters in which fundamental questions are raised, the field of inquiry is broadened through the Renaissance. In Chapters V and VI the history of our image in Byzantium and in thirteenth-century Italy is presented. Since the integration of the image in the West was accomplished by around 1300, this will serve as a chronological limit for this volume. In the subsequent era different factors play a role (cf. Belting, *Bellini*).

It is still necessary to explain why we employ the concept of the "portrait" when the word usually implies a likeness of a living model. For a portrait, the faithfulness of the reproduction, whether a fiction or not, is obligatory, and thus it is more relevant to the "True Face of Jesus" in St. Peter's in Rome (fig. 30), the so-called "Veronica" or Vera Icon whose authenticity was affirmed by the legends of its origin (fig. 6).[5] The portrait panel in Rome, fixed to the reproduction of the historical physiognomy of Jesus, set a new standard for the degree of likeness a "portrait" could achieve.

The Imago Pietatis can only be considered a portrait if we employ a different concept of likeness. According to the old opinion of mimesis teaching, likeness is the suggestion of reality, the appearance of life. Psychic activity, which the viewer perceives as a sign of life, even to the extent of experiencing movement, also enters its domain. In our image the traces of physical suffering make the figure resemble a true man who can be contemplated in close-up. The sight of a corpse, which usually engenders aversion rather than a desire to draw near, could only be endured because of the awareness that the dead man was alive. With its rhetorical gesture of accusation and indictment, the image invites identification. The mimetic capacity of the viewer, to which the Imago Pietatis appeals,

Fig. 1 Vienna, Albertina. Miniature, ca. 1150: The Trinity

presupposes the viewer's (mimetic, as it were) desire to imitate or "resemble" in life the human Jesus—which of course was revealed in the image. "Our ability to rediscover resemblance is nothing but a vestige of the once powerful compulsion to become and act alike."[6]

Our image suggests the presence of a corpse touched by suffering. The experience of proximity which it offers is an experience of likeness. Jesus offers a "pitiful image." He appears in a state in which the viewer can obtain affective access to Him. Like a portrait it offers the pictorial close-up of a half-length figure. Our image also descended from a portrait if we may regard the icon as a portrait. Compared to the Crucifixion and the crucifix it was semantically more complex and offered a different form of experience. The person depicted is freed from any historical connection and is staged as an individual figure. It is not sufficient to speak of a turn from the *historia* to the *imago*.[7] While the Imago Pietatis is an altered *imago,* it displays the person depicted in a specific state, *in forma pietatis*.[8]

While the portrait, according to conventional usage, is its own subject or content because the person depicted "himself forms the theme,"[9] in our case it must be understood as a form of expression. It was not as much a new pictorial content as a new pictorial form that came to light in the Imago Pietatis.

The crucifix was a forerunner of the Passion portrait. It initially portrayed the Passion "objectively," as it were, before offering itself to the Passion's affective re-experience. In the trinitarian group image called a "Mercy Seat" the crucifix is associated with the Father under the image of the sacrifice which was offered. A miniature with this theme (fig. 1) is described as follows in the manual of Sicard of Cremona (1160–1215): "In some [mass] books the majesty of the Father and the cross of the crucifix are portrayed so that it is almost as if we see at present the one we are calling to, and the Passion which is depicted imprints itself on the eyes of the heart" (majestas Patris et crux depingitur Crucifixi, ut quasi praesentem videamus quem invocamus et passio quae representatur, cordis oculis ingeratur).[10] The representation of God the Father is differentiated from that of the Passion. One is to be understood as a likeness, the other as a situation. But in our case the Passion is no longer a scene or *historia* but the state of the "speaking" figure of Christ in which, without displaying action, an *imago* is newly interpreted.

Indeed, even in the twelfth century the crucifix was contemplated affectively, even though it still did not visibly reflect this reception (fig. 3). This is corroborated by another, equally remarkable source from this period. Around 1170 Theodoricus speaks of an *imago Crucifixi* above the entrance to the monastery behind the Latin addition to the Holy Sepulcher in Jerusalem which was "painted in such a way that it imbued every beholder with deep remorse" (ita depicta ut cunctis intuentibus magnam inferat compunctionem).[11] No doubt this refers to a mosaic representation of the dead Christ which the Latin patron had appropriated from Byzantine iconography (fig. 4). The difference in western iconography may explain why the form of depiction was experienced as something extraordinary. Indeed its importation into the West is a significant date in the prehistory of the Imago Pietatis.[12] But how the Jerusalem crucifix appeared is less important

6   *Introduction*

than how the viewer reacted to it. In order to guarantee the affective reaction, a written speech was added to the image which controlled the communication with the viewer: the crucifix addressed the believer in the familiar form as a partner and appealed to his sympathy.[13]

The "speaking image" was originally a topos of the legends of miracles that alleged magical powers for particular images. The reception of the image anticipates what the image (through its own visual means) achieves only at a later date. This also applies to the Jerusalem crucifix, which was regarded as a devotional image before it could be one in the formal sense. That this occurred in the Latin East should be noted with particular interest because the encounter with eastern memorial shrines, relics, and images, opened new avenues of religious experience that contributed to the development of an affective religiosity. The Imago Pietatis was initiated by an eastern image, the icon.

The psychological implications of the new religiosity with which the devotional image was in accord are just as complex as the social conditions from which the religious individual developed his self-awareness. What took place in the thirteenth century was one of the most comprehensive transformations European society ever underwent. While the symptoms were often only visible in images at a later date, the impulses to modify images reach back to the thirteenth century. The emancipation of the citizen in the civic republics and his mobility in a field of operation enlarged to include the eastern Mediterranean are characteristics of this process. The initiation of lay religious activity through the preaching of the mendicant orders is more a consequence of, than a reason for, the changes of this period. Within the framework of increased participation in religious life for which *new* forms of affective activity unconnected to theological structures and language were discovered, the image came to play a new role. Instead of an abstract ordering it offered a plastic mode of perceiving the religious world and was applied to direct sensory experience. The participation of the laity in the functions of public life and in the cult practice of the Church, though unorganized, grew both quantitatively and qualitatively with astonishing speed. The next turning point to which we turn our focus manifests itself through the social crisis and religious changes during the Plague of 1348. Religious productivity was directed along different lines that postponed the need for supplying religious reality. The third turning point is summed up by the concept of the early Renaissance. This can be seen, for example, in the new control the artist had over his work, as a consequence of which the art of the image became its function (cf. Belting, *Bellini*).

Chapter I
New Forms of Existence
of Images in the Middle Age

The framed panel has become so much a part of our conception of art that an investigation into its raison d'être must be justified.[1] Such an inquiry is only possible once we realize that during the medieval period the independent panel painting was for a long time a rarity which could only exist in certain *forms* and under certain *conditions.* Thus we can speak of forms of existence of the panel which were at the same time the conditions of its existence. The panel needed a function in order to be accepted, a material or a symbolic, that is, social function. One could also speak of functional *forms,* but such a concept would suggest too strongly that the image is connected with an external purpose in the narrower sense, a circumstance which is true only in special cases.

The rarity of the painted panel in the West up until the thirteenth century is not the result of an interrupted tradition, but rather a sign that it possessed no real function. The panel had a modest place among the pictorial media as long as there was no demand for it. We therefore have to ask how and why this demand arose, and in what way it shaped the subsequent development of the panel painting. Indeed, it is not at all a simple matter of substituting one medium for another as the material vehicle of the picture. The medium of the portable panel, which can be experienced as a separate object, has at its disposal semantic qualities that are not available to other media to the same degree. Two observations will illustrate this point.

In its early history, the panel was the vehicle of a sacred portrait which was the recipient, so to speak, of the adoration paid to the "cultic person" depicted. Thus the panel either exhibited the "cultic person" for public veneration or made "him"or "her" available for private devotion. In the cult image we encounter the independent painted panel for the first time. It was placed in a "shrine" or on the altar, as in Rome, and could be set in motion almost like a living person during a procession.[2] While in the West the cult image had been

Fig. 2a, b London, National Gallery, and Budapest, Museum of Fine Art.
Sienese Diptych, mid-13th c.

previously a plastic sculpture, this changed, especially in Italy, with the importation of icons. The icon of the Virgin is the chief evidence of this fact.

However, narrative pictures were accepted by the art of panel painting only hesitantly, and rarely without change in their narrative structure. The scenic *historiae* had their place on church walls and in manuscripts. In both instances they were tied to a context and depended on it, both in reality and semantically. They relied either on the law of the series, which subordinates the individual image to the whole course of the narrative, or on the text of the book, which not only explains the image but legitimizes it as well.[3] It is evident that both conditions are suspended as soon as the scene becomes the subject of the painted panel. Isolated from the narrative cycle, the scene loses the context that makes clear its narrative message.[4] If it were not to become incomprehensible, and therefore mute, the previous manner of presentation had to be replaced with a new one. The flow of action, in which the individual scene is only transitory, had to be arrested and a new "static" reading established that made the image intelligible to the beholder. Consequently, the painted panel would have had only a limited usefulness if the images themselves had not been altered.

The second observation concerns a thirteenth-century Italian diptych which displays on one of its panels (today in London) a portrait of the Virgin and on the other (today in Budapest) a depiction which can be described neither as the Crucifixion nor as a crucifix, but which contains elements of both (figs. 2a, 2b).[5] The isolation of the crucified Christ from the Crucifixion shows that there was no intention to depict a scene. In fact, one is reminded of the "painted cross," an oddity within the scope of the cult image which merges both cross and painted panel (fig. 3).[6] On the other hand, the background, no less than the mourning angels, is a characteristic feature of the Crucifixion panel as it had developed in eastern icon painting (fig. 4).[7] Even as an object, the winged diptych is a product of icon painting. Our double panel appears to reproduce an icon, yet with a noteworthy modification: the protagonist is isolated from the Crucifixion scene and transformed into an *imago* which in its underlying idea, if not also in scale, corresponds to the adjoining *imago* of the Virgin. This is an adaptation to a new function. The interpretation of the subject changes when it is transferred to the panel. This syntactical change accompanies of a parallel change on the semantic level; the confrontation of the Mother and Child with the crucified Christ invites theological contemplation, which the viewer

The Image and Its Public

Fig. 3 Bologna, San Domenico. Painted cross by Giunta

could accomplish by means of affective "empathy."

The conflict between the schema of a Crucifixion scene and the format of a painted cross illustrates the problem of adequately expressing new functions of images in a new medium. The same problem arises in connection with narrative panels having a single subject. These are considered classical devotional images which are "abbreviated in form and plurisignate in content."[8] For example, the panel of Giovanni da Milano in the Accademia of Florence cannot be clearly identified as depicting either the Deposition or the Lamentation (fig. 5).[9] It has a different appearance from that which it would have in a strictly narrative context. The devotional image is a further type of the medieval panel.[10]

The reformulation of the narrative image on the single panel is much more than simply a practical matter. Parallel alterations in wall painting and book illumination show that the practical disadvantages of the panel do not alone explain the course of events in question here. Rather, a general process had begun that was altering the structure of pictorial art. In other media as well, representations assume the appearance of panel paintings without any practical need to do so.[11] The framed panel is therefore only the "symbolic form" of a new, independent image which was sought after everywhere. The manner in which the image was received changed, and the image itself adapted to this change. For it was a social product which presupposed and responded to the mental and visual expectations of its public.

Of course, the painted panel has one important characteristic that cannot be reproduced in other media. Because of its material, enclosing frame and its transportability, it makes evident in an especially striking manner the autonomy of the image from its surroundings (fig.7). The size, because it is endlessly variable, also plays a role in achieving this effect. In a small size, produced at a low cost, the intimate panel made paintings accessible to a new public, and did so to a degree that would be surpassed only later by mass-produced prints (fig. 10).[12] As a replica of a public cult image, it brought about an increased participation in the institutionalized veneration of the image.[13] And finally, legends about images and reports about the rites associated with images indicate that the "portable image" could almost be experienced as a living person, as if it were the depicted person himself and not merely his likeness that was being displayed in the processions.[14] Definitions of the image's reality from the theological point of view had only a slight effect on this experience.[15] For our investigation, the important point is that the "ambling cult image" clearly increased the public's sensitivity toward the image in general.

On one such "cultic saunter," in 1216 the Roman Vera Icon of Christ performed a miracle in the opinion of its devotees by suddenly standing on its head (fig.6).[16] The miracle was interpreted as a divine recommendation to use this particular image as an instrument for the supernatural transmission of grace. When the pope granted a ten-day indulgence to anyone who directed a special prayer to this image, he created the genre of the miraculous image, in the version known as an "indulgence image." This was yet another type of the image in the Middle Ages.[17] The miraculous image, though not itself a devotional image, fostered the latter's development because now the authority of the Church had recognized that the image could also serve to convey the redeeming grace which previously could only be obtained through relics and the sacra-

Fig. 4 Berlin,
Staatliche
Museen.
Mosaic icon
of the
Crucifixion,
Byzantine,
13th c.

ments. Devotion and institutionalized prayer for salvation could
both be addressed to the same image, which invited contemplation
and at the same time was suited to receive supplicatory veneration.[18]
The importation of numerous new cult images from the East during
the thirteenth century supported the public's increasingly active
response to certain images (see. Appendix C).

One must be aware that there was an interaction between the
new sensibility to images in general and the new attention to panel

New Forms of Existence of Images   15 painting. In its various types, the painted panel became instrumental in effecting a qualitative structural change in religious art. Its production, the conditions for which were, for the most part, created only at that time, underwent a rapid quantitative increase during the period in question.

This structural change which the image underwent, attested to by the "career" of the independent panel, can be understood only in a larger context. The image is given a communicative quality which it previously neither had nor needed to have, enabling it to function as a document of a supra-individual and objectively given world order. High Gothic art is the background before which the change becomes visible. While "measureless" for the individual, the closed and classified pictorial systems of the façades and windows of Gothic cathedrals represent an objectively pregiven world system, which at the same time was interpreted as a value system.[19] The believer stood before this *ordo* not as an isolated individual, but took his place in it as a member who did not have to be persuaded to do so, but who through his own study and "reading" confirmed his membership. In Giotto's Arena Chapel in Padua, however, we encounter another situation.[20] There the painted surfaces, which can be grasped perspectively only from a single viewing point, present Christ's life as a spectacle to the individual, which allowed his personal observation and empathy. The cathedral window, though transparent, was a closed field whose arrangement was no less important in its total content than that of each individual pictorial unit. Paradoxically, the mural picture in Padua is, as it were, an "open" window, allowing the viewer a plastic perception of the divine events, so that he seems to understand the world through his own observation. Illusion itself here has content. Through the new resources of the picture in which the event is brought to life, the illusion is created anew in the consciousness of the individual viewing the picture. The new pictorial rhetoric emerging here serves the new narrative function of the image.

In the narrative literature of the thirteenth century, which shows man in his world, one can observe a similar change. The great epic works of the early thirteenth century, whose milieu was the court, were followed by the novellas whose milieu was the private sphere. J. Szöverffy distinguishes the "objectivizing" idealism of the one literary genre from the "subjectivizing" tendency of the other.[21] The decline of the communal ideal of a supra-individual system of values promoted the development of a personal worldview on the

The Image and Its Public

Fig. 5
Florence,
Accademia.
Lamentation
by Giovanni
da Milano.
1365

GIOVANNI DA MILANO

New Forms of Existence of Images

part of the laity, whose social and religious roles became the object of continual reflection.

The laity demanded its rights in private or corporate religious practice as well, and in that way set its stamp on the explanation of the Christian faith given by the Church. In all spheres, a "naissance de l'esprit laïque" took place during the thirteenth century, as G. de Lagarde explained in his work bearing that title.[22] The laity is neither nonreligious (though perhaps anticlerical) nor confined to the lower classes; rather, it represents all social estates other than the clergy. Its self-assertion in the face of ecclesiastical institutions manifested itself also, especially in the forms and desiderata of religious practice, as the religious brotherhoods prove. The physical barrier between the clergy and the people within the church naves symbolizes the separation of two spheres in public life. The thirteenth century, which was characterized by an incessant change of traditional society, generated the process by which late medieval society came into being. The decline of the universal powers: the empire and, shortly thereafter, the papacy, belongs to this scene no less than the rapid rise of the urban communes.

Even within the Church—if one may limit "Church" to the narrower sense of "church of the clergy"—a radical change is taking place that is reflected in the social history of the religious image. We shall examine later the role of the mendicant orders, whose members, even though they were laymen, preached to the people and expressed criticism of the Church through their ideal of poverty. For theology, the "via moderna" of the nominalists and, on the other hand, of the mystics provides access to new possibilities of experiencing the world in which knowledge and belief can diverge. The "principle of direct experience which the nominalists employ with regard to things in nature," is directed by the mystics "to God and His works."[23] The empiricism which nominalism was in time to develop removed the obstacle posed by the reality of the pure concept from the path of personal observation of the visible world as a reality *sui generis*.[24] The intuitive vision of God that mysticism promised afforded personal participation in the invisible world as a reality accessible to the psyche, far removed from the communal worship of the Church.[25] Alongside philosophical rationalism, which also has its roots in the thirteenth century, mysticism is only another, though complementary, response to a world experienced in a new way. Positivism in logic and the negative theology of the "dark" God are compatible doctrines. Turning toward and turning away from the world mutually intensify each other in the self-experience of the individual, who reacts to external experience, whether positive or negative, more and more intensely. In this context it is possible to see that object-realism and mystical concept-realism,[26] while antagonistic within the religious image, are, if anything, related ways of assuring the reality of the world.

Fig. 6
Woodcut, 1481. Presentation of the veronica.

The new function of the image of which we have spoken is thus the product of a historical change which first brings into being the viewing subject that makes new use of the image. But before discussing the social characteristics of this new image, we must consider its genesis within an even larger framework of the development of European pictorial art.

Early Christian art, especially in the East, had passed through a cycle which repeated itself under different conditions in the high and late Middle Ages, particularly in the image's cultural function for its audience. From the sixth century onward, the official art of the Church, which had presented the Christian faith systematically as objective reality, increasingly gives way to the cult and votive image articulating the subjective concerns of individual or collective viewers. Kitzinger speaks of raising the image which, as icon, became the object of a rapidly growing cult, to a "higher order of potency."[27] In the Iconoclasm of the eighth century this development reaches a crisis. When it was restored to respectability after that Iconoclasm, the icon was no longer the same as before. It was taken under management by the Church and regulated in such a way that it borrowed its reality from the liturgical practice, whose order it represented. That also meant a theological use of the icon, through display of the doctrines of faith in a symbolic pictorial reality or a panegyrical coloring. The mystical language of liturgical texts connected abstract theology with the concrete visual reality of the liturgical act, the ritual. A similar mystagogical function was assumed by the icon, which for that reason was accessible to the viewer only in formulations over which he had little influence (but see p. 110). The icon is characterized by a system of references used by the Eastern Church. Its concept is linked to the liturgical status of the panel in Byzantium (see Chapter V).

In the West, if one excludes such Byzantine enclaves as the city of Rome, the development had taken a different course. Central and Western Europe had adopted early Christian art first as a kind of foreign language. Its official character was a mirror of its function as an instrument of the Church's preaching and of cultural orientation. Later, the High Scholastic era developed an internal reference system of correspondences with regard to content as well as formal elements, depicting the divine world order in a manner more didactic than psychological. In his ecclesiastical handbook, Durandus, who summarizes this phase much later, classified these painted programs in their entirety strictly according to didactic viewpoints.[28] In this phase, High Medieval church art is comparable to that of the "golden age" of early Christian pictorial art. Admittedly, in contrast to the latter, it acquires a complexity whose ordering structures only a theologian could comprehend, but which the layman had to accept as a fait accompli.

The aesthetic organization of pictorial art also reaches a high level of complexity in this period. Solutions were tested that later were to acquire, under different conditions, a surprising significance in the reception of the Gothic in Italian monumental painting. But for our investigation another historical development is much more important. This is the importation of the eastern icon, which initially stood in the greatest possible contrast to the conventions of High Medieval art.[29] In the distinctive reality of its portraiture, it was as foreign to the West as Christian-Classical art had been to the areas outside the homelands of classical civilization in the early Middle Ages. In the icon's pictorial rhetoric, the immediacy of the cult image, whose origin lay ultimately in classical culture, was still preserved. The rapidity with which it gained acceptance and vogue, particularly in Italy, raises questions that we shall pursue here.

In the West, the icon awakened associations most readily with those cult images which were familiar as sculpture, and which also appeared in mystery plays. A good example is the substitution of a panel painting of the Virgin for the sculptural group in the nativity play that took place in thirteenth-century Padua.[30] Icons which were

The Image and Its Public

Fig. 7
Florence,
Uffizi.
Rucellai-
Madonna by
Duccio, 1285

New Forms of Existence of Images

partially identical with early Byzantine panels continued to be venerated in Rome.[31] The importation of new icons from the East immediately invited speculation on their mysterious origin. Their strange appearance and eastern provenance ensured these icons the status of authentic relics, a belief that was enhanced by legends surrounding them.[32] In a sermon delivered in 1306 the Dominican Fra Giordano da Rivalto spoke of the importation of old pictures from Greece in which the saints "are depicted exactly as they appeared in real life." For example, there was a picture of the crucified Christ made by Nicodemus who "was present" at the Crucifixion, or the portrait of the Virgin which Luke had painted from life: "consequently, the old images imported from Greece long ago . . . possess . . . the greatest possible authority . . . and as proof are just as compelling as Scripture."[33] Even where certain icons had belonged to the usual inventory of an ordinary church in their native land, a new cultic status was now granted to them that made it possible to classify them.[34] Their transfer into another society broke the ties between their form and their original function, permitting them to acquire a new function.

Social factors also play a role in the integration of the icon into western religious art. The proliferation of religious confraternities in the form of lay brotherhoods created the need for cult images that these groups could possess as their own. The brotherhood was neither a part of the church hierarchy, nor did it develop its own internal hierarchy.[35] Consequently, the cult image became the titulary and focus of a community that required a recipient for its cultic activity (fig. 7).[36] Such a use of the image, a kind of self-representation of a community through a cult image, continued in the public as well as in the private sphere. On the one hand, in the city-states the cult of images was established particularly early, satisfying there the desires for autonomy and identity of political entities. These desires were also expressed in the dedication of towns to the Virgin, as their patroness. It was possible to visibly represent the heavenly authority in the form of its image and to have it reside, as it were, in a particular town.[37] Moreover, in the cult of the Virgin, owing to the lack of bodily relics, the painted panel acquired a material function that should not be underestimated. On the other hand, the image cult of the lay confraternity extended itself, with fluid transitions and constant spreading, into the familial sphere. Family chapels within a parish or monastic church allowed individual families to acquire their own "cult centers" on an equal footing with the brotherhoods.[38] The entry of the image into the individual's household

The Image and Its Public

was then only a matter of time (fig. 26). Of course, the official Church did not stand idly by as this development occurred. Since it was the oldest possessor of cult images, it was in a position to furnish its own images with the power to confer grace, the social significance of which is made sufficiently clear by the institution of the indulgence. But in the images with the power to confer grace, whose origins coincide, and not accidentally, with those of the cult images in the lay associations, one can see perhaps a kind of competing product, to simplify matters somewhat (figs. 14, 108). Of course the official Church also tended to integrate and incorporate the practices of the lay cult into its own. It perhaps even surpassed what the latter could offer, and in this way took over into in its own practice what at first had merely developed alongside it.

One example of this seems to be the early altarpiece, the history of which has been studied by H. Hager.[39] The altarpiece, which is of paramount importance for the rapid diffusion of the painted panel, had evidently been installed on the main altar of a church only during a second phase of its existence. Certainly, liturgical changes, like the celebration of mass in front of the altar, and architectural changes, such as the elimination of the apsidal conch (a traditional place for images) in Gothic structures, helped in creating the function of the altarpiece. These changes, however, are only secondary factors of the process integrating the previously autonomous cult image into the regular liturgical inventory, a process which nevertheless could not prevent the further dissemination of the semipublic and private cult image. It must be kept in mind that the veneration of images took place not only in the public sphere, but also in the semi-public (that is, confraternal) and private spheres. The diverse kinds of cult images testify to this.

In this connection, cultic devotion has to be distinguished from those liturgical practices in which images were merely included. Cultic devotion is a function conferred upon a particular individual image by some agent who is able to organize that devotion. It could serve the communal or ecclesiastical public, a professional or private association, or even an individual person.[40] Of course, cultic devotion only becomes evident when it acquires an organized form, a condition which is fulfilled only by public and confraternal cultic worship. If the cultic worship was performed by a community, or was open to pilgrims, it required an institutional framework in order to manifest itself at all. But it is a common error to believe that such cultic practice necessarily determined the form of the cult image, for example by forcing it to be impersonal and hieratic in appearance.[41] The cult image does not have a stable, unchanging form of appearance, since it fulfilled expectations which were themselves subject to change. The impact of changing visual conventions was limited, however, by the postulate of a persisting identity of the cult image, especially of those images with a long tradition. Nonetheless, Bernardo Daddi's panel in Or San Michele in Florence, evidently the third image to fulfill that cultic function, attempts to come to terms both with the postulate of identity and that of an attractive, lively modernity of expression.[42] A special case is that kind of miraculous image which, resisting all pressures for change, is fixed in the status of an exemplar.[43]

In general, the interchange between the public and private spheres is a factor that must be borne in mind. What can be called public and the manner in which it expresses itself are also subject to historical change.[44] In the late Middle Ages the individual, who has an identity beyond the definitions of his social ties, receives from a popularized mysticism instruction for the use of private images within his expected religious training.[45] Consequently, the assumption that personal models of piety reacted upon public cultic worship and its images is not in need of proof. If one may term the private cultic worship "devotion," then devotion reacted upon the practices and upon the images of public cultic worship.

Two examples will illustrate the points we have discussed. The first one exemplifies the key role of the Marian brotherhoods in the recognition and diffusion of the monumental altarpiece, the maestà. Its incunabulae are two works in Siena created a year apart: the Madonna del Bordone, which the Florentine Coppo di Marcovaldo painted in 1261 for the Servites, and the S. Bernardino Madonna, which a Sienese master (Guido?) completed that same year, carrying out a commission from the Compagnia di S. Maria degli Angeli (fraternitatis b. Marie semper virginis, according to the original inscription). Even the dimensions of Coppo's image (2.20 x 1.25 m), which the other image also possesses, were at the time almost without parallel. Soon thereafter they were surpassed and even doubled by Duccio's Rucellai Madonna (1285), which again was commissioned by a brotherhood of the Virgin, the Laudesi of S. Maria Novella in Florence (fig. 7).[46] The size and beauty of the panel (ad pingendum de pulcherrima pictura quandam tabulam magnam) were expressly stipulated in the contract. The Laudesi ventured an extraordinary financial commitment, surely for the sake of their social prestige. All these images, whose innovations soon became the norm, were cult images serving the confraternal

24

cultic worship of the "association" that had wanted to create a monument for itself. Thus we hear of a lamp which was hung before the Rucellai Madonna and was said to have burned unceasingly.[47] These monumental panels tend to give a powerful presence only to the "cultic person," either by suppressing supplementary features or by relegating them to the painted frame, as was done to the brotherhood's Dominican patron saints in the case of the Rucellai Madonna. More important, no fundamentally different tone is struck with the tender sentiment of the Rucellai Madonna, than by the small devotional image of Duccio's Madonna of the Franciscans, however much the intimate relationship with the depicted clients plays a role in the latter. The monumental image for public veneration is given no less human features and affective accessibility than the private devotional image. The most important difference between the two panels, in addition to their size, is the direction of the Virgin's gaze to a general audience in the monumental panel, while in the other panel she addresses her regard to three donors who share the picture with her. In the first case, she presents her foot, prominently exhibited on a footstool, to the confraternity assembled in front of the panel. In the other case, her foot is in the hands of one of the three Franciscans on whom she turns her gaze.

The second example illustrates the influence that public opinion exerted on the official image cult by means of the state, and the fluid boundaries between private piety and institutionalized cultic veneration of images performed in the name of the polity. In 1360, following an initiative of the citizens of the town who in Siena petitioned the government of Siena to commission the painting of an image of the Virgin at the Porta Camollia.[48] The text speaks of the necessity of the "office of piety" (officium pietatis), in which the "worship of the divine [mysteries]" (cultus divinorum) manifested itself. They adjured the town government not to neglect the well-established "rite of this kind of piety" (ritum devotionis hujusmodi). By that they meant the venerated images of the saints, who attested to the "practice of this piety" (devotionem pietatis hujus) at street crossings everywhere in Siena. The citizens, it was said, were permeated by a deep veneration for the image of Mary, who was acknowledged by all who knew the city-state as an "extraordinary protector and shield" (refugium singulare). And several citizens, no doubt the petitioners, thought it was important that this veneration also be practiced and demonstrated (demonstrari), evidently by means of the proposed image. Piety and cultic practice, private and state interests merge here. In both spheres matters are viewed from the same perspective, however much the forms of fulfillment of the intentions in the two spheres may have differed.

The connection between the public use of images and private piety was established early in the mendicant orders' policies concerning images. In this regard they had the most progressive attitude found within the Church. As early as the thirteenth century, through sermons and the presentation of images, the faithful were urged to an emotional piety that could be performed privately and at the same time guided publicly.[49] The painted panels of the crucified Christ and the Madonna, which played a central role in the mystic veneration of the Passion and of the Virgin then being promulgated, were instruments as well as objects of religious education, particularly as potential cult images (figs. 3, 81).[50] An organized image cult did not become the norm; nonetheless, the miraculous "speaking" crucifix of S. Damiano in Assisi was doubtlessly an early cult image.[51] Panels showing Saint Francis were placed on the altars of the order's churches and, in their alleged miraculous ability, took the place of reliquaries.[52] The panel in the Louvre signed by Giotto, which shows the order's patron saint receiving the stigmata of Christ, is the tradition of the pure "portrait icons" of the saints.[53] It makes clear how mutable a cult image could be, if its capacity for development was not restricted by its status as the exemplar of an image.

From the mendicant orders, who also tended to the religious needs of several lay confraternities, there emanated strong impulses for the use of private images. An early source documents the existence of private images in the cells of a Dominican monastery in the mid-thirteenth century (fig. 28).[54] The small Madonna of the Franciscans by Duccio is a striking example of the use of personal devotional images by the mendicants: it appropriated the iconic schema of the Virgin of Mercy, which had had currency among the crusaders (especially in Cyprus), and fills it with a newly formulated sentiment expressing the burning devotion of the frati toward their patroness and anticipating the response to it from the heavenly partners.[55] Thus the work manifests, in the medium of the image, the attitude of expectation which motivated the image's owner. Its high quality and costly execution give the small panel the degree of perfection of an object of the "precious arts," that is, a product of those working in metal or ivory. Since the personal life of the religious orders' members was also organized religiously, images were given a prescribed function in the religious organization of their life. In contrast, the "bedchamber images" of the burghers can be traced back only to the late trecento. But it is important to note that the personal cultic veneration of an image was really fulfilled only

The Image and Its Public

through its personal possession. Thus the cult image became a private image. The important results of this change become evident when the private patron becomes able to determine the appearance of his image through negotiation with the artist.[56]

Chapter II
The Portrait of the Dead God
(Imago Pietatis)

The history of the Imago Pietatis can be developed in a meaningful way only after we have defined the image that has historically borne this name. A small Bohemian double panel from the second quarter of the fourteenth century, now in Karlsruhe, provides a suitable example of the image of which we are speaking (fig. 8).[1] It shows a pair of half-length figures which exist independently in two separate pictures, yet are related to one another. To the right appears the half-length nude figure of a dead man. The head has sunk to the shoulders. The eyes are closed, the arms folded, as if in preparation for burial. A kind of parapet bears the legend "The Mercy of the Lord" (Misericordia Domini). Thus the figure represents Christ under a specific aspect, as the Lord of Mercy. In the left-hand panel we see Christ once again, this time alive as a child playing in the arms of his mother, who, however, directs her attention to something else. She looks past the playful child to where her adult son is shown dead.

Of the two half-length figures, whose union in the diptych must have had a special reason, only the Virgin turns to her partner. Her depiction by the painter appears to have been a spontaneous creative act; nonetheless, her painter in fact made use of an iconic schema. Known under the name of the Pelagonitissa, this archetype is characterized by the child's contorted posture.[2] Obviously it has been transmitted in the instance we are considering through an intermediary, a Venetian painting which we may regard as the direct model. The slightly older Leningrad diptych, a Venetian work of the early fourteenth century, gives us some idea of what that intermediary picture looked like (fig. 9).[3] In the Venetian diptych, Mary's complement is the Crucifixion. This juxtaposition of images appears to be the older of the two and is known from examples originating in the dugento. It clearly had the same theological meaning as the other.

In the model of the Bohemian panel, the Crucifixion had already been replaced with the Imago Pietatis. Thus, the model was similar in this respect to the diptych by Tomaso da Modena, which was brought to the Bohemian court of Emperor Charles IV after

Fig. 8 Karlsruhe, Kunsthalle. Bohemian diptych, mid-14th c.

Fig. 9
Leningrad,
Hermitage.
Venetian dip-
tych, early
14th c.

1356.[4] The combination of these two half-length figures is not at all rare in fourteenth-century painting. A diptych from the circle of Barna da Siena, at present in the Museo Horne in Florence, is a pertinent example (fig. 10).[5] Like a diptych by Pietro Lorenzetti in Altenburg,[6] its portrayal of the Virgin shows a modern feature that the Venetian diptych does not employ: the turning of her gaze toward her dead Son. In both of the Sienese panels the visual relation is subtly achieved by Mary looking simultaneously at her newborn Son and, behind him, at her dead Son whose Passion she already foresees, fully in accordance with the prolepsis of Symeon's prophecy (p. 114). The Bohemian panel, instead of following this Sienese variant, reproduces an iconic schema which was not suited for this relationship among the figures. It is also different from the Sienese panels with regard to the figure of Jesus; those panels perhaps adopted the crossing of Jesus' hands from the Pisan retable of Simone Martini.[7] The figure of Christ in the Bohemian panel, just as the motif of the folded arms, has prototypes in Venice, namely, in the circle of Paolo Veneziano (fig. 11).[8] Thus the Bohemian work would seem to be a response called forth by a Venetian diptych. If its model had the same small size, it too was intended for private use.

The Karlsruhe panel provides still more information which helps to shed light on the tradition of our image-type. A single detail expresses an important difference between it and the Italian prototypes. Only in comparison with the Italian panels do we notice that in the Bohemian panel Jesus turns almost imperceptibly toward his mother, and as he does so draws attention to the gaping wound in his chest. The forefinger of his left hand is raised to this spot, making a gesture which only a living person can make. In the Italian examples, this contradiction—the portrayal of a corpse that acts—is unknown. In these pictures the dead Christ is clearly dead, a circumstance which makes his upright posture all the more strange. The Bohemian artist, in contrast, annuls this definitive passivity by allow

The Image and Its Public

Fig. 10 Florence, Museo Horne. Siennese diptych from the circle of Barna, 14th c.

ing the dead man to make a gesture betraying that he is not dead and can therefore not only receive pity, but can grant it as well. Jesus begins a subtle dialogue with the viewer who is attuned to this nuance. In this shift of emphasis the whole difference between the Mediterranean and transalpine conception is revealed.[9] Through its alteration, the Italian type proves itself to be an import into Bohemia. Even in Italy it had not been indigenous, but had been taken over from a Byzantine icon. If that is the case, we must first analyze the type in the place where it was created. But it is still premature to take this step. First we must determine whether it is at all a question of an Italian type.

In the Karlsruhe diptych and its model, the half-length figure of the dead Christ, which we provisionally call a "type," formed a figural pair with the Madonna, a pair of figures. The Sienese panels and the work of Tomaso da Modena offer the same variant.[10] Other

Fig. 11 Venice, San Marco. Detail from the Pala Feriale by Veneziano

examples are easily found in W. Kermer's catalogue of extant diptychs. The early Venetian Stoclet panel from the dugento also was part
of a diptych (fig. 101).[11] All these cases involve works of a small size,
barely larger than approximately 30 cm in height.

But the diptych is not the only context in which we encounter
the type now under discussion. In another group of works it is the
center of a triptych, flanked by Mary on its right and usually by the
apostle John on its left. Significantly, this context occurs principally
in the socle-friezes of composite altarpieces, that is, of predellae.
Giotto's retable in Bologna and that of Simone Martini in Pisa
(1320) are early examples.[12] The triptych group is known from
tombs as well. In a recently discovered funerary fresco in the cathedral of Prato, it is a substitute in another medium for a sarcophagus
relief.[13] As early as the dugento, it appears without a funerary context in the frescoes of Mosciano near Florence (fig. 106).[14] In Paolo
Veneziano's well-known formulation on the *Pala Feriale* of San Marco
in Venice, commissioned in 1343–1345, the group forms the center
of an icon frieze, and John, instead of being the youthful apostle
standing under the Cross, appears as the aged evangelist (fig. 11).[15]

Xyngopoulos long ago recognized the three central panels in
Paolo's frieze as a reflection of an independent triptych,[16] an exam-

34   *The Image and Its Public*

ple of which has been published by Van Os (fig. 12).[17] With its mixture of Byzantine and Venetian traits, it occupies a key position in regard to the reception of the original icon in Venice. The bust of Christ with severed arms is unqualifiedly the norm for the corresponding type in the East (fig. 49). Mary and John stand with their gestures of mourning in the pictorial tradition of the Crucifixion. Paolo, although modifying these gestures and introducing another variant to the Christ-type, evidently has used just such a triptych as a model. Its former diffusion in Italy is demonstrated by numerous echoes in other media. In this triad Mary is the lamenting woman who mourns her Son, and not the Mother of God with her Child, who represents a separate theme. Like the companion figure of John, she was universally familiar from the three-figured Crucifixion scene. The secondary figures are both reduced to half length, and the crucified Christ is replaced by another type. It is, however, not the Crucifixion, but another icon of Christ which seems to be a presupposition for the triptych.

Such a view is confirmed by a third group of works in which this figural type appears without the context of the diptych or triptych. This is especially common in the case of miniatures. In the pictorial appendix to a Franciscan devotional book in Florence our type alludes to an independent panel with which the viewer was familiar (fig. 105).[18] At another place in the same book, this type illustrates a pseudo-Bernardine text from the mystic writings on the Passion that treats the crucified Christ (fig. 38).[19] On Giovanni Pisano's lectern in the Staatliche Museen in Berlin, two angels display the Christ-type wrapped in the shroud, which is not completed as a full figure in the space available below (fig. 31).[20] The shroud, which served as evidence of the Resurrection for the Marys at the Tomb, simultaneously refers to both the Tomb and the Resurrection. But this context, unlike that of the diptychs and triptychs, constitutes a kind of commentary which offers the half-length Christ in a special view; thus, the context was added to the half-length figure after the fact.

A similar procedure is used in a Venetian panel of the thirteenth century from Torcello (fig. 103).[21] In a less suitable way, elements from the Crucifixion, which appear to be added ad hoc, are assembled around the half-length figure. The inconsistencies of scale may have been tolerable, in view of the conventions of the painted cross. However, it is evident that the artist in Torcello is carrying out two operations which, as it were, translate his prototype into a different language. The one operation facilitates the understanding of the panel by "presenting" to the viewer the figure of Christ together with allusive elements from the Crucifixion. The other operation is of an aesthetic nature and counterbalances the isolation of the Christ figure in the prototype by means of subordinate motifs. Thus the prototype required a double change in order to become understandable. The difference between the prototype and the response to it obviously means that each originated in a different cultural sphere. We shall come back to this point later.

In this connection it is especially interesting that the image in Torcello was from its outset a single panel. It is precisely this fact which may have led the painter to his interpolations. If we exclude these, we are left with the remarkable conclusion that the half-length Christ in the model had been created not only as an isolated *figure*, but also as a single *panel*.

When the isolated figure appeared in a larger unit, such interpolations were not needed. We learn this from a Venetian triptych in Trieste which was produced in Paolo Veneziano's atelier for a community of Poor Clares (fig. 13).[22] In the right panel, the type we are investigating appears as an isolated quotation which does not conform to its neighbors even in its scale. Its immediate neighbor is a quotation as well: she reproduces the cult image of the Virgin of Mercy.[23] The juxtaposition of the unequal pair permits the pictorial function of both figures to be explained reciprocally. The figure of Mary provides the western filiation of an icon by visually interpreting the protective function of the Virgin's cloak. The identity of the popular cult image lies in its authentic image form. The meaning of the Virgin of Mercy is bound to the type of the mother with an outstretched cloak. By identifying themselves with the people under the Virgin's cloak, the Poor Clares graphically expressed that they addressed themselves through cultic means to this "picture within a picture." The bust of Christ is placed on one and the same level with this figure of Mary. Also in this case, the figural type is in the literal sense the distinguishing characteristic by which that meaning and provenance of the type can be identified. It is a functional form that is as appropriate for acquiring a cultic status as is the functional form of its neighboring figure.

The most famous single panel exhibiting our type is the mosaic panel in S. Croce in Gerusalemme in Rome, which, according to the "cult propaganda" of the Carthusian order residing there, is supposed to have appeared to Pope Gregory the Great during mass (fig. 14).[24] Here the idea of the Imago Pietatis was revalued by the declaration of the panel to be an authentic original of the image and endowing it with generous indulgences as a miraculous image. But this legend is no longer acceptable, for we know that the panel is a Constantinopolitan mosaic icon from around 1300, which prob-

The Image and Its Public

Fig. 12
The Hague, private collection. Venetian triptych

Fig. 13 Trieste, Museo Nazionale. Venetian triptych, 14th c. (detail)

ably arrived in Italy around 1380, where it could no longer have an effect on the diffusion of the image-type corresponding to it. Consequently, it is misleading to continue to speak of a "Gregorian archetype."[25] It is more sensible to call the corresponding image-type the portrait icon, or simply the Passion portrait. An original icon, the panel in Rome, gives testimony in another specimen of that work which the artist of Torcello used as his model. And after its arrival in the West, it could continue to exist without difficulty with other functions and in other contexts.

With this our first round of investigations has been completed. We have found a firmly established type, which could thus also have been exported to Bohemia. Already symbolizing certain meanings that "protected" its form, the frequency of its occurrence in the Veneto is as striking as its similarity to eastern icons. The conclusion that it was introduced through icons is obvious.[26]

But how are we to define what we call a "type"? Iconographical schemata, which were restricted to a single or dominant meaning (for example, the Eucharistic Christ), had not yet come into being.

The Image and Its Public

Fig. 14 Rome,
San Croce in
Gerusalemme.
Byzantine
mosaic icon,
ca. 1300

For this reason I would like to speak of formal *variants*. Within the scope of these variants the Passion portrait persisted as a type which was confined neither to a single formal variant nor to a single meaning, especially since an undisputed original, such as the miraculous image in S. Croce in Rome, did not exist yet.

Among the pictorial conventions of the West, the Imago Pietatis was experienced as an image of a different kind.[27] The close-up depiction of the picture's subject offers physiognomic accuracy, while the depiction of suffering and death introduces a psychological quality into the description given by the portrait. Not limited to a particular biographical situation (the Deposition, the Lamentation), the image was able to symbolize the full range of the meditation on the Passion. In this respect we can speak of a functional form with which the Imago Pietatis was provided. Was it a devotional image?

Chapter III
Functions of Medieval Images

It was Erwin Panofsky who liberated the concept of the devotional image from its confinement to the nunneries of southwest Germany. In 1927 he argued that, by virtue of its form and content, the devotional image qualified as an instrument for religious contemplation by an individual.[1]

But a conceptual definition is serviceable only if it provides criteria. Criteria are distinctive features, and here we encounter our first problem. Does the Imago Pietatis exist in a form in which it is not yet, or is no longer a devotional image? In Panofsky's system, the pictorial type that we have analyzed is still not classified as a devotional image, but only precedes the latter's actual development. Only at a subsequent stage of the development, after supporting and embracing coactors have been introduced who set the main figure in motion and change its psychological expression, is Panofsky willing to call our icon-type a devotional image (fig. 15).

In his system, the pure portrait icon must first be infused with life before it can enter into dialogue with the viewer (fig. 10). This required a whole range of carefully calculated changes—changes of the *imago* and the *historia*, that is, of the two basic categories of western art which are discussed time and again in the pronouncements of the Roman Church on images.[2] In other words, Panofsky argued from two, and only two, preexisting kinds of images, which he considered sufficiently defined by the terms that had been historically used to designate them, and described them as representational and narrative images (fig. 16). The *imago* portrays and thereby represents the person portrayed. Panofsky called it a "cultic representational image," thus adding a functional notion to the generic concept (fig. 25). The *historia*, which Panofsky referred to as a "scenic historical image," appeared to be more lively because it narrated and, in the opinion of Gregory the Great, also taught.

In Panofsky's view, these images together produced a third kind on which they bestowed their virtues, thus extending the existing boundaries of images. The narrative image bequeathed movement and expression of life, the representational image tranquillity and timelessness, hence duration which is suited to quiet contemplation. In other words, the new image overcame both the rigidity of the cult image and the restless activity of an image that only narrated. The result was the "devotional image," undefined spatially and temporally, in which two old traditions merged into a new category of images.

From a genetic perspective, both parents were still recognizable within the child whom they had begotten (fig. 5). The point of departure for the development we are examining must be a scene of the Deposition that has been stripped bare of a literal description of the event, as in the case of Giovanni da Milano's panel in the Accademia of Florence.[3] Or it could be, as in the case of Masolino's painting in Empoli, a single picture showing Christ after his Passion, enriched in Masolino's work by gestures and secondary figures from the Deposition, which has been shifted from the mode of external movement to that of internal emotion (fig. 15).[4]

But Masolino's image does not stem from representational images such as look down upon us from the apses of Romanesque churches. That would be tantamount to equating the icon with the western representational image. It is precisely this error that Panofsky committed. The reference system has a lacuna. It lacks the icon, which was not taken seriously as a pictorial category *sui generis*. Consequently, Margaritone's hieratic *maestà* of the Virgin and the animated intimacy of Lippo Memmi's Madonna and Child (both in Washington) had to be discussed under the same rubric (figs. 16, 17).[5] Lippo Memmi, however, created an image that was not developed out of Margaritone's, but rather presupposes an altogether different, eastern icon of the Virgin.

For the West in the thirteenth century, the icon was a new experience, and certainly not only as the medium of panel painting, but as a particular portrait form *en buste*. Durandus offered a rather strange explanation for this portrait form. The Greeks, he said, in order to prevent evil thoughts, did not depict figures below the navel.[6] In any event, he felt obliged to explain the half-length portrait icon, and in his explanation he identified it as a Byzantine import.

In Panofsky's system, however, the imported icon was omitted. It could not find a place alongside the *imago* and *historia*. An entire phase of the devotional image's early history of the devotional image was thus ignored, namely, that phase in which the image still had the form of an icon, while already having the function of a devotional image. In that phase the icon, so to speak, transferred its form to the devotional image, but that form lost the content that

The Image and Its Public

had been tied to it. It thus became available for a new content and a new function. To the West the iconic form was foreign, but also captivating. As a devotional image, the Imago Pietatis did not have a form that had come into being in its own right, but rather usurped a foreign one.

The panel in Torcello and the lectern of Giovanni Pisano present the original icon-type to the viewer with additional formulae which function as a visual invitation to meditation and worship (figs. 103, 31). To this purpose, the triptych in Trieste puts the figure in a position equal in value to that of the Virgin of Mercy (fig. 13).[7] With a similar intention, the statutes of a Laudesi brotherhood of Bologna, preserved in a manuscript from 1329, add this icon-type to that of the b r o t h e r h o o d ' s

patroness, the Virgin of Mercy, and they expressly call it "forma pietatis" (fig. 18).[8] Here we have the proof that in its new function the former eastern icon was accepted as a devotional image, and as such was even given a name of its own.

If that is so, the problem arises of how the form of an image

Fig. 16 (left)
Washington,
National
Gallery of Art.
Madonna by
 Margaritone,
13th c.

Fig. 17 (right)
Washington,
National
Gallery of Art.
Madonna by
Lippo Memmi,
14th. c.

relates to the image's function. The problem is best illustrated by the dilemma we now face, namely, that we must distinguish between icon and devotional image with regard to function, even when we cannot yet distinguish between them with regard to form. Originally, the icon was integrated into the Byzantine liturgy and possessed an ontological reference to the identity of the person portrayed; this person's image was, so to speak, his only possible physiognomy. In contrast—if one follows Panofsky—the devotional image continually changed in accordance with the viewer's expectations and needs. How is it that the devotional image could borrow its form from the icon, which was used so differently?

This question illustrates, first, that the relation between form and function is more complex than Panofsky assumed it was, and, second, that function is more complex than it appears to be in the triadic schema: representing–narrating–rendering the viewer empathic. We shall examine both of these matters more closely in two brief discussions.

First, Sixten Ringbom has rightly determined that "the half-length portrait icon of eastern origin" was "the devotional image *par excellence*" before it was either modernized or was superseded by the "scenic close-up."[9] He saw its psychological advantages in an intimacy which allowed the viewer the experience of dialogue and at the same time "inspection" of bodily details that were familiar to him as objects of cultic vener-

Fig. 18
Bologna, Bibl. Com. dell'Archiginnasio, Fondo Ospedale MS 52. Statutes of 1329

ation such as Christ's wounds, Mary's limbs (fig. 108).[10] Even in its early form, in which it had been brought to the West, this portrait icon appeared a *specific* enough form to the contemporary viewer because it differed in appearance from all the other images he knew. For the modern eye, however, the equation between form and function is less apparent when an already existing form is usurped for a new purpose and use. When this happens, the equation rarely remains limited to the situation in which it had been developed originally. The form is an instrument or symbol of a function, but not its mirror. The interaction between form and function is more complex than hitherto assumed.

Critical voices doubted whether the devotional image, as a pictorial class of its own, had a distinct form which was specialized for the function of devotion. R. Berliner argued that even scenes were used as devotional images (fig. 25).[11] We can go a step further. All such historical categories of images were themselves subject to changes. Any such form, as a way of experiencing a content or an object, is bound to a changing interpretation of content.[12] Panofsky's classification does not take into account this diachronic aspect. The *imago* no longer remains mere representation, but portrays in that lively manner which seemed restricted to the devotional image. The *historia* no longer merely narrates an objectively pregiven content, but retells it in a way that also seemed characteristic of the devotional image. The literary parallel is the new recounting of the stories of the Bible in the *Meditationes Vitae Christi,* which are both devout *and* realistic because it is rich in detail and dramatic.[13] The principle of psychological realism also applies to the scenic image. It leads ultimately to the principle that Alberti proposes for every *historia,* namely, liveliness.[14]

Two early examples from the thirteenth century, almost contemporary with the *Meditationes Vitae Christi,* illustrate how a former *imago* was reinterpreted as a narrative devotional image, and how a former *historia* was recast as a stationary devotional image. They are found in the same Franciscan devotional book in Florence in which we have encountered the portrait icon of Christ of the Passion (fig. 20).[15]

The depiction of the Enthroned Virgin with Child quotes a large-sized, Tuscan panel of the Virgin, which had become customary on altars at that time.[16] The only surprise is that it now has become part of a pictorial biography of Christ. The picture's position between the Massacre of the Innocents and the twelve-year-old Jesus in the Temple invites a biographical reading of the image. The *Meditationes* describe the intimacy of Mother and Child in detail. They also call for a "beautiful...meditation" on how the Holy Family did "live all this time."[17] In short, we see in the drawing a familial image within the historical situation of Christ's childhood, basically a *historia,* which can be understood as a scene only from the context (fig. 19).

A second drawing in the same book is clearly a scene because it depicts the Crucifixion.[18] But the intense pathos of the accompanying figures is striking. It is so dominant that the scene becomes a picture conveying the mood of *compassio.* The comparison with a slightly older miniature in a Franciscan missal belonging to the Vatican Library reveals the new "key" of this drawing (fig. 21).[19] It depicts not so much the objective event as the subjective experience of it in the grief of the witnesses. Panofsky's definitions of the devotional image hold good for this drawing, even though it is a matter here of a scene. It is of decisive importance, however, that the scene does not remain a scene *alongside which* the devotional image arises,

46   *The Image and Its Public*

Fig. 19
Florence,
Bibl. Med.
Laurenziana,
MS Plut.
XXV.3, fol.
373v. Ma-
donna (Emilia
1293–1300)

but is for its part subjected to continual change through which it can become suitable, also with regard to its form, to serve as a devotional image.

Both the reinterpreted *imago* and the recast *historia* are, as it were, stations at which a meditation can linger. The *Zardino de Oration* (1454) recommends that the faithful make use of such stations in order to attain an "inner vision" of the Passion: "Move slowly from episode to episode, meditate on each one, dwelling on each single stage and step of the story. And if at any point you feel a sen-

Fig. 20
Florence,
Bibl. Med.
Laurenziana,
MS Plut.
XXV.3, fol. 366.
Crucifixion

sation of piety, stop: do not pass on as long as that sweet and devout sentiment lasts."[20] As early as the thirteenth century, the dissolution of the narrative sequence into stations of contemplation was already a literary principle in the *Meditationes*. Once the narrative account given in the Bible was valued as a source of nothing more than raw material for what the faithful wanted to contemplate, this new view

48   *The Image and Its Public*

Fig. 21 Forme,
Bibl. Vaticana,
Cod. Reg. Lat.
2048, fol. 129v.
Crucifixion:
Missal, 13th c.

cannot have been without consequences for the realm of visual depiction.

Is it at all legitimate to distinguish the devotional image as defined by Panofsky (both formally *and* functionally) from the scene?

The criticism of this thesis culminates in Ringbom's book. His objections to it are as follows: Not only could something that does not look like a devotional image (for example, the scene) have functioned as one, but something that did not function as a devotional image may look like one.[21] Depictions that in reality symbolize a theological notion or mystery of faith can look like devotional images. One example of this is the use of the Imago Pietatis for symbolizing a church bearing the title of "The Sacred Body and Blood."[22]

Ringbom therefore proposes to abandon Panofsky's functionally as well as formally defined concept of the devotional image. In its place he introduces a term, "devotional image," which designates the function without the form, and another, "*Andachtsbild*," which designates the form without the function.[23] But *Andachtsbild*, which is merely the German equivalent of "devotional image," does not provide a second term at all, and, in addition, does not define what it ought to define, the pictorial form.[24]

It is not advisable to distinguish between "devotional image" and "*Andachtsbild*." As we saw, the relation between form and function is complex and, moreover, unstable. Function can change an existing pictorial form, and the pictorial form can assume new functions. Thus it is better to use a somewhat imprecise term than to separate form and function when their interaction is so crucial.

Ringbom's position is best explained by his intention of tracing the "development of the dramatic close-up" in the fifteenth century. This is a "form which combined the vividness of the narrative...with the portrait character and direct appeal of the traditional icon."[25] Such a formulation sounds similar to Panofsky's, but applies to close-ups from scenes which are, however, not themselves scenes. According to this view, Mantegna's *Presentation of Christ in the Temple* (now in Berlin) was not developed out of a scene, but out of a Madonna in profile and is to be understood as an "annotated" image of the Virgo Purificata (fig. 22). In a formal sense, the image has narrative features, and in a functional sense is to be understood as a "devotional image."[26]

The Lamentation in the oeuvre of Giovanni Bellini is also a "narrative without time (fig. 23)." The Berlin panel, as a scenic close-up, differs from the panel in the Brera which is presented to us as an "expanded fourteenth-century formula" of the Imago Pietatis.[27] In fact, the Brera, image follows a fourteenth-century model even more closely than Ringbom knew (fig .24).[28]

But it is a fundamental difference of the Brera picture from its prototype which is the point of Ringbom's conceptual operations.[29] The old "*Andachtsbilder*" were "conceptual representations of a set of accumulated theological notions built around the figure of Christ" or "static, ahistorical agglomerations of symbolical elements."[30] It is the new "devotional images" which first develop "a coherent narrative" in the form of "expressive close-ups of the group of the Saviour surrounded by mourners."[31] Like their forerunners, they were

Fig. 22 Berlin, Staatliche Museen. Presentation in the Temple
by A. Mantegna

objects of private devotion, but only now did they receive a form appropriate for that function.

Certainly, images from the trecento look different, but that does not mean that they symbolized only theological content. In this regard Panofsky was the more accurate observer. The trecento images also perform a psychological function, but in combination with other semantic functions in accordance with the complex understanding of image and symbol in the Middle Ages.[32] In contrast, specialization is a symptom of quattrocento art. On the one hand, the scenic devotional image is now enlarged thematically by the transferal of new themes to panels. The result translates into reality two prerequisites of the independent painted panel that we have already discussed, namely, the selection of a scene and reading it in a static way (p. 12). On the other hand, the new devotional image now explores objective (that is, artistic) means for depicting emotion. It promises a "natural" close-up of the holy persons, in an ever new, original way, in the "window-opening" of the frame. But it is only fulfilling in new ways the old desiderata of the devotional

Fig. 23 Berlin, Staatliche Museen. Lamentation by Giovanni Bellini

image, which are exactly its precondition. The market in which panel paintings with new compositions found their customers was first created by the social function of private devotional images.

We now return to the question of whether devotional images should be distinguished from *historiae*. The answer may be given in the positive, if we argue within the long span of historical development. In the beginning of this development, certain images changed, probably due to the influence of icons, into "scenic stations of devotion" either through a remodeling of the scene *in toto* or through the depiction of a selected part of a scene. By isolating the main figures of a scene, some images, together with their form, "adapt" themselves to being viewed in a certain religious manner, that is, to serving contemplation. An example is the so-called *Pietà Fogg* in Cambridge, Massachusetts (fig. 25).[33] Only according to the letter is it a *scene* of the Lamentation; in spirit it is a *Pietà group* in a scenic context. The "unnatural" presentation of the corpse is not a shortcoming of the picture, but rather its purpose. Here the painter

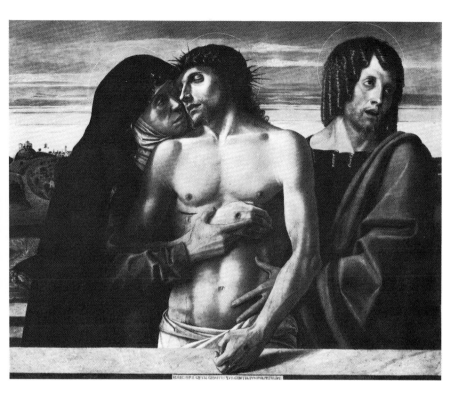

Fig. 24 Milan, Brera. Lamentation by Giovanni Bellini

does not adhere to the principle of "accurate" description, but instead maintains for the viewer the expressive power and dominance of the main figures, even at the cost of "correct" reproduction. Object-illusionism and the depicted subject's expressive power, two demands of mimesis, are in conflict with one another here.

The theory of art in the quattrocento clearly formulated both demands, and contemporary practice reconciled them with one another. Here we have reached the other end of the span of development within which the devotional image and the *historia* are located. Their difference, which had often been blurred in the intervening period, is again dramatized. They increasingly differ from each other to the same extent to which the *historia* becomes more "technical." Certainly, according to Alberti, the new *historia* also was to stir the heart of the viewer by putting him in a certain affective state.[34] However, its closed reference system, which rationally arranged the parts of the image according to optical laws, moved farther and farther away from the open reference system on which the devotional

image was dependent. Here *open* means incomplete in the factual narration, unconnected within the internal pictorial syntax, while being bound to an external viewer. One could almost speak of a technical (in the double sense of *techné* as art and science) and a psychological perspective. They coincide in Masaccio's *Trinity*, but otherwise become opposed tendencies. Certainly the *historia*'s further history, which Ringbom has traced, is the fusion of both perspectives. The resulting unitary perspective combines the perfect illusion of the window-image and its experience of intimacy with the mood of the figures (fig. 23).`

The affirmative answer to the question whether the devotional image can be formally distinguished from the *historia*, confirms that the former is a type of image in which form and function have interacted, not in a linear way but in stages of reciprocal influence. Once again we encounter the problem of determining the function of the devotional image, indeed of understanding what an image function is or can be.

Second, as we saw, the function of an image relates to its pictori-

54   *The Image and Its Public*

rial form in very com-
plex ways and mirrors
a social practice which
must itself first be
explored before it can
explain the image.
"Devotion" is consid-
ered a function of the
devotional image.
Panofsky distinguishes
the devotional image
from the representa-
tional image and the
historia, which he
understands as image
functions. He refers to
the triadic schema
considered a function
of the devotional
image. "represent-in-
struct-emotionally at-
tune," which, as a
locus classicus of
medieval theories of
the image, was still
taught by theologians
of the Renaissance.
The schema desig-

nates functions that made the image permissible and perhaps even
useful in the eyes of the theologians. The image, according to this
schema, could teach especially the illiterate, serve as a reminder of
the constant presence of the mysteries of faith, and finally, as Balbus
said, stimulate a feeling of pious devotion *(devotionis affectum),* which
was produced more easily through the eyes than through the ears.
The schema had been known ever since the time of Gregory the
Great.[35] In the late Middle Ages, empathy with the subject matter of
religion received more attention; nevertheless no third term was
introduced, in addition to *imago* and *historia,* to designate an image
specialized for effecting it.

The schema, to be sure, contains only three basic situations in which the image was accepted by *theologians*, and is not a catalogue of images and historical uses of images. For this reason, it is not sufficient to appeal to the schema in order to define the devotional image. Of course, the devotional image serves the viewer's empathy, but it is not necessarily specialized for this purpose, nor does it form an independent class of images that can be easily distinguished from their surroundings. How did it relate to its function or, to be more precise, to its functions?

Panofsky understood function in a linear way, as something psychological, and associated it with the individual mind and the individual's capacity for mystical experience. Among the current definitions of the devotional image,[36] the prevailing tendency is to situate it in the private sphere at a distance from the collective cult of the ecclesiastical liturgy. It is thus conceived of as an instrument of personal, noninstitutional piety. As we shall see, this conception is only partially correct. Such a definition blocks our view of devotional images that are not only to be experienced affectively, but are to be contemplated cognitively as well, namely, as the pictorial symbol of a cult or mystery of faith.[37] Above all it leads from the basic schema of general uses of images to a time-bound and therefore social-historical phenomenon: lay or private devotion. This devotion developed only after the thirteenth century, even though its types of piety were "prethought" earlier by theologians such as Anselm of Canterbury and Bernard of Clairvaux.[38]

Ringbom has given a concise account of the history and the forms of this new devotional practice. The *prie-dieu*, the Book of Hours, and the *petit tableau* become the tools of this new devotional practice (fig. 26).[39] They are to be found primarily in the household and in a family's private chapel. The layman develops a private prayer life for which new kinds of texts and new kinds of images are produced. In this private life of prayers, the mysteries of faith are felt more than analyzed. According to the piety promulgated especially by the mendicant orders, feeling and acting are the means of participation in ecclesiastical life for the new social groups, above all the theologically untrained laity. It is in this context that the devotional image receives its function. On a preverbal level, it promises more than texts could. Whenever the individual is instructed to produce within himself "inner images" of historical and supernatural matters of faith, greater value is attached to material images (fig. 27). They are also recommended by a popularized mysticism which can invoke the surprising resemblance between the "images" revealed in visions and existing religious images—which in reality

The Image and Its Public

Fig. 27
London,
Courtauld
Institute
Gallery. Brugge
diptych, late
15th c.

was due, of course, to the fact that the material images were reexperienced in the visions, that is, claimed as the viewers' own experiences.[40]

Within this framework, the devotional image is frequently spoken of. It is the "petit tableau de devocion," and Heinrich Seuse used it for "andaht nach bildricher wise."[41] In the domestic sphere, certain images which "move the spirit to piety" are recommended to the merchant Francesco di Marco Datini of Prato.[42] Prayers were to be said before the images "devotamente," "mit andaht."[43] It was not enough to form them with the lips. The viewer had to engender in himself a certain emotional state: devotion, then to devoutly contemplate the images, which in turn helped to produce the devotional state. The suggestion of a reciprocity between the viewer and the person depicted in the image, which A. Neumeyer called an "exchange of gazes" (*Blickaustausch*),[44] is vividly described in a history of the first Dominicans written before 1269 and cited by O. von Simson: "In their cells they had before their eyes images of her [the Virgin] and of her crucified Son so that while reading, praying, and sleeping, they could look upon them and be looked upon by them [the images], with the eyes of compassion [*oculis pietatis*]."[45] Now, "piety" is a reciprocal attitude, especially in the understanding of the Imago Pietatis. Images intended for use in cells such as this Dominican source mentions survive from the Carthusian monastery of Champmol; they depict, following the same schema, the

Crucifixion in which the roles of the *passio* and the *compassio* are assigned to Christ and to Mary, and include the Carthusian viewer symbolically and graphically within the image (fig. 28).[46]

Image devotion was not restricted to the monastery, but was at home in various social units of lay society, and may even have originated within them. The mental state of "devotion" was a standard of personal religiosity for which precepts or stereotypes were available. Thus so-called private devotion was also a collective role in which even the various degrees of perfection were programmed. In Italy, it was essentially a fruit and a remnant of religious mass-movements whose ecstatic piety was channeled into the stable paths of daily prayer. I have in mind the great flagellant movement of 1260, which had so enduring an effect on the rise of the lay confraternities. The statutes of the Compagnia di S. Maria della Vita of Bologna call it the "time of general piety" *(tempore generalis devotionis)*.[47] Their text is provided with the classic devotional images of the Virgin and the Passion which, however, reproduce in their pictorial form—nota bene—in one case an icon and in the other a narrative, the Scourging of Christ (fig. 83).[48]

This cursory sketch of devotion in general and of image devotion in particular permits us to formulate some tentative conclusions. Devotion is a collective style of affective religiosity that brought into existence an analogous style of contemplation of images. The images were expected to reciprocate the believer's mood, and, if possible, even generate it. The viewer and the person depicted in the image were related to one another mimetically. The viewer tried to assimilate himself to the depicted person and demanded back from the latter the quality of aliveness which he himself possessed. This mimesis, which was intended to bring about the ecstasy of the individual viewer, nevertheless in the long run drew the sacred into the human sphere, which in any case dictated the level of communication. In a move countering the progressive abandonment of images, which mysticism demanded from the individual, the image became more and more corporeal and communicative, as the individual wished his partner in dialogue to be.

Just as devotion was a convention, so too it created corresponding pictorial conventions in the devotional images. Of course, these did not remain confined to the original functional domain, but informed viewing conventions so generally that they also modified, for example, public cult images. Therefore, the problem of distinguishing different image functions and correspondingly different functional images, is a problem of priority, of determining when a

58   *The Image and Its Public*

Fig. 28
Cleveland,
Museum
of Art.
Crucifixion
panel from
Champmol
by Jean de
Beaumetz,
1388

pictorial invention was used originally, and when it was employed for other purposes. Private devotion had not only colored public cultic forms, but had also drawn upon them, because it ultimately needed objective contents that were beyond the whims of the individual. Any rigid classification would fail to grasp the complexity of these interrelations. In any event, conventions tend to spread without being constrained by functional restrictions.

In all these cases function is understood, as we have stated, as the use of images or the need for it, that is, as a collective attitude in the sense given to the term by social psychology. It is necessary to distinguish from this conception another function of the image that not only corresponds to a general mode of experience, but is also an objective connection of the image to a purpose. This function thus represents either a specialized use or a restricted application of the general pictorial function with a narrowly defined meaning. In order to reveal its message, this applied function needs to be associated with a specific context.

When we look back at the examples through which we have so far come to know the Imago Pietatis, we see that they provide an entire catalogue of delimited situations in the sense we have just mentioned. The small-sized, portable diptych of the Casa Horne was obviously a private image (fig. 10); the triptych in Trieste, on the other hand, was the cult image of a convent of Clarisses (fig. 13). On the *pala feriale* of Paolo Veneziano and on the Pisan retable of Simone Martini, the Imago Pietatis appears, without a change of form, in a great altarpiece (fig. 31); in the relief of Giovanni Pisano, it is an image on a pulpit. In the Roman mosaic icon, it was regarded as a relic and accordingly was employed as a miraculous image, hence in a secondary function in which it did not have its origin (fig. 14). If, as we believe, not only this one specimen, but the pictorial form of the Imago Pietatis in general was imported into the West as an icon, then its function there as a devotional image was likewise ancillary at first.

Further situations in which this pictorial form appears are easily found. The Imago Pietatis appears on patens, on paxes, and on tabernacle doors, as a pictorial symbol of the Eucharist, or on private sepulchers where, in the name of the deceased, it summons the bereaved to supplicatory prayer to "Our Lord of Mercy," who had led the way in death. The restricted notion of function is useful for interpreting specialized images. With its help, the form of the miraculous image, which it was forbidden to change, and which therefore remained outside the general development of the image's form, can be understood. On the predella of an altar retable, the Imago Pietatis functions as a reference to the sacramental Christ by means of, and only by means of, the location of the image (fig. 35). During the early quattrocento, at the latest, the pictorial formula of Christ shedding his blood was developed to serve this purpose. Independent of its context, this formula exclusively possessed the sacramental meaning.[49] We know its meaning, as well as its connection with the Mantuan relic of the Precious Blood, only from such cases in which the context or the function of the images in question can be reconstructed.

That brings us to a third use of the notion of function. Whereas

The Image and Its Public

Fig. 29 Cambridge, Mass., Fogg Art Museum. Christ with arma by Roberto di
Oderisio, ca. 1355

in the first case the notion refers very generally to the social-psychological function of the devotional image, and in the second case to the connection of individual images with certain specific functions, in the third case function designates, on the semantic level, the relationship of a particular meaning with a particular pictorial form. The meaning is then a function of the pictorial form, and the pictorial form is its expression. This state of affairs occurs when an image, without explicating itself, as in the second case, by being linked to external purposes, is intended to communicate specific meanings that are not understood *eo ipso*.

An example is the expansion of the Imago Pietatis through the so-called *arma*: instruments from, and shorthand references to the Stations of the Cross, which are scattered over the entire picture.[50] The Imago Pietatis, as in R. Oderisio's panel in the Fogg Art Museum,[51] is then expanded with regard to its meaning (fig. 29). In the cartographic glossing of the main figure, the viewer could memorize individually the Stations of the Cross implied by the portrayed figure and simultaneously perform the veneration of the *arma* and the stigmata to which religious usage obligated him. Literal object-realism and mystical concept-realism are united in one and the same image and, in iconic and ideographic communication of meaning, they offer two different approaches which the user knew well. The prayer texts current at that time offered models for reading *and* experiencing such an image.[52] They had prepared the way for the close-up detailed presentation of actions and persons (for example, in the veneration of the individual stigmata or of individual tortures of Christ), and thus created social conventions for the reading of such an image. The beholder of today who wants to reexperience the reaction of the viewer at that time, does not possess the latter's interpretive model and therefore fails to understand the image's code. He also has problems with encountering simultaneously psychological illusionism and abstract symbolism, which he is accustomed to assign to fundamentally different classes of the image. At that time both could serve the purposes of the devotional image, as well as, for example, visually present a theological concept. If the concept itself was supposed to be mystically experienced, then the "illusionistic" image of devotion could be used. In other cases, the contemplating subject was expected to contribute with his own imagination what the image lacked in terms of illusion. In this regard, the generality of a pictorial form could even be advantageous, as Baxandall believes.[53]

The Image and Its Public

Fig. 30 New York, Morgan Library, MS 729, fol. 15r. Book of Hours of Yolande of Soissons: Veronica

In Oderisio's image, the accompanying figures of Mary and John show how complex the semantic structure of such a panel is. Through miming and gesture, they delineate for the viewer the mood of pity into which the latter wants to put himself, and complement the *arma*'s articulation of meaning with an articulation of psychological meaning as "guiding figures" that enhance the expressive capacity of the main figure. We will not, however, deal with the expressive function of pictorial language until the next chapter.

Various definitions of the pictorial function have been introduced and differentiated from each other. In this discussion, the devotional image can only be a subordinate concept because it articulates very generally the pictorial expectations of a historical public. In this case function is a category of social psychology. The private devotional image is only a special case or an applied function that is, so to speak, specialized. The private image could be the domain in which pictorial form originated that then "migrated," as well as the secondary area of its diffusion. From the standpoint of art-historical research, it is important to stress the interactions between the various social levels of the image cult (public, confraternal, and private), as much as the migrations of established pictorial forms from one functional area to another.

Thus, the devotional image could possess from its beginning a cultic status that was institutionalized by being semantically tied to a public cult, the veneration of the Blessed Sacrament or of a relic, say, or through its use in a cultic association, such as a confraternity. In the *Book of Hours* of Yolande of Soissons, the veronica was, according to its function at that time (granted, a secondary function), a devotional image that the private possessor contemplated (fig.30).[54] But originally it was a miraculous image or a relic image that the Church had provided with an indulgence. Thus, the image shifted from public to cultic private worship.[55] Like the Imago Pietatis, which had been imported as an icon, it did not possess "innately" the form of the devotional image. However, the Imago Pietatis developed such a form because, in contrast to the veronica, that image did not exist in an authentic original. Only in a later phase would the Imago Pietatis be provided with indulgences. Since its reality was likened to the reality of Christ's existence in the Sacrament, at an early time in its history it drew to itself supplicatory prayer and the expectation of salvation. As we have said, the functions of devotion, as an act of contemplation, and of supplicatory prayer, as an institution for assuring salvation, merged when an image invited contemplation by its form and petitionary veneration by its cultic status.

Chapter IV
Realism and Pictorial Rhetoric

The devotional image has generally been understood in psychological terms, that is, as an image appealing to the viewer's emotions and suggesting the experience of a personal dialogue with the depicted individual. While this may be true, it is impossible for us to understand the image spontaneously as if it were addressed to us, because that would presuppose the same basic psychological disposition for both the medieval and the modern viewer. In order to reconstruct the reality the image expresses, we must first know what reality it refers to. For the image conveys only as much reality as the viewer was able to recognize in it. However, the understanding of the image was tied to changing historical circumstances. Here we shall try to gain access to that reality which the medieval viewer could discern in the Imago Pietatis.

Two examples furnish the questions with which we can begin. The first is Giovanni Pisano's lectern in Berlin, which we discussed earlier (fig. 31).[1] The other is a small, early fifteenth-century household altar, probably German, also in Berlin (fig. 32).[2] While the lectern certainly should not be simply regarded as a devotional image, it does exhibit the theme of such an image to the public. The lectern belongs to the functional sphere of public cultic worship. The extent to which the public and private spheres intermeshed in the use of the Imago Pietatis no longer needs to be proved. It is, however, the official cult that will best introduce us to the reality the image was intended to convey.

As a cultic depiction of reality, the relief on the lectern "represents" Christ reposing in the sepulcher. Two angels display the dead body by holding the shroud with which Christ was wrapped in the tomb. With faces presumably expressing lamentation, they direct their gaze out of the image toward the community to whom they are displaying Christ. The image makes a number of statements that are not intelligible in themselves. Why only a half-length figure of Christ? Why is he being displayed? Why by two angels? Why should the shroud play a role in the pictorial syntax?

Since Christ is depicted as the Imago Pietatis, he expresses all the meanings attached to that iconic type. The angels are not com-

Fig. 31 Berlin,
Staatliche
Museen.
Lectern from
Pistoia by
Giovanni
Pisano

prehensible in this context, because in the Bible they are not mentioned until Easter morning. Of course, on Easter morning their role is the same as in the image: they display the burial shroud. But on Easter morning the shroud, the evidence of Christ's Resurrection, was empty. Therefore, by displaying the dead Christ, the image is *prima vista* false or it runs the risk of being read incorrectly. But this is unlikely; rather, the image's viewer was capable of understanding it correctly. But what is the correct meaning of the image?

Since the relief represents the biblical Mysteries as they were enacted in the Passion and Easter liturgies, the correct interpretation is obtained by substituting cultic reality for biblical reality.[3] These rites began with the adoration of the unveiled cross and the crucified Christ on Good Friday. This was immediately followed by the extraliturgical burial (*depositio*) of the cross which was wrapped in a "shroud" and led in procession to its entombment in the "tomb of Christ." On Easter morning the raising (*elevatio*) of the cross took

place, "representing" the Resurrection, and the rites were concluded with the public "visit of the women to the empty tomb" (*visitatio*).
The boundaries between the liturgy and the Passion play, an interpolation into the liturgy, are not always clear. Now, we would like to
see the *elevatio* of the crucified Christ in the relief, something for
which the shroud and the angels (though not their lamenting
expression) would be well-suited. But why is Christ not portrayed as
living? The cross was, after all, "elevated" already on its way *to* the
tomb. The answer to our question, however, can only be found if we
once again change interpretive planes.

The cultic staging of the Passion made use of the sacramental
reality of Christ by employing the consecrated Host in addition to
the cross or in place of the cross. A Zurich *ordo* from 1260 argued in
vain against the "absurd" practice of burying the sacramental Body

of Christ, as if the latter were dead.[4] Nevertheless, as a practice, the entombment of the *corpus Domini* in a burial shroud continued to spread, becoming even more a topic of current interest as it entered into the discussion about the real presence of Christ in the Sacrament, which, since the twelfth century, had been regarded as the tangible reality of Christ's flesh.[5] All difficulties in interpretation disappear if we may see in the Imago Pietatis a likeness of the Host. Then, without literally reproducing particular rites, the image refers to the raising of the Host or to its burial, or to both. Indeed, it possibly transcends the context of the Passion liturgy and evokes the "elevation of the Host," which followed the consecration of the bread in every mass at that time.[6] Then, the image would have graphically united the real presence in the Sacrament with the reality of the historical Body of Christ—or with Christ's death in his sacrifice and his life in the Resurrection. Thus, a technique would have been selected that R. Berliner might have considered an example of "the freedom of medieval art" to be more complex than conceptual language.[7] But the argument presupposes that just this figure of Christ could designate the Sacrament, or, in other words, (1) that the viewer recalled the rites involving the Sacrament and could decode the reality conveyed in the image, and (2) that the Imago Pietatis was familiar to him as a pictorial formula for the Sacrament. Here we pause and turn to the second example.

The small altar in Berlin, very probably a German work from the early fifteenth century, is also a presentation of Christ, but in this case only one angel plays a role (fig. 32). The pictorial realism differs here from that of the lectern image, inasmuch as the angel grasps the enshrouded dead body under the arms and rationally accounts for the body's pose by holding it upright. But this only makes the presented reality all the more problematic, for there is no biblical situation in which Christ, as a corpse, is held by an angel. What situation is beingdepicted, if not a biographical one? The only biographical context in which Christ, as a corpse, lies in the arms of others is the Descent from the Cross, an event in which, however, no angel took part. Furthermore, the angel presents the dead Christ as if wanting to present him to us. This angel is not only displaying Christ generally, but is, as it were, offering to give him over to us. This angel has been identified as the one of the mass's epiklesis, who, according to the text of the prayer, bears the sacrifice offered on the altar up to the heavenly Father.[8] But why does the supporting figure offer to us the sacrificial figure that stands for the Host? One cultic situation in which the believer does in fact receive the Body of Christ is Communion.

Fig. 33
Montalto.
Reliquary of
Sixtus IV
(Paris ca.
1400)

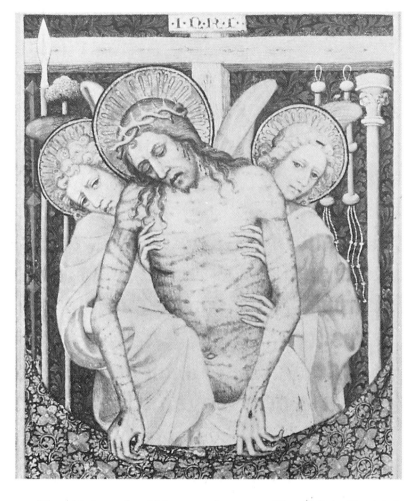

The widely read, mid-fourteenth century *Vita Christi* of Ludolph
of Saxony is a key text for information about historical and cultic
reality, about Christ's Descent from the Cross and Communion. In it
we read, "For it is far greater [for people] to receive the Body of
Christ from the sacrificial place of the altar than it is to take him
down from the sacrificial place of the cross. For those who did the
latter received him in their arms and hands, while the former
receive him in their mouths and hearts."[9] The text does not state
the connection between the Descent from the Cross and
Communion for the first time, but it does offer us a suggestion for
understanding that connection by explaining the visual gesture of
invitation made to the viewer with the reception of the Sacrament in

The Image and Its Public

Fig. 35 Pisa, San Francesco. Marble altar by Tommaso Piseno

Communion, and vice versa. This is more than merely known symbolism, which is read into the image. By being able both to understand the gesture of offering, literally and to refer it to himself, the viewer was able to experience the image in a way that gave the pictorial rhetoric its specific significance.

It has long been known that the real sacramental existence of Christ offered a means for grasping the way in which the Imago Pietatis could be understood. That existence made it legitimate for the image's depictive realism to portray simultaneously both historical and cultic reality. A vision of Angela of Foligno, who lived at the beginning of the fourteenth century, throws light on the store of ideas, on the basis of which our image could be interpreted. "At the display of the Host during mass," she saw an image of the crucified Christ, looking "as if he had just been removed from the cross."[10] Many other texts of this kind could be cited. The transformation of the sacramental Body of Christ into his visible Body was the experi-

Fig. 36
New York, the
Cloisters.
Fresco from
Florence,
14th c.

ence of Christ's doctrinally assured presence in the Sacrament. Through autosuggestion, Angela converted known reality into visible reality. The beheld figure of the divine victim as he was after his Descent from the Cross presupposes material images that were understood in the same way that Angela understood her vision. In these images, which were, for their part, related back to the Descent from the Cross, the Sacrament literally became visible.

The legend of St. Gregory's Mass, according to which the Host was transformed before Gregory's eyes into the living Christ of the Passion, must be seen in this context.[11] This legend, too, subserves the desire to compensate for the consecrated bread's deficiency of reality through its visionary transformation into a visible bodily form. Significantly, the mosaic icon of the Imago Pietatis of S. Croce in Rome, which we have already discussed, was considered to be a true likeness of the living image that Pope Gregory beheld (fig. 14).[12] As a relic, that icon again authenticated the pictorial type that

Fig. 37 Pescia,
Oratorio of
San Antonio.
Descent from
the Cross,
13th c.

already had a "specialized" reference to the sacramental Christ.

Now, does the small altar in Berlin, which was our point of departure, depict Christ not only in the Sacrament, but—as the texts suggest—also as he was following his removal from the cross? And further, does it belong at all in the context of the Imago Pietatis? The first question can be answered with the help of the famous reliquary of Sixtus V in Montalto, which was made as an altarpiece ca. 1400 in the workshop of a Parisian goldsmith (fig. 33).[13] It provides an important preliminary stage, if not the prototype, for the composition of the Berlin altar. This work appears in the 1457 inventory of Cardinal Pietro Balbo as "a large, silver-plated altarpiece on which Christ, having been taken down from the cross, is borne in the hands of a large angel."[14] This is surely no interpretation ex post facto. It is the sacramental Christ, already evoked by the location of the altarpiece, who is portrayed in the image of the victim removed from the cross.

The two small altars in Berlin and in Montalto lead us away from Italy geographically and away from the Imago Pietatis compositionally. But it has long been known that their pictorial form has its roots in the Italian pictorial tradition of the Imago Pietatis. In a pocket-sized Amsterdam triptych, which, like the panel in Montalto, was created in the Parisian milieu ca. 1400, the two canonical accompanying figures of Mary and John point to this tradition.[15] In a miniature from the *Très Belles Heures de Notre Dame*, commissioned by the Duc de Berry around 1382, the "Angel Pietà,"[16] this time with two supporting angels, is linked through the half-length figure of Christ with the same Imago Pietatis of which the Amsterdam and Montalto examples have retained the position of the arms (fig. 34). A stone retable of Tommaso Piseno in S. Francesco in Pisa gives evidence of the Angel Pietà on Italian soil (fig. 35).[17] In Venetian quattrocento painting it became a popular pictorial form, starting from the time it was fashioned by Donatello on the tabernacle door of the high altar in the Santo in Padua.[18] Perhaps we can retrospectively add G. Pisano's pulpit lectern to this enumeration as well.

If we agree that the Berlin altar is in the tradition of the Imago Pietatis, and that its allusion to the Descent from the Cross is clearly a topos, then the occurrence of this topos in the earlier Italian examples can also be demonstrated. In addition, we will investigate a particular gesture that the Imago Pietatis adopted beginning in the second quarter of the trecento: widespread arms stretched straight out (fig. 36). This gesture alters the half-length portrait, relative to the original formulation, and appears to introduce into the portrayed figure's death the contradiction of vital activity. The gesture is derived from the Descent from the Cross, or rather, from a certain formulation of it. We find this gesture in a great number of life-sized wooden sculpture groups from the Italian dugento depicting the Descent from the Cross. One example among many is the group of S. Antonio in Pescia (fig. 37).[19] It shows Christ with his feet still nailed to the cross. His unsupported arms are angled out symmetrically from the body. Mary and John seem on the point of taking his hands and kissing them.

The group, which places the crucified Christ in the scenic context of the Descent from the Cross, has not been studied with regard to its cultic function, but various pieces of evidence indicate that it was introduced by confraternities into the Lauds and probably into the Passion plays, and carried around in processions and publicly displayed by them.[20] Christ's gesture is peculiar; it is actually one of embracing. The metaphor that the crucified Christ embraces the believer had been presented previously in the *Vita* of Saint Bernard.[21] It appears again in the famous hymn, *Planctus ante nescia*, which was sung in accompaniment to the Lamentation of Mary and the Passion plays: "Rush to the embrace! While he hangs on the tree of the cross, he offers himself with outstretched arms to the loving for a mutual embrace."[22] It is possible that the Lamentation of Mary was performed before such sculptural groups as those from which the Imago Pietatis quotes the gesture under discussion. The gesture, a familiar motif from the Deposition, in this way assimilates the icon to the image of Christ's Descent from the Cross (see also p. 151).

The analogies between the sculpted Descent from the Cross and the painted Imago Pietatis become even more numerous as soon as the painted figure of Christ is enlarged into the three-figured Lamentation. They now also include the gestures of Mary and John who hold, venerate, and display Christ's hands. Fra Angelico's famous Lamentation in Munich expresses, as it were, a reverence for the old cult image, and a Lamentation from Ghirlandaio's circle (fig. 94; bequest of the Lanz collection, now in Groningen) alludes just as clearly to the schema, for example, in the version of the group in S. Miniato.[23] Both quattrocento images only become intelligible once their allusion to the group sculptures of the dugento is noted.

However, the Imago Pietatis was already understood in the sense of the Deposition before the appearance of this gesture. In the Florentine devotional book of the dugento that we have cited several times, it accompanies a pseudo-Bernardine text that speaks of Bernard's being strongly embraced by the crucified Christ (fig. 38).[24] The half-length figure of Christ in front of the cross, to which he is, however, not nailed, could be construed in the West, as in Byzantium, as a portrait of the Messiah brought down from the cross. In a subsequent stage of the image's evolution, this interpretation was translated into a visual presentation. Thus the image was adapted to the understanding of it that had already been current prior to the change.

But does the image also signify the sacramental Christ? Such an interpretation is compellingly suggested to the viewer if the image's

Fig. 38
Florence,
Bibl. Med.
Laurenziana,
Plut. XXV.3,
fol. 183v
(Emilia
1293–1300)

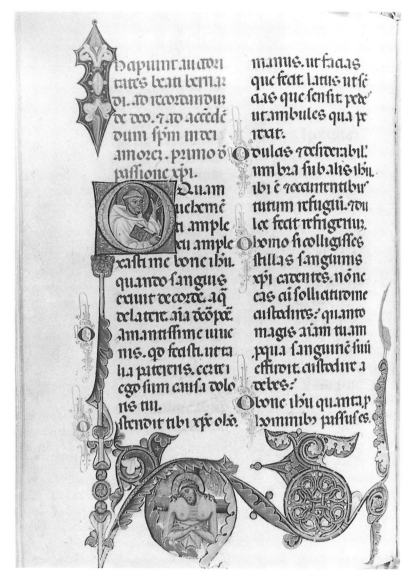

location links it to the Eucharist. Situated in the center of a predella, the Imago Pietatis is physically and symbolically connected to the sacrificial site of the altar. And it is precisely here, and also above the sacramental niche, that the gesture of an embrace was most frequently to be found. On a Venetian retable, such a figure is presented by John the Baptist as an image of the Sacrificial Lamb (fig. 39).[25]

Fig. 39
Boston, I.
Stewart
Gardner
Museum.
Venetian
retable,
15th c.

The passage from John, "This is the Lamb of God," is adjoined to the image on a bronze tablet (fig.40) serving as a pax that was made by Hans Multscher (ca. 1458–1460).[26] On a panel by Giambono (ca. 1432) in the Metropolitan Museum of Art in New York, the liturgical character of the half-length figure standing in the tomb is indicated by a richly embroidered corporal that serves as an altar cloth; the

Fig. 40
Cleveland,
Museum of
Art. Bronze
panel by Hans
Multscher

corporal signifies the equivalence between the sarcophagus and the eucharistic altar (fig. 41).[27] Finally, the embracing gesture is shown in miniatures from the articles of a Venetian brotherhood from ca. 1500; here the figure is placed in a chalice borne by two angels.[28] A lost picture by Sittow, which presumably depicted the Angel Pietà, is described in the inventory of Charles V as the "Holy Sacrament carried by two angels."[29]

With this we have come full circle, and it proves to be the case that Angela was only expressing a convention when she beheld the *corpus Domini* in the visible form of Christ descended from the cross. The physical presence of the sacrificed Christ in the consecrated Host upon the altar experienced more visibly in the image of the sacrificed Christ than in the aniconic, although physically present, sacramental "original," the Host itself. The allusion to the elevation of the Host in the relief of G. Pisano's pulpit lectern (fig. 31) and the allusion to the reception of the Host during Communion in the image on the Berlin altar (fig. 32) were only possible once the viewer was prepared to experience the reality of the Host in the image and the visibility of the image in the Host. The cult gave the stage directions, so to speak, for this way of perceiving the image and the Host. The elevation of the Host and its presentation to the communicants are projected back into Christ's Passion. Since the viewer of the image was also a witness to the "cultic gestures" that united liturgical and historical reality, he could find these gestures in the image. The artist was told to select such gestures from a common experience with which he was able to convey the reality of the image.

The doctrine of the real presence in the Sacrament, which suggests that the living Redeemer persists in Christ's slain and sacrificed

The Image and Its Public

Fig. 41
New York,
Metropolitan
Museum of
Art. Panel by
Giambono,
ca. 1435

body, explained the figure of the dead, yet active Christ, which otherwise made no sense at all. This is also true when an image does not portray the Sacrament as such (on the predella or on the tabernacle), but serves the functions of a devotional image or epitaph. The figure of the "God of Mercy," in which the Redeemer and Comforter held a dialogue with the viewer, relies on the same reality of Christ's presence in the Host. An example of this is the "Pietà

Fig. 42 Pisa. Tomb of Archbishop Scarlatti (died 1363)

with two angels"(fig. 42), as it is called in the contract, on the tomb of the Pisan archbishop Scarlatti (d. 1362),[30] as is also an epitaph in Bourges[31]—an Angel Pietà in a private funerary context (fig. 43). In the latter work, the presentation of Christ is significantly strengthened by the presence of the drawn-back curtain. The viewer, symbolized by the figure kneeling in prayer, experiences the Imago Pietatis as his own private vision.

The "presentation gesture," as we find it in the Bourges panel, introduces a new argument. It helps to understand subtle references to both cult objects (the Sacrament) and cult acts (the ritual of the Lamentation beneath the cross) (fig. 43). It is generally accepted that, from the thirteenth century onward, religious images began to "speak." They undertake to persuade the viewer, through their own proper means, of the presence of what they represent. The functional sphere in which these images developed their pictorial rhetoric is the domain of the ecclesiastical cult. Here an analogous change of representational acts and forms took place that gives evidence of the presence of a public with new expectations and demands. These included the much discussed "need to see,"[32] which has not yet been sufficiently elucidated sociologically. This need is also apparent from a new mediating activity of the cult, which increasingly tended toward the visual exhibition of the cult objects and theatrical presentations of what the cult was about. In short, the public at least wanted to see what it was supposed to believe, and in this way it could participate in the reality of the cult.

Before we draw conclusions from the aforementioned processes

The Image and Its Public

occurring within the cultic sphere, we shall give a sketch of them by means of three examples. We begin with the exhibition of the sacramental Host. During the early thirteenth century, the raising of the Host, by which the priest displays the transformed bread to the people, became a fixed element of every mass.[33] This display has the quality of a demonstra-

Fig. 43
Bourges, Musée Jacques Coeur. Epitaphios, late 15th c.

tion that the transformation has occurred, and the sense of a summons to worship the Eucharist. In passing, it might be noted that the elevation of the Host in the context of the paschal rites is documented at an earlier date; in those rites it symbolizes Christ's Resurrection from the dead.[34] While the Host had been presented to the faithful since the early thirteenth century, it was first exhibited, or as it is usually put, exposed, beginning in the early fourteenth century.[35] The *elevatio* occurred inside, while the *expositio* occurred outside the mass; the latter thus made the Sacrament available for private devotion. Between these two points in time there lies the early development of the cult of the feast of *Corpus Christi*, which presented the *corpus Domini* more as a relic than as consecrated bread and made it the focus of new cultic activities (for example, processions).[36] The feast existed in the bishopric of Liège beginning in 1264, but gained general acceptance in the Church as a whole only from 1317 onward, and in some Italian cities even later. This fact explains why some pictorial forms of sacramental symbolism appeared later in Italy than in the North. But the tendency to exhibit the Host is documented early in Italy as well. Accounts of bleeding Hosts excited the popular imagination, and visions furnished patterns for this imagination that served to fill the new cult with life.

Like the Host, the relic was also the object of a ritual exhibition that developed increasingly detailed means of achieving theatrical effect. Here it is difficult to arrive at precise dates. While the exhibition of relics is documented since Christian antiquity, its manner underwent historical change. In the late Middle Ages, fixed exhibition dates become mass gatherings of pilgrims. The exhibition sites were platforms in front of the church from which the relics are brought forth. The stage, the "*Heiltumsstuhl,*" and the exhibition ceremonies are documented as early as 1239, when the Constantinopolitan relics arrived in Paris.[37] The mass literature and mass graphic arts profited in the fifteenth century from this practice of exhibiting relics. As early as the late twelfth century, the image relic of the veronica (Vera Icon) was exhibited in St. Peter's in Rome on the balcony of its relic ciborium (fig. 6).[38] In Paris in the thirteenth century, French kings displayed a fragment of the True Cross to the populace, evidently from the open loggia in the upper floor of Ste. Chapelle.[39]

The form given to the reliquary is a further symptom for the new exhibition of the cult object. Beginning in the early thirteenth century, relic ostensories appeared having glass cylinders that made the relic visible. These had been preceded by the "talking reliquaries" that indicate the physical form of the relic (head, arm, and so on) by the shape of the container (fig. 44).[40] The ostensories, which are not only receptacles, but also showcases of their contents, fulfill the postulate that reality attains to full existence and is proven only in visibility. Why visibility suddenly became important as evidence for the existence of reality is a question that cannot be answered quickly.

Presenting becomes universally the gesture that both invites and proves: it is an invitation to look at what is presented, and it proves the reality of the presented object through the beholding of it. The act of exhibition makes use of the new reliquary form of the "display" container.[41] However, this new kind of reliquary is not just physically transparent, but is itself provided with a presentation gesture. When two bearing angels assume the role of exhibitor, such a reliquary displays its contents continuously. On twelfth-century reliquaries from the Meuse region, the angels bearing the relic of the True Cross are still within an iconographic context, inasmuch as they are part of the image's proper content.[42] Beginning in the thirteenth century, they become independent presenting figures. Two somewhat later examples may illustrate this. A Byzantine panel reliquary in the Louvre is displayed by two kneeling angels, and an ostensory in S. Domenico in Bologna is shown by two standing angels, so that the static relic is presented to the viewer in a perpetual act of exhibition (fig. 45).[43]

The Image and Its Public

The display of the relic with a gesture of presentation is a rhetorical element that we also find in the rhetoric of the images previously discussed. The two angels on G. Pisano's lectern display the Imago Pietatis in the same way as the analogous figures supporting an ostensory display the relic (fig. 31). This is also true of the angels of an altar frontal in Aquileia (ca. 1330), who hold a clipeus with the Imago Pietatis between them-

Fig. 44
New York,
Cloisters.
Reliquary

selves,[44] and of the image of the Angel Pietà in the *Très Belles Heure s de Notre Dame* of the Duc de Berry (fig. 34; see also p. 74).

The comparison of such images with reliquaries acquires additional importance for our argument when we recall that the relic ostensory preceded in time the eucharistic ostensory, with regard to the form of the container as well as the rituals of exhibition and procession. Against this background the relationship between relic and Eucharist is manifest. The understanding of the images profits from their comparison with the cultic utensils. Of course, the comparison does not lead to an equivalence, for the image is governed by different laws and must integrate the main figure and the supporting figures into a pictorial context. The aniconic relic does not require to the same extent the integration of its supporting figures with itself.

Nevertheless, the analogy existing between exhibitory reliquaries and exhibitory images is remarkable. One could speak of veritable *imagines monstrantes*. The gestures of invitation and presentation that the images make are more than simply internal changes of form for which we may give credit to the "progress" of art. They perform a communicative function by presenting an object of worship, so to speak, with exclamation marks. And they refer to a reality that could be experienced by everyone in the functional sphere of the cult. It is no accident that the main figures of religious images are also the titularies of the most important cults (those associated with feasts, rites, and so on). The frequently cited psychology of the devotional image relates back so strongly to the "staging" of the public cultic worship, that the private element, stimulative though it was for certain motifs, seems to operate secondarily.

One must be aware of the reciprocal relation between the reception of the cult and the reception of the cult image in order to be able to appreciate the psychological rhetoric that developed in the image. In fact, when seen from this viewpoint, the much studied problem of the structural changes in the devotional image appears in a new light. The demonstrative gesture is not so much the form taken by a private dialogue as it is a means of enacting the subject matter of the cult. By inviting the faithful to behold and to venerate, the gesture takes on the character of a summons.

This insight yields a new approach to understanding the Mother-and-Son group that in Italy was called the "Pietà," a name also used there for the Imago Pietatis (fig. 46).[45] "Pietà" is a key word of the songs of lamentations from the literature of the Passion and means not only the pity of the viewer for the dead Christ *and* his mother who weeps for him, but also the hoped-for pity of Christ and his mother for the viewer concerned about his own salvation. North of the Alps, the mystical contemplation of the Pietà found often used metaphors in which, for example, the dead body of Christ lying in the lap of his Mother was entreated to place itself in the "lap of the soul."[46] Here we would like, at least for the Italian examples, to propose a different, but complementary view. As is well known, the Pietà group consists of a figure bearing and a figure borne, of Mother and Son. Mary is, so to speak, the monstrance for the exhibition of the sacrificed Christ whom she displays, and with whose piteous appearance she awakens the pity of the viewer. Mary as the "throne of wisdom" is an old topos. With the child-sized figure of the body on her lap, which figure we shall discuss later, the connection with this topos is still maintained. But an early Italian example of the two-figure group with Christ's body shows that a different pictorial impulse was possible, for, significantly, it does not yet employ Mary, but has instead an angel as the figure supporting the "displayed" body of Christ (fig. 47). With its unbiblical association of corpse and angel, the early fourteenth-century Roman fresco in St. Paul Outside the Walls recalls the contemporary pulpit lectern in Berlin. Here as well, the subject matter of the cult (that is, the Sacrament) and cult practices (that is, rites) may have provided the

The Image and Its Public

Fig. 45
Bologna, San
Domenico.
Reliquary

reality to which the image refers.[47]

It is well known that the canonical group of the Mother with her dead Son in her lap, as an import from Northern Europe, gained acceptance in Italy only slowly.[48] Italian painting was, however, rich in other formulae in which the Mother displays her dead Son. On Simone Martini's Pisan retable and on R. Oderisio's panel with the *arma* (fig. 29), both of which we have already discussed, she appeals plaintively to the viewer and displays Christ in the form of the Imago Pietatis. In a Paduan grave fresco by Altichiero, she is depicted twice, once holding Christ out to the viewer in a way similar to the angel on the Berlin altar, and once displaying him to the viewer with an ample gesture.[49] An unforgettable Mother-and-Son group that formulates the idea of the Pietà in an original way was created by Jacopino di Francesco on a trecento retable in Bologna (fig. 48).[50] Here Mary embraces her Son, who is already lying in the sarcophagus, and appeals to the viewer to have pity on both Christ and herself. The words of the accompanying text: "Look and see, you who pass by, and ask yourselves, if there is any sorrow like my sorrow" (Lamentations 1:12), are to be understood as spoken by Mary (see Appendix B).[51]

Jacopino's composition brings us to a final aspect of the representation of reality and the reality of the representation. Here the role of the supporting figure is not limited to holding and exhibiting; rather, that figure presents the object of the sacrifice and lamentation in a declamatory pathos that at first seems unsuitable for cultic exhibition and for this reason may suggest a relevance to private petitionary prayer. Nevertheless, it is with this rhetoric that the image leads us back into the functional sphere of the cult. In one "variety" of the cult, we are literally given instructions about how to understand the means of communication used in the image. The lamentations of Mary or *planctus* at the foot of the cross, which had been composed originally as independent hymns, were introduced into the Good Friday liturgy no later than the early thirteenth century.[52] A thirteenth-century rubric from Toulouse explains that they were sung by two monks from a pulpit covered with cloths, as an antiphony between Christ and Mary, and that the cloths also offered protection from the crowd, which was usually moved to a state of great agitation by the songs.[53] Part of the staging of these hymns was the almost total darkness that betokened Christ's abandonment. Only a single candle still burned, symbolizing Mary, who alone remained true to her Son.

In a fourteenth-century rubric from Friaul, we encounter the Lamentation of Mary dramatized in the form of a play that took place before the crucified Christ after the liturgical adoration of the cross. Two actors in mourning-dress played the roles of Mary (*sub typus b. Virginis*) and John.[54] A fourteenth-century Planctus text from Cividale furnishes detailed stage directions on how the singing roles should be accompanied by stylized but dramatic gestures.[55] In the play, Christ was a sculpture. The living members of the cast, however, make use of gestures replicating the repertoire of the gestures appearing in the images. Thus Mary and John turn "to the people" and with "raised" or "outstretched arms" show them the crucified Christ "as the Sacrificial Lamb." There is significance in the dialogical relation between the parts assigned to Mary and John. They speak, sigh, and shed tears with one another as well as to the people and over Christ, and thereby correspond to the pictures in which they stand on either side of the Imago Pietatis or the crucified Christ. Equally important is the division of the strophes in speaking parts and their established accompaniment by certain gestures.

The Image and Its Public

Fig. 46
Paris, Luart
Collection.
Pietà by
Giovanni da
Milano

Further, Mary is given the same text from Lamentations that was joined to the images. When Mary then continues, saying, "Weep with me!" another actress has already prepared the audience by asking, "Who would not weep when he sees the Mother of Christ in such sorrow?"[56] Jacopino's retable in Bologna and Oderisio's panel impressively express the weeping in the image. In addition, Mary's gestures of helplessness and her wan complexion, which are topoi in pictures of the Crucifixion, are all mentioned in this or other texts.

Realism and Pictorial Rhetoric

Fig. 47 Rome,
Bibl. Vat.
Barb. Lat.
4406, fol. 133.
Fresco from
St. Paul out-
side the Walls,
early 14th c.

In vernacular texts, the Lamentation of Mary culminates with the plea, "Have pity on me!" (*Pietà vi prende*), which reminds us of the Italian name of the image of the Virgin with the dead body of Christ.[57] Finally, in the play of Cividale a further intensification is achieved when Mary points to the wound in Christ's side.[58] This is just what she does in Giovanni da Milano's picture of the Deposition in the Accademia of Florence, which is nothing else than a trecento version of the Pietà (fig.5).[59] The usual contrast between the rhetorical activity of the mourning figures and the mute passivity of the crucified Christ (Imago Pietatis), which distinguishes the Passion plays from the literary tradition of the dialogue between Christ and Mary, appears here also. The Imago Pietatis could remain unchanged for such a long time as a pictorial formula because it did not portray the actor, but the addressee of the actors. In Italian pictures of the Lamentation, the dramatic situation of the lamentation for the dead Christ continued for a long time to be a compositional model, and the living-dead "Man of Sorrows" of transalpine art did not alter this model until late.

We can now draw some conclusions from all these observations on cult ceremonies and the accompanying cult plays. The question we posed at the beginning of this chapter was directed to the reality depicted in the image and the communication of it to the viewer. With regard to this question, how significant is it that the devotional image recalls, in the mimicry and gestures of its lamenting figures, the performances of the Lamentation in the "sacred representations" (*sacre rappresentazioni*) of the cult plays? And what significance

Fig. 48
Bologna,
Pinacoteca
Nazionale.
Polyptych by
Jacopino da
Francesco, ca.
1360 (detail)

lies in the fact that in the trecento the Imago Pietatis was supplied
with a gesture that is a quotation from the sculpted groups of the
Deposition from the dugento? The cult plays and the life-sized
groups, which both deal with the events of the Passion, reveal a relationship that cannot be ignored any longer. Finally, what significance can be attached to the fact that our images contain formulae
of presentation that were drawn from such practices of cultic activity
as the elevation of the Host and the receiving of Communion and
embodied in reliquaries or sacred vessels (that is, in the supporting
figures of ostensories)?

Realism and Pictorial Rhetoric   89

Time and again, our attention is directed to the functional sphere of public cultic worship in which the conditions for experiencing religious reality were institutionalized. The reality here was that which the cult "represented." What this reality lacked in evidence was compensated for by faith. But the ritual activities, the relics, and the images, suggest this reality more powerfully, the more the reality was presented graphically and the more emotional stimuli were offered. The excitement of the audience was so great at the climaxes of the rite or play, that the actors had to protect themselves from it. An interaction between the audience's expectation and its fulfilling cultic experience was the force propelling this development. The increasing number of reports of visions from the thirteenth century onward is eloquent testimony of the desire to experience the reality offered in communal cultic worship in a more personal way. The demand for such reality grew at a rate that the cult was no longer able to satisfy.

With regard to the images, this insight leads to the conclusion that the argument for the origination of the devotional image in private contemplation was idealistically exaggerated. Further, the separation between the communal cult and personal piety, which appropriated "the great themes of theology and liturgy as personal experience,"[60] has placed much too great an emphasis on contrasts. The devotional image did not originate in the seclusion of the individual's own room, but rather presupposes a collective experience of reality: in its subject matter it presupposes the objective reality of what the cult was about, and in its forms it presupposes the subjective experience available in the staging of the cult. In the songs of lamentation and the cultic plays of Holy Week, frontiers of psychological realism were explored in a way hardly possible in other areas of medieval culture. And in the devotional images, a pictorial rhetoric was developed that served this psychological realism and prepared the way for a new role and use of images as such. Texts and images complemented and corroborated each other in articulating the experience of a newly and personally accessible reality.

Chapter V
The Icon of the Passion
in Byzantium

The Problem

The Imago Pietatis was an icon before it became a devotional image. It received its pictorial form from the icon, as an import from the East, as it were (cf. Chapter VI, Section "The Cross and the Descent from the Cross...").[1] We could be content with this observation, as long as it can be substantiated, and proceed immediately to the icon's legacy to the West. But then we would miss an entire phase in the history of the image, a phase in which the icon itself requires explanation. For it raises questions insofar as it is a rather recent creation in the long history of eastern panel painting,[2] serving semantic functions that had developed rather late in the history of Byzantine liturgy.

In order to make a proper assessment of our particular icon, it is necessary to free ourselves from a number of clichés. Neither the widespread opinion that time "stood still" both in icons and in the liturgy, nor the distinction between official liturgy and private piety will stand up under close examination.

In what follows we·shall be speaking of a portrait icon of the Passion in order to designate the *form* of depiction as the characteristic distinguishing our icon (fig. 49) from other images of the Passion, such as the image of the Crucifixion. The portrait, as we understand it here (see the Introduction, p.6), will prove to be a functional form that also serves to explain the emergence of the image. However, it is a question of a special kind of portrait. Our icon cannot be assigned to either of the two genres that eastern panel painting developed: it is neither a pure portrait icon, lacking any element of action, nor a scenic icon, in which the action is dominant. It combines the close-up of a bust image, such as the icon of the Pantokrator (fig. 51), which belongs to the first genre, with the nakedness and sunken head of a corpse, as these are found in the icon of the Crucifixion, which belongs to the other genre. Yet it differs from both of them. The Pantokrator icon, one of the oldest images made in the East, makes a simple statement by reproducing the appearance of God in a portrait of Christ as man, thus bearing witness to a central christological dogma. The Crucifixion icon cap-

Fig. 49
Kastoria.
Bilateral icon
of the Passion,
12th c.

tures the act of redemption as a historical event on Golgotha (fig. 4). The Passion portrait is not a timeless likeness of Christ, nor does it narrate an action. Certainly, the way the figure is posing does contain an element of action; however, this moment of action cannot be identified with any of the known stations of the cross. Since Christ is clearly not nailed to the cross, his upright position is not a reference

Fig. 50
Kastoria.
Bilateral icon
of the Passion,
12th c. (reverse
of fig. 49)

to a particular biographical situation, but rather calls for another explanation.

The icon about which these observations are made comes from Kastoria and dates from the twelfth century (fig. 49). It is thus one of the oldest panel paintings of the Passion portrait.[3] In the context of the present investigation, it is interesting that on the reverse side

Fig. 51 Nicosia,
Cyprus. Icon of
the Panto-
krator, 12th c.

of this icon there is an image of the Mother of God that also requires explanation (fig. 50). Oddly, the young Mother, who one would think would be pleased with her Child, has such an expression of suffering that one might want to call her the Mother of Sorrows, although the reason for her sorrow is not clear at first. In order to understand this apparent paradox, it is necessary to relate what is expressed by the figure of Mary to the image of her dead son on the front of the panel, about whom she appears to be thinking while she is still holding him as a child in her arms. An antithesis is thereby formulated that is, however, still not an explanation, but rather requires an explanation. The answer lies in the homilies and hymns especially composed for the liturgy of the Passion. This is where we find the Lamentations of Mary, those ritual songs containing the recollection of Christ's childhood as a fixed topos and employing the contrasts between long ago and now, between birth and death, happiness and sorrow, as a rhetorical device in order to intensify the lament's effect. We will return to these matters. The antithesis expressed by this two-sided icon is a characteristic feature of the ritual Lamentations of Mary, and it supplied the icon not only with a meaning, but also with a practical function, namely, subserving this lament and personifying it. If the Marian side of the icon must be explained liturgically, the same is true of the side with Christ. It, too, must have played a role in the liturgy. But what role?

Other Images of the Passion

Before we pursue this question further, the scope of the inquiry

Fig. 52 (left) Rome, Bibl. Vat. Mus. Sacro. Cover of a Byzantine staurotheke, 10th c.

Fig. 53 (right) Oxford, Magdalen College, Cod. 3, fol. 104v. Icon with the title "Apoka-thelosis" (deposition): drawing (after Velamans)

should be broadened to include other, analogous images that were employed in the Passion rites or at least can be interpreted within such a context. First, there are those images that reproduce histori-cal events of Good Friday, namely, the Crucifixion and the Deposition. At an early date, the cross and Crucifixion icon already appear as cult objects or feast images associated with the Passion rite.[4] The "notion of the cross as a quasi-scenic element of the Passion ceremonies," as Pallas has shown, is an old one.[5] Painted crosses with images have also recently come to light in the East.[6] In the Hagia Sophia in Constantinople, two crosses were venerated that will play a role for our arguments: a "golden Crucifixion," twice-life-sized and situated behind the altar; and, located in the area of the treasury (*skeuophulakion*), a cross "on which all the symbols of the Passion [that is, the *arma* τὰ σύμβολα τοῦ πάθους τοῦ κυρίου] are mounted."[7] Both crosses are documented from the tenth century onward. The latter cross, in addition to serving as a reliquary for the *arma*, itself functioned as a relic, since its size was said to replicate

Fig. 54 Nerezi,
Macedonia,
Church of the
Panteleimon.
The Lamen-
tation, 1164

the measurements taken of Christ's body in Jerusalem.

Naturally, the Crucifixion was at first part of the liturgical feast cycle and, as a *historia*, a narration, it illustrated an event of the Passion. However, from the tenth century onward, there was a Crucifixion icon in Constantinople attributed to Nicodemus that the Emperor John I Tzimiskes transferred from Berytos in 975.[8] The authenticity of the depicted scene, which was guaranteed by an eye-witness to the Crucifixion, conferred on the icon a cultic status, such as otherwise befitted only the relic and the veronica. Finally, the Crucifixion entered materially and symbolically into a relationship with reliquaries of the True Cross that heightened their reality. The cover of a *staurotheke* that was produced in Constantinople in the tenth century, evidently as a gift for the Church of Rome, and incorporated into the treasure of Sancta Sanctorum, shows a depiction of the Crucifixion that not only acquired a liturgical authority through its context, but also made use of liturgical texts in its account of the event (fig. 52). As R. Cormack has shown, the figure of Mary can be explained by means of a Good Friday sermon of Bishop George of Nicomedia in which the motif of the kissing of Christ's limbs is already developed.[9] The language in which the event is recounted in the sermon and the manner of experience in which it is brought to life strikes a "realistic" note that was then taken up by the artist. For his part, the painter composes and presents the scene in the mood of the liturgical texts. In addition to the Crucifixion, the Descent from the Cross, too, probably became at an early date the subject of a separate icon, and it is likely that as such it was introduced into the liturgy of the Passion. The monastery of the Lavra on Mount Athos had an icon of the Deposition (*imaginem Christi e cruce depositi*) donated by Emperor Nikephoros III Botaneiates (1078–1081) that is early evidence of the depiction of this subject on a separate panel.[10] Examples of such panels that have been preserved, such as an icon in Kala, Georgia,[11] and anoth-

Fig. 55
Belgrade, Muzej Srpske pravoslavne crkve. Aer-cloth from Fruska Gora, ca. 1300

er in the Stoclet collection in Brussels,[12] date from the twelfth and thirteenth centuries. Perhaps ivories of the tenth and eleventh centuries, as represented by the specimen of the Kestner Museum in Hannover, reflect the existence of still earlier images that were possibly designed as "group icons" showing several stations of the Passion.[13] Lastly, the title "Deposition" (*Apokathelosis*), which appears on several examples of our Christ of the Passion, points to an icon having this subject, the function of which was taken over by the portrait (fig. 53).[14]

The Entombment, as the third station representing the events of Good Friday, did not appear in works of art until the eleventh

The Icon of the Passion in Byzantium   97

century and was immediately recast into a scene of mourning for the dead Christ, that is, into a threnos, or lamentation, by Mary, even though the title "Entombment" (*Entaphiasmos*) survived (fig. 54).[15] This "new" scene of middle Byzantine painting apparently did not become an independent icon, or at least had little effect, for it is preserved only in the context of wall paintings and the minor arts. Thus, it is more important to consider its "career" in light of the liturgical texts that suggested the manner of its composition, that indeed brought about its emergence as an image at all. As H. Maguire was able to demonstrate, it was the aforementioned homily of George of Nicomedia, a ninth-century text, where poetic language was translated into the painted poetry of the Lamentation.[16]

The rhetorical antithesis of joy and sorrow that we know from the self-contradictory icon of Mary from Kastoria (p. 93), is given in embryonic form in the homily in the description of Mary kissing the wounds of the motionless corpse, the silent lips of the creator of speech, and the closed eyes of the maker of light. Addressing her son in the first person, she tells him that she is now embracing as a corpse him whom she once pressed to her breast as a child. The image also takes on the mood of the retelling of biblical events in liturgical texts. But I would like to proceed two steps further. The homily of which we are speaking became an established component of the monastic liturgy of Constantinople at the latest in the eleventh century, namely, as a reading in the "Office of the Passion" of Good Friday,[17] and this service was followed in the evening of the same day by an "Office of the Threnos," whose subject matter was the ritual Lamentation of Mary at the tomb of her son.[18] The emergence of the Threnos image, a product of the new rite, reflects a change in the liturgy and at the same time a change in the religious experience that was conveyed through the liturgy. Cult objects, too, that were declared to be original relics from the Passion, seem to have enkindled the religious imagination and in this way enriched the formulation of images. The anointment stone used in the anointing of the dead Christ, which in the twelfth century was put on display in the Pantokrator monastery in Constantinople, was not only an authentic adjunct of the biblical event, but also was understood as an iconic reliquary, since it was said to still show traces of Mary's tears that had fallen upon it.[19] We first hear of the relic subsequent to the development of the ritualized Lamentations of Mary, which provided the impulse for the origination of the Lamentation scene. The Lamentation did not acquire a liturgical function. As we shall see, it ceded that function to the Passion portrait, which, as a

The Image and Its Public

two-sided panel or diptych, would become the true feast icon of the Threnos.

In addition to the depictions of the Crucifixion, the Deposition, and the Lamentation, we at last find a representation of the dead Christ without a scenic context. In this quality it comes close to, and, indeed, stands in a causal relationship with the Passion portrait. This time, however, we are not concerned with a panel painting, but with an image on cloth. Its later name, *epitaphios*, causes misunderstanding.[20] The cloth or velum that covered the eucharistic bread and wine—the aer—was called the *Amnos aer*, or "cloth of the Lamb," when an image had been placed upon it (fig. 55). The thirteenth-century specimen in Belgrade, which we cite as an example, appears at first only to reproduce the historical shroud of Christ, but in point of fact it refers to the Eucharist, for the reclining figure of the dead Christ, like the Host on the paten, is covered with a liturgical velum (p. 124). A knowledge of liturgy is required to understand the image as the visual expression of a liturgical function. We shall return to this point later (p. 127).

The *Amnos aer* provides us with another independent portrayal of the Christ of the Passion, in addition to the Passion portrait. The former is a full-length image on cloth; the latter, a half-length panel painting. The first, as we know, was employed in the liturgy; through its functional form, the second will signal to us that it has a liturgical use. But we have not only two different images, but also two different liturgies in which the images could appear. One is the so-called Divine Liturgy or eucharistic celebration of the mass, the rites of which were set firmly in a symbolism drawn from the Passion. The other is the liturgy of the Passion between Holy Thursday and Holy Saturday, whose commemoration of the Christ's sacrifice was embedded in eucharistic symbolism. The constellation made up of two images calling for a liturgical explanation and of two liturgies able to supply such an explanation is our point of departure. I am greatly indebted to D. Pallas's *Die Passion und Bestattung Christi in Byzanz* (see Literature Cited in Abbreviated Form) and often refer to it, without, however, always sharing its conclusions. My argument, which seeks more to understand the functional than the theological features of the images under discussion, is intended to promote the study of images more as historical than as iconographic evidence.

Aspects of the Liturgy of the Passion

It was in the Passion rites and not the eucharistic celebration of the mass that the Passion portrait found its first use. I would like to enlarge upon this statement with a few general comments. A history of the Middle Byzantine liturgy is yet to be written. Since only a few editions of liturgical rules exist for this period,[21] chronological questions are still a ticklish matter. But the real problem lies elsewhere. It would be incorrect to speak of "the" liturgy. Within the framework of the rites of the Passion (and certainly elsewhere as well), the liturgy of the "Great Church" (that is, the Hagia Sophia) exhibits fundamental differences from that of the monasteries. It remained constant from the ninth century onward and adopted elements from Palestinian rules to a relatively large extent only in the thirteenth century.[22] Its conservative character allowed little room for liturgical innovations. In the monasteries, however, the situation was different. There the infiltration of numerous elements from the Palestinian rules occurred in waves and at an earlier date.[23] Beginning in the tenth and eleventh centuries, monasteries appear to have introduced a rapidly growing number of new texts, rites, and even entire offices. But once again a distinction is necessary. It would be incorrect to speak of "the" monastic liturgy, inasmuch as there were no generally binding rules for monasteries, not even in Constantinople. The Byzantine institution of "personal" monasteries owned by families prevented any uniform observance. Thus, we must distinguish between large monasteries on the scale of the Stoudios monastery and semiprivate family-owned monasteries, in which the variety and flexibility of liturgical practices—often laid down by the lay "founders" in the typika—were extremely great. This is especially true of the eleventh and twelfth centuries, which saw a boom in the founding of new monasteries by the aristocracy.[24] While these considerations prohibit us from generalizing what we know, it is still possible to draw certain conclusions, in agreement with D. Pallas.

Let us take as an example an eleventh-century typikon, a set of liturgical rules, for the monastery of the Mother of God the Benefactress (*Evergetis*). It begins the celebration of Good Friday with an early morning service, with which the participants "begin the Holy Passion."[25] In this office, which we can call the "Office of the Passion," the aforementioned homily of George of Nicomedia "on the Threnos of the Mother of God in this hour" was read aloud, as dictated by the typikon, dating from 1131, of the Greek monastery of the Savior in Messina.[26] In both monasteries, the homily was preceded by the singing of the Theotokia and the hymn (*kontakion*) of Romanos Melodos: "Come, let us praise the one who was crucified for us" (Τὸν δι᾽ ἡμᾶς σταυρωθέντα).[27] In the kontakion, Mary speaks to her Son both on the *via crucis* and while he is on the cross, calling him a lamb "led to sacrificial slaughter." Christ reproaches Mary for crying and thereby ignoring the necessity of the Passion.

In the Constantinopolitan monastery, the Good Friday hours were concluded with an office—it, too, newly instituted—as a compline (*apodeipnon*) that can be termed a service of rogation and consolation (*presbeia* or *akolouthia parakletike*).[28] It contained two choral pieces that are of interest: the troparion "Noble Joseph" (*Ho euschemon Ioseph*) and the "song of lamentation [*kanon threnodes*] of the Mother of God." The former contemplates the Deposition and the Entombment: "The noble Joseph took your holy body down from the wood and wrapped it in pure linen and fragrant herbs; then he attended to it and placed it in a new tomb."[29] The latter song is probably identical with the canon of Symeon Metaphrastes that is supposedly uttered by Mary (θέλων σου τὸ πλάσμα) and is concerned with the events occurring between the death on the cross and the Entombment. It contains the following passage, that is of interest for our subsequent discussion: "With the bowing of your divine neck you sleep, my Savior, on the cross the life-bringing sleep. The whole of creation is shaken to its foundation, and the heavenly hosts of angels tremble when they see your suffering in the flesh."[30] Thus, we find in the typikon of Constantinople two new offices containing mystagogical elements and psychological realism in rich profusion: the one commemorates what happened on the cross; the other, the subsequent Deposition, Lamentation, and Entombment.

The funerary theme reappears in a third Passion office that is identical with the early morning service of Holy Saturday.[31] The Holy Saturday rite already includes a solemn entry into the church that is interpreted as a procession to Christ's tomb by the repetition of the troparion "Noble Joseph" and the chanting of the *Trisagion*.[32] However, the fully developed ritual of the *Epitaphios Threnos* is still lacking. Apparently, this ritual was completely developed only in the fourteenth century.[33] In Hagia Sophia, it was only in the thirteenth century that the Holy Saturday rite became at all an important office in the reproduction of the Passion. We hear of it for the first time in a sermon by Patriarch Germanos II (1222–1240) that was delivered on this occasion.[34] Some decades later (ca. 1305), Patriarch Athanasios I (1289–1293 and 1303–1310) wrote a number of letters for the purpose of obtaining the adoption of the rite at court and among the people. He invites his correspondents "to venerate and to proclaim in the mother of churches the all-holy sacrifice" (τὴν παναγίαν σφαγήν) and the life-bringing entombment (τὸν ζωηρὸν ἐνταφιασμόν).[35] In another letter, he exhorts the emperor to be an example to his subjects and not only to participate

Fig. 56
Halberstadt, Cathedral treasury. Reliquary of St. Demetrios, Byzantine (detail) (after Wentzel)

"in the inconceivable and ecstatic [ceremony of the] entombment," but also to mourn the Passion of Christ with a "compassionate soul" and to "join in the song of lamentation of the Mother of God."[36] The expansion of the liturgy to include Holy Saturday morning had thus still not gained acceptance in Hagia Sophia at this time. The terms "sacrifice" and "entombment" in the first letter obviously refer to the protagonist and subject matter of the rite and not, as Pallas suggests, to icons, although the latter were certainly not absent. A sixteenth-century Slavic ritual, which was translated from a Greek source, mentions for the first time in connection with Hagia Sophia an icon that was set up on a lectern in the middle of the church on this occasion and received, as it were, the ritual lamentation of the congregation, recited in Mary's name.[37] The epitaphios cloth (*plastanica*), which this source also mentions, was held above the cleric carrying the gospel book during the entry into the church, before it was deposited, together with the book, on the altar at the end of the ceremony. While the funerary chant "Noble Joseph" was being intoned, the book was hidden from sight. In this realistically performed funeral procession, at the end of which the gospel book is covered with the burial linen, the last phase in the development of the final stage of the Passion offices is attained.

In the Slavic ritual the icon was called *Unynie Gospoda nashego*. In this appellation we may see, as did Pallas, a paraphrase of the Greek title *"Akra Tapeinosis,"* or "Deepest Humiliation" (that is, of God), taken from Isaiah 53:8, which the icon had received in the course of its history.[38] As early as 692, a general council had called for the portrayal of Christ's human form, with the instruction that the full magnitude of God's humiliation in the Incarnation and Passion should be made visible in the image.[39] The icon at first carried only the title "borrowed" from the Crucifixion: "King of Glory" (*Basileus tes doxes*).

The Image and Its Public

With its soteriological dimension, this designation of God and the Messiah as triumphing in the Passion invites us, certainly, to make fruitful interpretations of the icon. Nevertheless, it must not be understood as a title establishing meaning that was especially given to our image.[40] We shall return to the function of the icon in the liturgy.

This brief overview has distinguished among three offices in which icons could be employed: the morning "Office of the Passion" and the evening "Office of the Threnos" on Good Friday, followed by the early morning service on Holy Saturday, whose gradual development as a ritual entombment was the last of the three to be completed. In contrast, both of the Good Friday offices were already fully evolved in the eleventh century, but only in the monasteries, or rather, in certain monasteries. In the semiprivate institutions established for the material security and religious activity of the aristocracy, there developed a rich spectrum of new rites, and consequently it was in these monasteries that the demand for icons originated that could be employed in the new rites.

The Emergence and History of the Passion Portrait

The new rites of the Passion, which are recorded as early as the eleventh century, created new functions for icons. To state the matter succinctly: the cross and the Crucifixion icon alone could no longer satisfy the requirements of the new contents of the liturgy. Either a number of icons were needed, including those showing the Deposition and the Lamentation at the tomb, or else a new kind of icon whose content was so complex and form so plurisignate that it could function in several different offices. It is only the Passion portrait of Christ that fulfilled such requirements (fig. 49). The cross behind Christ in that portrait, just as later the tomb, is an addition that, through its significance, symbolically links the depicted figure to the events of Good Friday, without, however, narrating any single one of those events. To use a metaphor from the liturgy, in the Imago Pietatis Christ is sleeping. The metaphor of sleep, which is supposed to present sensibly the paradoxical simultaneity of human death and divine life in the one person of Christ, appears frequently in liturgical texts. We find it not only in the *Kanon Threnodes* of Good Friday (p. 101), but also in a homily on the Lamentations of Mary usually attributed to Symeon Metaphrastes,[41] as well as in a sermon of Patriarch Germanos II (1222–1240), in which the cross on which Christ sleeps is compared to the bed of Solomon, as the latter is described in the Song of Solomon 3:7.[42] In a 1281 treasury invento-

Fig. 57
Leningrad,
Public Library,
Cod. Gr. 105,
fol. 65v.
Gospel
manuscript
from
Karahissar
(Cyprus?), ca.
1180 (after
Willoughby)

ry from Dubrovnik, an icon is mentioned "in which Christ was [depicted] as sleeping" (in qua erat Christus, sicut dormivit).[43] The death-sleep of Christ is also the subject of a second type of icon. The metaphors of the *Physiologus* of the lion that sleeps with open eyes and of the lion cub born dead that is awakened to life after three days, are implied in the image of the reposing (*anapeson*) youthful figure of the waking Emmanuel that owes its name *Anapeson* to a liturgical text.[44]

In contrast to the *Anapeson*, the Passion portrait makes the death-sleep of Christ directly perceivable, instead of referring to it allegorically. Since it is not tied to a definite situation, it fulfills the function of serving simultaneously the requirements of several different offices of the Passion. Further, the image is just as undetermined spatially and temporally as are the ritual Lamentations of Mary. It is thus especially well suited to be the addressee of her lamentations, and its expansion into a double image through the addition of an icon of Mary makes it a pictorial embodiment of the *Staurotheotokia*, in which the two protagonists of the Passion drama were left alone with one another in an analogous fashion.[45] The partnership of Mother and Son in the double image symbolized the dialogue of the liturgical community with its dead hero.

If the combining of the two icons in a double image is as important as I believe it is, then it provides us with an explanation for the choice of the portrait form for depicting the dead Christ. For as a half-length portrait, Christ is, in the formal sense, the counterpart of the portrait of Mary, and in the double portrait the partnership of

The Image and Its Public

the pair is expressed pictorially (fig. 50). A functional form emerged that differs from the narrative scene of the Threnos not in content, but in the pictorial language employed (fig. 54). Christ offers himself as the recipient of a liturgical lament that was no longer part of a biblical situation, but instead took place in the present and within a Byzantine church. The close-up view of Christ's person simulates contemplation as an act performed by the viewer. Here we have the psychological dimension that the

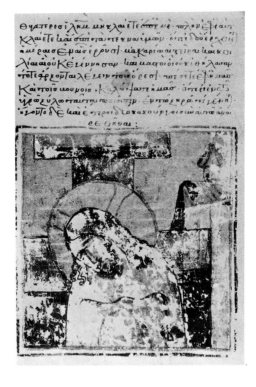

Fig. 58
As fig. 57.
Cod. Gr. 57,
fol. 167v.

portrait possesses, according to our definition of it (p. 6). The icon was an invention that competed with the narrative scene of the Threnos and served another function.

The portrait of the dead Christ no doubt benefited from still other experiences. I am thinking of the "original" of Christ's shroud. Shortly before 1204, it was displayed every Friday in the Blachernai church in Constantinople and, so we are told, raised itself up of its own accord so that one was given a good view of "le figure [de] Nostre Seigneur."[46] It surely was one of the "burial cloths" (*epitaphioi sindones*) that Nicholas Mesarites, as custodian of the palace relics, had inventoried, also shortly before 1204.[47] It was probably identical with the "Shroud of Turin," traceable in the West beginning in 1353, which contains two impressions of a human corpse in a burial pose.[48] The existence of the "authentic" features of the dead Christ justified the introduction into religious art of a corresponding portrait icon. Although the relic of the shroud was not, as Pallas believes, the prototype of the panel painting, it may have prepared the way for the latter. Only later did it perhaps transmit the crossed hands of the burial pose to the Passion portrait. An

Fig. 59
Meteora,
Monastery of
the Transfi-
guration.
Diptych, late
14th c.

example of this is the small mosaic icon (ca. 1300) that made its way in the fourteenth century to S. Croce in Gerusalemme in Rome (fig. 14). This icon reproduces the position of the hands of the figure on the shroud, but does not do so in a literal sense.[49]

The death portrait was a rarity in icon painting and, as it contradicted the nature of the icon, was always tied to special conditions. A parallel to the death portrait can be found in some reliquaries of St. Demetrios, a specimen of which was carried off from Constantinople to Halberstadt in 1204 is reproduced here (fig. 56).[50] It

Fig. 60
Meteora,
Monastery
of the Transfi-
guration.
Diptych, late
14th c.(other
half of the dip-
tych in fig. 59)

attests to the existence of an analogous icon in the church in
Thessaloniki where the saint is venerated. The icon seems to have
been kept in the ciborium above the tomb. The crossing of the arms
on the chest recurs in a variant of the Passion portrait of Christ that
is now in Moscow.[51]

Notwithstanding possible references to other images, the
Passion portrait is to be understood above all as the visible expression of a ritual function. The existence of this function must be
proven, however. It is documented for the first time in a gospel

The Icon of the Passion in Byzantium   107

Fig. 61 Pec, Macedonia, Church of St. Demetrios. Fresco of Demetrios in prison, early 14th c.

manuscript that was once in Karahissar and is now in Leningrad, which has recently been dated to the 1180s (figs. 57, 58).[52] Within the framework of a cycle of illustrations of the New Testament, two miniatures replace a narrative scene, the Crucifixion, with the reproduction of an icon of a half-length figure, the Passion portrait. Therefore, the icon that they reproduce was so widely known at this time that allusion could be made to it. Further, it had the same significance as the Crucifixion whose place it appropriated. It could be substituted for the Crucifixion because it had already been introduced at this time into the Good Friday liturgy in place of the latter. In the manuscript, two reading selections from that liturgy, Matthew 27:35ff. and Luke 23:33, appear beside the icon. The clumsy addition of the tomb as a domed structure in the second miniature bespeaks an experimental stage in the functional adaptation of this icon, whose allusion to the Entombment is not really successful (fig. 58). The addition of the tomb confirms that the cross is also an addition. The latter, like the half-length portrait and the lowered head, refers back to the Crucifixion, the liturgical function of which was assumed by our icon.

Further evidence for the function of the icon is furnished by a Cypriot panel of St. Paraskeve, whose personality developed from a personification of Good Friday. On this fourteenth-century panel, the saint carries the Passion portrait in her hands as an icon of the

108   *The Image and Its Public*

feast.[53] The title *Deposition*[54] (*Apokathelosis*), which the icon at times adopted, only makes sense if it was supposed to refer the viewer to a rite having this subject matter, or to its equivalence with a painting of the Deposition, which again directs us to Good Friday.

A late fourteenth-century diptych in the Monastery of the Transfiguration, in Meteora, Greece, offers a further indication in this context (figs. 59, 60). On the verso sides of the two panels showing the dead Christ and the lamenting Mary, the following instructions were written in an eighteenth-century script: "On the Holy and Great Saturday, this old founder's icon [εἰκών...κτητορικὴ καὶ ἀρχαία] of Christ [or of Mary] is to be stood on the *epitaphios* together with the icon of the Mother of God [or of Christ]."[55] The text could be repeating the instructions of the monastery's founder, probably Joseph Uros Palaeologos, and if so, it dates back to before 1381. Like the sculpture laid in the tomb in the West, the icon on the shroud made visible the presence of Christ in the tomb. The connection to the Holy Saturday rite corresponds to a late phase of the liturgy. Nevertheless, our question is answered. The function of the Passion portrait in the Passion liturgy of Holy Week has been demonstrated, and we may turn our attention to other questions.

The Meteora diptych does not place the paired Christ and Mary on the front and back of a single panel, but on a double panel. This arrangement appears to have been characteristic of privately owned small-sized icons, among which the Meteora example belongs by virtue of its size (ca. 28 x 24 cm). The two mosaic icons in S. Croce in Rome (19 x 13 cm) and in the Tatarna monastery (fig. 73; 17.5 x

Fig. 62
Moscow, Tretjakov Gallery. Half of a diptych, 13th c.

Fig. 63
Moscow,
Tretjakov
Gallery. The
Vladimir
Madonna,
Byzantine ca.
1100 (after
Onasch)

12 cm) may have originally been diptychs as well, and in fact, in fifteenth-century parchment copies, the Roman icon is supplemented with an image of Mary to make a diptych.[56] The small, early thirteenth-century diptych with the pectoral cross that belonged to the Georgian Queen Tamar (1184–1213) and is in Tiflis, was also an object of private piety.[57] But it makes different use of the diptych form by connecting the Passion portrait with Mary and John to make a paraphrase of the Crucifixion. The private use of the Passion portrait, this time as a single panel, is illustrated by a fourteenth-century fresco in Pec, in Macedonia (1337–1345). Saint Demetrios, shown here in prison, receives consolation from a small panel with our image hanging on the wall, which evidently was a personal possession of the prisoner (fig. 61).[58] Another private use is recorded for the burial of Byzantines, in which the icon of the dead Christ was laid on the breast of the deceased.[59]

One must not make such a rigid distinction between the liturgical and private use of icons as is customary. In any case, the semiprivate monasteries owned by the aristocracy, which clearly transmitted many impulses to the liturgy, permit no strict differentiation, and for its own part, private usage profited from a liturgical practice to which it had previously given impetus. The subject matter of private piety, too, was influenced by the liturgy. What had become established in the liturgy could in turn modify private piety. The founder's diptych at Meteora permits no unequivocal distinction

Fig. 64 Nerezi,
Macedonia,
Church of the
Panteleimon.
The Lamen-
tation, 1164
(detail)

between liturgical and private use in the family monastery. We must
see both in a relationship of interchange.

The Meteora diptych, however, contains still more information.
Not only does it place Mary at Christ's side; it also alters her appearance. Instead of the self-contained Mother-Child group, a lamenting
figure appears that we, drawing upon an eleventh-century poem by
John Mauropous, could call the "Mother of the Passion."[60] Although
she was invented for the diptych, the lamenting figure is reminiscent
of that Mary who stands under the cross. In the pair of figures that
thus originates, the members are spatially and psychologically related to each other like a pair of actors on the stage of the Passion rite.

In order to see the invention of the "lamenting woman" in con-

text, an excursus into the history of the image of Mary within the framework of the Passion themes is required. The "lamenting woman" of the Meteora diptych is anticipated by one of the halves of a thirteenth-century diptych that today is in Moscow (fig. 62).[61] Both figures of Mary are in almost literal agreement with each other, with the exception of the earlier figure's gaze, which is directed to the viewer, thus causing a rhetorical interlinking of the gaze and the figure's gesture toward Christ, and thereby establishing a link between Christ and the viewer. Perhaps the first mention of the "lamenting woman" is to be found in John Mauropous's poem about a "weeping Mother of God." A similar grieving figure was introduced into the Lamentation scene. The iconic "lamenting woman" was a functional pictorial form in that, as an independent figure, she offered the congregation an intensified identification through emotional empathy.

The creation of the "lamenting woman" may be compared to that of the Virgin *Eleousa*, already documented in the eleventh cen-

Fig. 66
Lagoudera,
Cyprus,
Monastery
church, south
wall. Madonna of
the Passion, 1191

tury, whose "original" was kept in the church of the same name built by Emperor John II Comnenus (1118–1143).⁶² The most famous example of it is the so-called *Vladimir Madonna*, a twelfth-century image from Byzantium famous because of the intimate contact between the faces of Mother and Child (fig. 63).⁶³ This poetic motif received its literary formulation not in the texts of the Christmas liturgy, but in those of the Passion liturgy. A well-known example of this is a homily of Symeon Metaphrastes in which the Lamentations of Mary are intensified by tender recollections: "Then I dipped my lips into your honey-sweet and dew-fresh lips. Often as a child you slept on my breast, and now you lie in my arms as a corpse."⁶⁴ Here we approach as closely as is possible to the language of the image. Furthermore, in the icon the lyrical motif also retains its function of referring to the Passion. Mary's elegiac gaze into the distance attests to that, and it is no accident that a sacramental interpretation of the

The Icon of the Passion in Byzantium   113

Fig. 67
Lagoudera,
Cyprus,
Monastery
church, north
wall. Symeon
and John the
Baptist

sacrifice on the cross is painted on the reverse of the image.

The scene of the Threnos and the figure of the Eleousa, which both show Mary cheek-to-cheek with Christ, have related meanings and use a similar language, but stress different things (fig. 64). The Threnos scene, like the literary text, employs anamnesis, in that Mary recalls the time of her happiness as a mother. The Eleousa employs prolepsis, in that Mary anticipates the time of her maternal sorrow that Simeon had prophesied during the Presentation of Christ in the Temple. The protohumanistic ethos, as Pallas explains, lies in the insight Mary finally gains, that mankind's salvation necessarily presupposes the Passion.[65] The soteriological argument was also supposed to make an impression on the viewer, who was offered in Mary a model for spiritual catharsis and inner training in reasonableness.

The liturgical image expands the dimension of visible reality by communicating a theological argument and supplementing it with an ethical statement. Like the images discussed previously, the Eleousa is both an instrument and an object of mystagogical contemplation. The "new interest in pathos and human feelings,"[66] which has been observed in the art of the twelfth century, had deeper roots. A growing lay public appears to have developed a new need for religious and affective activity that changed art. And the semiprivate liturgy of the small personally owned monasteries contributed to many clichés in which the educated Byzantine could express himself.

The Eleousa, however, was no more the first icon of Mary with

The Image and Its Public

Fig. 68
Moscow,
Tretjakov
Gallery.
Mandylion
from
Novgorod,
12th c.: reverse
side (after
Onasch)

Passion symbolism than the "lamenting woman" was. The famous *Hodegetria* icon in the Hodegon monastery, allegedly an "original" image painted by St. Luke, had perhaps been reinterpreted even earlier when it was made into a two-sided icon through an image on its reverse side of an event from the Passion, possibly the Crucifixion.[67] In a replica in the Sinai monastery, which I would like to attribute to the Constantinopolitan artist Manuel Eugenikos and date to the 1380s, the Hodegetria is part of a diptych, whose other half depicts the Deposition.[68] Early Italian diptychs also attest to the supplementing of the Hodegetria with subject matter from the Passion. In the miniature of a twelfth century Octoechos manuscript in Messina, the Hodegetria is physically and symbolically connected with the cross and the tomb of Christ (note the caption *taphos*) to make a theological synopsis (fig. 65).[69]

In this connection it must be recalled that Symeon

Fig. 69
Moscow,
Tretjakov
Gallery.
Mandylion
from
Novgorod,
12th c.: front
side

Metaphrastes, author of ritual songs of lamentation, resided and did his work in the Hodegon monastery and thus may have taken part in stimulating the reinterpretation of the icon.[70] But the Hodegetria, as a pictorial relic, could not be altered, even though its semantic and liturgical function changed. Only its successors were changed. The Hodegetria from Kastoria, which, together with a Passion portrait of Christ, forms a two-sided panel, expresses grief though its mimicry, and two angels are ready to receive the Sacrificial Lamb from her arms (fig. 50).

The icon of Mary from Kastoria employs an artistic, or rather, a psychological syntax in order to express in a pictorial formula the Mysteries of the Incarnation and Christ's sacrificial death. The Octoechos miniature uses symbolic, or rather, ideographic means in order to make this statement. The famous Passion Madonna of the *Amolyntos* (Unblemished) type proceeds in yet another way, combin-

116   *The Image and Its Public*

Fig. 70
Jerusalem,
Greek
Patriarchate.
Gold frame of
an icon,
Constanti-
nople, 12th c.

ing psychological and ideographic means. One of its early examples
is the fresco, painted in 1192, of the titular icon of the Arakos
monastery near Lagoudera in Cyprus (fig. 66).[71] The name caption-
ing the image, Mary of the Annunciation (*Kecharitomene*), which
should be understood here symbolically, refers back, along with the
icon's form, to the titular icon of the monastery of the same name
in Constantinople, founded by Emperor Alexios I Comnenus
(1081–1118).[72] The image is as complex as an entire sermon, but its
theological arguments end in a presentation of a human ethos that
accepts and transcends predetermined human destiny. Mary's
thoughtful look and the didactic gesture of the Child attest to this.

The Icon of the Passion in Byzantium   117

Fig. 71 (left)
Novgorod,
Museum.
Steatite icon
from
Novgorod,
12th c. (after
Bank)

Fig. 72 (right)
Sinai,
Monastery of
St. Catherine.
Crusader icon,
13th c. (Michi-
gan–Princeton
–Alexandria
Expedition to
Mt. Sinai)

Having this quality, the image was well suited to serve as intercessor for the living and the dead in the donor's family (note the inscriptions).

The interplay of realistic, allegorical, and symbolic statements in the image may be illustrated with four examples that can also document the liturgical and soteriological components of the Passion theme. Mary's arm position resembles a liturgical spoon (*labis*) on which the Sacrificial Lamb reposes; thus the image employs a metaphor documented in this context by literary sources (Pseudo-Methodios).[73] The reclining pose of the young Emmanuel *anapeson*, who is asleep and at the same time awake (p. 104), anticipates and symbolizes Christ's sleep of death in the tomb.[74] By indicating another plane of reality and time, his pose is a perfect example of the prolepsis of the Passion. The same level of meaning is made explicit by the image's spatial relation to two figures on the opposite wall: John the Baptist with the proclamation of the Lamb of God (note the scroll), and Simeon holding in his arms the Lamb of God, of whom John is speaking (fig. 67). Like John, Simeon is a prophet of the Passion, which he foresees while announcing it to Mary. A last motif in this image of Mary makes patent the hitherto encoded pictorial semantics. Two angels present to the Child, who is still resting in Mary's arms, the implements of the Passion. We find the two angels with *arma* analogously depicted on an adoration of the "cross with the symbols of the Passion" (p. 118) that forms the reverse of a

Mandylion icon (portrait of Christ) from Novgorod (fig. 68).[75] The Mother -Child group and the cross became, so to speak, interchangeable: the one emphasizes the Sacrificial Lamb; the other, the sacrificial altar, to use the language of the liturgy.

Selecting from the repertoire of related pictorial formulae what best corresponded to the intentions in a given case was a question of preference. From this we can conclude that the educated Byzantine responded to the cross references between different images, which, for their part, reflected the analogies among various texts and rites. Thus we gain insight into a creative phase of Comnenian icon painting of the twelfth century, a period from which little has survived. A complex pictorial structure that is simply saturated with theological and panegyrical motifs makes accessible to us the behavior of the viewer in responding to images such as the Eleousa, the "mournful Hodegetria," and the Passion portrait of Christ, which, though they have become nearly impenetrable for us, were explicit enough for contemporary viewers (fig. 50). In this pictorial structure, the themes of the Passion have only an apparent dominance. In reality, they are as much linked to the themes of the Incarnation and the symbolism of the Eucharist as they were in the liturgy. The analogy between them, and simultaneity of events and of persons, which were separated in time and space, only for a chronicler, became just as important here as in the liturgy. Thus the images reflect a reality which otherwise could also be found only in the liturgy. They require from the viewer an attitude and an interpretive ability that could only be developed through liturgical practice.

The Novgorod icon with the Mandylion of Christ (fig. 69), of

Fig. 73
Tripotamon, Greece (Tatarna), Monastery. Mosaic icon, ca. 1300

which we have so far spoken only of the reverse side, is one of many icon forms that served for the Passion liturgy. As its style indicates, it reproduces a Byzantine model of the early twelfth century. The "true face" of Christ, whose "original" was kept in the palace chapel,[76] was considered factual proof of the reality of Christ's human life and therefore possessed semantic analogies to the Mother-Child group. Further, this icon reproduces two pictorial relics, namely the "true face" and the *Arma* cross replicating the measurements of Christ's body (p. 95). Consequently, it was well suited to be a Good Friday feast icon. But as such, its type met with little success. Perhaps this was a result of the conflict over the canon of the Feast of the Mandylion, which was abandoned soon after 1100 as a response to heretical doctrines.[77]

In the framework of the Passion liturgy, only the Passion portrait seems to have been victorious in the competition with other icons. Up to the early thirteenth century, however, it was clearly only one of many others that were either lost or changed to such an extent that the early history of their function can hardly be recognized any longer. Two-sided icons in particular were eminently suited for use in the liturgy and its processions. Their two sides joined together two concepts or two persons that played a role in the liturgy (figs. 49, 50). We have seen this in the example of Christ and Mary, the two protagonists of the ritual Lamentations of Mary on Good Friday. The pillaging in 1204 of most of the cult images and relics that were Constantinople's pride changed the history of icon painting. In the years following 1204, icon painting was not only reduced quantitatively to a smaller repertoire of themes and forms, but was also restricted qualitatively in its creative vigor. Its proverbial immobility is characteristic only of its history in late Byzantium.

In summary, it must be emphasized once again that it was the liturgy of the Passion in which the Passion portrait of Christ, as a counterpart to an icon of Mary, acquired its first function. It may have made its debut early in the repertoire of relevant icons of the Passion. Anna Comnena's (1083–ca.1148) icon of Christ the "bridegroom" (*nymphios*) and judge, who "sleeps the sweet sleep," was perhaps an early example of it.[78] But perhaps the princess was describing a sleeping boy of the *anapeson* type who could be interpreted in a similar manner (p. 104). We can, however, adduce pictorial evidence to prove the age of our image. The two-sided icon from Kastoria (figs. 49, 50) is a specimen of our icon just as much as the miniatures of the Karahissar evangeliary (both twelfth century). But the most important extant twelfth-century specimen has not yet been mentioned.

The Image and Its Public

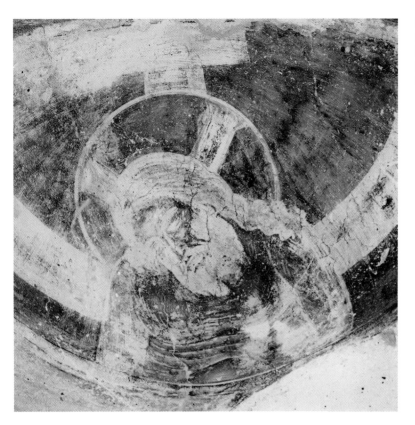

Fig. 74
Gradac,
Serbia. Left
side choir,
ca. 1271

It is a small icon that came to the Church of the Holy Sepulcher in Jerusalem only in the eighteenth century (fig. 70).[79] Its gold frame covers everything except the painted figure of Christ. We must analyze this icon carefully because it was long considered a work that originated in Jerusalem and more recently a fourteenth-century Georgian product. In reality, it is one of the rare masterpieces of the goldsmith's art from twelfth-century Constantinople. In its splendor and style, it can be compared only with the famous Nikopoia icon of Mary in San Marco in Venice, which, according to tradition, was plundered from the carriage of the Byzantine general before the walls of Constantinople in 1204.[80] The painted Christ figure in the Jerusalem icon, which was painted over in the eighteenth century in a way that distorted its meaning, must be imagined in the style of the obviously contemporary painted figure of Mary in San Marco. Unfortunately, the outer frame of the Jerusalem icon is a later addition and therefore of no use to our interpretation. Yet

Fig. 75
Leningrad,
Hermitage.
Byzantine
enamel, 12th
c. (detail)

enough remains to give us an idea of the appearance of the Passion portrait, the outlines of which remain visible. Here we receive an impression of one of the most costly specimens of our icon ever produced, which a private patron, apparently a member of the court, had commissioned. Like the inscription from the cross and the lamenting angels, the close-up view of the figure, conceived of as a shoulder bust, identifies the icon as an early version of the image that refers explicitly only to the Crucifixion and not yet to the Entombment.

Another early specimen is the small stone icon recently excavated in Novgorod (fig. 71). As A. Bank demonstrates, it too dates from the twelfth century, and it furnishes evidence for the transferal of our image-type to small works of art, on which the image could serve as an amulet.[81] A small icon made in the middle third of the thirteenth century, and belonging to the Sinai monastery, is stylistically related to Crusader art and thus directs attention to a milieu that surely played a great role for the reception of the Passion portrait in the West (fig. 72). Like most specimens of our type, it bears the Greek version of the inscription on the cross, *Basileus tes doxes*.[82]

The highest artistic rank among extant panels is held by two small mosaic icons dating from around 1300. One, which became known only in 1964, is in the Monastery of the Birth of Mary in Tatarna (now Tripotamon) in Aeolia(fig. 73).[83] The other was brought to S. Croce in Gerusalemme in Rome, apparently in the 1380s; there it was proclaimed the prototype of the Imago Pietatis

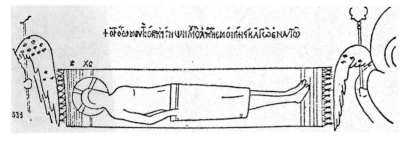

Fig. 76
Samari,
Greece. Apse
fresco, 12th c.
(detail)

(fig. 74).[84] Both are privately commissioned pieces par excellence, for the technically complicated miniature mosaic, costly in more than one regard, was produced only for a small, aristocratic clientele. In the descending lines of the figure's powerful but limp body, the icon in Tatarna expresses the heroic pathos of Hellenistic tradition. The drama of the *agon* undergone in dying is echoed in the powerful movement of the body's forms that recall classical images of gladiators. In contrast, the Roman icon is rigorously constructed in horizontal zones. The line of the arms is repeated in the muscles of the chest and the contour of the shoulders. The body serves as a pedestal for the sensitive head with its relaxed features. The crossbar of the crucifix, which is lacking in the other image, contributes to stabilizing the image just as much as the outline of the body, which parallels the frame. While the one panel still implies the death agony that Christ has gone through, the other relegates the dead Christ to the stillness of the grave. The distinctions are not only justified artistically; they also present variants of meaning in which a functional change is expressed. Without a definable biographical situation being established, the emphasis shifts from the death on the cross to Christ's repose in the tomb. Indeed, the Roman icon shows the burial pose with arms laid one atop the other and the hands crossed, the pose which almost became the norm for the later history of the portrait icon in the East. The sarcophagus, too, was now accepted as a pictorial motif.

In this second phase of the history of our image, which has not yet been treated, the portrait icon was introduced into wall painting. The transferal into another medium also meant a transference of the image into another functional sphere: the image now entered the sphere of influence of the "Divine Liturgy" and consequently became the vehicle of eucharistic symbolism. This process took place only gradually, however. As late as 1271, the image, as a fresco in the apse of the diakonikon of the Serbian church in Gradac (fig. 74), is the counterpart to an image of the lamenting Mary that is located in an analogous position in the prothesis chamber.[85] At this time, however, the portrait icon began a new "career," in which it took over the task of making the Sacrificial Lamb graphically present, principally in the prothesis, where the preliminary oblation of the sacrificial bread took place. There is no need to pursue further this second phase in the history of our image, as it has already been examined thoroughly by G. Millet, S. Dufrenne, and others.[86]

The Cloth-Borne Image of the Epitaphios

The history of the cloth-borne image, of which we have already spoken, also proceeded in two phases, but in the opposite direction: the velum bearing the image functioned first in the eucharistic liturgy and was transferred into the Passion liturgy only in the late Byzantine period. I would like to sketch briefly this process, which can now be accurately reconstructed for the first time. It is no longer necessary to puzzle over the liturgical use of this cloth, which was embroidered with the full-length image of the dead Christ.[87] In the "Divine Liturgy" it covered the bread and wine, especially during their preliminary oblation and their subsequent transfer to the high altar, the so-called Great Entrance.[88] The images confirm the liturgical function of the cloth. Since textiles are a fragile material, reproductions of the image in other media have been better preserved than the cloths themselves, especially in the case of earlier examples.

A Byzantine enamel in Leningrad and a fresco in the Greek church of Samari in Messenia attest to the existence of the cloth-borne image as early as the twelfth century (figs. 75, 76).[89] The enamel shows the dead Christ on a shroud that is flanked by two angels carrying liturgical fans (*rhipidia*). The composition distinguishes this image from the narrative Lamentation scenes and anticipates the pictorial formula of the embroidered cloths. The accompanying inscription: "Christ is presented here as an offering and also participates in the godhead" (ΧΡ πρόκειται καὶ μετέζεται θεῷ), expresses a eucharistic point of view. The fresco in Samari is similarly composed, but offers additional information. The inscription: "He who eats my flesh and drinks my blood..." (John 6:56), confirms the image's sacramental significance. The location of the image in the central apse, beneath an enthroned Madonna, underscores this pictorial meaning.

At the same place within the church program, in the central apse, we find another theme that appears in the same period and is first documented in Kurbinovo (1192). This is the *Melismos*, which we must discuss briefly, as its meaning is related to that of the cloth-

Fig. 77 Serbia, Markov Monastery. North side apse, 14th c.

borne image.[90] The name refers to the division of the Host in Communion, but the image depicts the liturgical sacrifice and dares to render the transformation of the bread into the body of Christ by means of a naked child. A kind of "x-ray photograph" makes the bread transparent so that what it is changed into is visible. The coincidence in time of the appearance of the Melismos and that of the cloth-borne image in the late twelfth century calls for a historical

The Icon of the Passion in Byzantium 125

explanation, which, however, has not yet been found. It hardly needs to be explained that both depictions present visually the liturgical sacrifice, each in a different way. The Byzantines, too, understood this. In the prothesis fresco of the Markov Monastery (1375), both are even united into a single image through the substitution of the dead Christ for the child without altering the composition of the Melismos (fig. 77).[91]

Despite their closely related meanings, the Melismos and the cloth-borne image were functionally different. The Melismos is a description of the performance of the sacrifice, while the cloth-borne image is a likeness of the Sacrificial Lamb lying in the grave. This latter subject is explained by the fact that the liturgical velum was understood as the shroud of Christ. But this symbolism was already old, and it does not explain why it was not presented visually until that time. As for the function of the cloth-borne image, it is understandable only from the function and symbolism of the cloth.

We must now go a step further and not only distinguish between the indirect and the still extant evidence of the textiles, but distinguish as well between two types of cloth-borne images having the same content and function. The one type is documented by the two twelfth century works that we have mentioned. We encounter it again in an only slightly expanded version on the now lost Andronikos Aer of Ohrid (ca. 1295), which, according to the inscription, the Emperor Andronikos II (1282–1328) donated to Ohrid in order "to be commemorated in the liturgy of the Shepherd of the Bulgarian"(fig. 78).[92] The inclusion of the four symbols of the Gospels, the chanters of the Trisagion, and an altar on which the aer along with the figure of Christ appears to be placed, indicates that the composition is not a creation of the Palaiologan period. Rather, its basic features, as shown by the two other examples, were fully developed in the twelfth century.

The second type of the cloth-borne image survives in only a single specimen (fig. 55). It is now in Belgrade, and according to the inscription, it was commissioned by King Uros II Milutin (1282–1321), at about the same time as the aer of Andronikos II.[93] The main difference from the first type lies in the frontal depiction of Christ, which alludes to the Shroud of Turin, understood to be the original of the image.[94] It deviates from that image relic only in that the body of Christ is covered with a liturgical velum. The depiction is thereby changed from a mere reproduction of the historical original to a symbolic image of the Sacrificial Lamb of the liturgy. Like the angels with *rhipidia* on the *Andronikos Aer*, the lamenting angels are to be understood as an allusion to the Cherubicon that

Fig. 78
Formerly in
Ohrid,
Macedonia.
Epitaphios
cloth of
Emperor
Andronikos II,
early 14th c.

was sung during the Great Entrance. On this occasion the cloth was also carried.

The cloth-borne image may have played a role for later variants of the iconic Passion portrait, but cannot have been its prototype, as Pallas believes.[95] It also had a different function. To put it briefly, in the eucharistic celebration, the *Amnos Aer* ultimately became a likeness of what, up to that time, it had only signified: a likeness of Christ's shroud. This must have occurred when the relic was still in Constantinople, and it is no accident that exhibitions of the relic are documented at the end of the twelfth century, that is to say, at the time when not only the cloth began to bear the image, but the Melismos, too, entered into the ecclesiastical program.[96]

In summary, it can be said that the cloth-borne image in both variants was employed in the "Divine Liturgy" and made its appearance during the Great Entrance, covering the offerings as they entered the church. The traditional mystagogical symbolism of this entrance as Christ's funeral procession gave the image on this occasion its semantic function. But there is one final piece of evidence for the function of the image-bearing cloth during the Great Entrance that up to now has remained unnoticed. Almost all the aeres have donor inscriptions that in reality are liturgical intercessory formulae.[97] They thus expressly refer to the custom first developed in the monastic liturgy of rhythmically interrupting the Cherubicon during the entrance of the offerings with liturgical commemorations for the living and the dead. This relationship speaks for itself.[98]

In the fourteenth century, at the latest, the cloth-borne image, like the Passion portrait, began a second career when it was introduced into the procession to the tomb on Good Friday. Its transfer into another function occurred when the liturgical development was ripe for it. The entrance into the church on Good Friday had gradually been changed into a funeral procession (p. 101). But what entered the church on this occasion? During the Great Entrance, it was the sacrificial offerings; on Good Friday, it was the gospel book that represented Christ. When the book was wrapped in the aer, the Good Friday procession looked just like that of the Great Entrance. The aer in San Marco in Venice, a fourteenth-century work, attests for the first time to the use of the image-bearing cloth in the Passion liturgy (fig. 79).[99] In this image the Christ figure very clumsily holds a gospel book, and that only makes sense when we learn that a gospel book was carried in the procession under the velum. Again a change of function brought about a change of image. At this point we can conclude our overview.

Concluding Remarks

The Byzantine history of our image has become a detailed mosaic of facts and a long-winded proof based on circumstantial evidence, because it was necessary to correct implicitly a number of widely held errors by means of counterevidence and to return the discussion to solid ground. Since this will be the basis for what follows, it had to be established as securely as possible in order to allow similarities to, as well as differences from the western history of the image to become visible in its history in the East. Both the similarities to the western images in the mood and the psychological function of the eastern images and the differences from the former in the latter's liturgical function. Now they come clearly into view. The chronology, too, has acquired sharper contours. The portrait icon in the Passion liturgy and the image-bearing cloth in the eucharistic mass, both products of their different functions were already fully developed in the twelfth century, independently of one another. Subsequently, they were both transformed and assumed into a different, or to put it better, an additional function. Thus the diachronic viewpoint is a necessary complement to the identification of the functional form in the composition of the image. In addition to the liturgical use of the images, a private use also becomes recognizable that was derived from the liturgical use, but that in its beginning had influenced the liturgy of the semiprivate, personallyowned monasteries in the twelfth century. Two other matters are even more important.

Fig. 79 Venice, San Marco. Epitaphios cloth, 14th c. (detail)

In the liturgical texts and images of Byzantium, the psychological realism, with its invitation to the viewer's empathy, anticipated the later development in the West and thus provided means of pictorial expression and structuring that could be used as soon as they had acquired a function under new conditions elsewhere. And lastly, the Passion portrait of Christ was conceived of as the counterpart to an icon of Mary, which complemented it, making it the perfect recipient and the personal representative of the ritual Lamentations of Mary.

Chapter VI
The Icon in the West: Its Reception during the Thirteenth Century in Italy

The Problem

The Imago Pietatis was one of the classic religious images in the later Middle Ages. Among Florentine artists at the end of the fourteenth century, it was considered the "most pious subject" (la più divota chosa) that one could paint.[1] Among Passion themes, it was periodically more popular and often more influential than the crucified Christ. Its history is characterized by the contradiction between a continuous metamorphosis of the pictorial structure and a main figure that remained constant. Unlike the crucified Christ, the half-length "portrait" of the dead Christ requires explanation (fig. 49). It first appeared in the West during the thirteenth century and quickly assumed so many functions and interpretations that it overtaxes traditional iconographic classification. Precisely this multivalency makes it a test case for an investigation of the change the religious image underwent during the Middle Ages.

The question of a "prototype" of this image, which Panofsky has raised, has already been answered in the present study. If there was a "prototype," it was the icon imported from the East. But it did not arrive in a single, historically significant specimen that could explain the image's subsequent development. Indeed, a "famous" specimen was first created in the miraculous image of S. Croce, and at such a late date that it had no impact on the main lines of the image's history (fig. 14).[2]

In the West, the icon became known through numerous examples and above all through diverse variants of the type that all became integrated into the western pictorial repertoire. During this process, the icon, while losing its previous eastern functions, entered into new functions and pictorial traditions which it encountered. The historical environment in which it became known and was appreciated now contributes more to the explanation than does the figure itself. And the means of assimilation into western images and to what was wanted of images in the West provide evidence about the way in which the process of assimilation took place. Therefore, both the environment and the procedure by which the image was adapted to its new environment must be examined. The problem that has been sketched here is the basis of the following discussion.

New Images in the Thirteenth Century

The first volume of the world chronicle that the monk Matthew Paris wrote before 1233 in St. Albans begins with a curious page of illustrations.[3] On it, three figures are assembled that seem to reproduce different painted panels: Mary with her Child in the upper half, and two Christ figures in the lower half, one depicted as living, the other as dead (figs. 80a, 80b). What is the significance of this assembly of images? The living Christ is depicted once again, in the second volume of the *Historia maior*. There, the context identifies him as a veronica. The accompanying text contains the office that had been newly instituted in honor of the famous portrait of Christ in St. Peter's in Rome, [4] and the chronicler reports a miracle by which the veronica is said to have established itself as an authentic portrait of Christ in 1216.[5]

If one of the three half-length figures in the first volume of the chronicle reproduces a famous exemplar, however inexactly, then both of the neighboring figures appear in a new light. The dead Christ corresponds in its close-up to the Byzantine Passion portrait (cf. the Jerusalem gold panel) and may be the first known Imago Pietatis in a western context (fig. 70). If I am right about this, we would have, in this proximity with one another of the Imago Pietatis and a veronica, a striking example for the distinction between two different icons of Christ: the "true likeness" and the image showing the experience of the Passion. The frontispiece would then be a collection of sample icons.

In form, all three half-length figures of the English miniature were reduced to a common denominator. They appear in the schema of the independent portrait icon. The new pictorial genre, which initiated a new kind of pictorial experience, was no doubt borrowed from eastern panels that streamed into the West in great numbers after the conquest of Constantinople in 1204.

In addition, the institution of an image cult by the pope was an occurrence of a new kind. Indeed, it was so novel that Matthew Paris included it in his world chronicle. Images now were allowed to do not only what relics had previously done, namely, to work miracles; now the same abilities were attributed to images as formerly to relics, namely, to convey grace and to grant remission of punishment for sins, that is, indulgences.[6] The reproduction of the veroni-

The Image and Its Public

ca in the English chronicle was necessary because one had to pray before the image in order to experience its effect. The value of an image was greatly increased when it was made the object of cultic worship, and other images, indeed all images, profited from this proceeding. They were seen with new eyes.

And finally, it is no accident that the miracle which privileged the veronica in Rome occurred at the moment when its fame was threatened by the competition of imported eastern "originals." Although the veronica had already existed for quite some time, a new constellation of historical circumstances was required for it to be invested with a status that the eastern relic images had first made attractive. It probably first became a painted relic at this moment, while before it had merely been an imageless cloth relic.[7] The increase in the veronica's importance, together with its transformation into an image, was the Roman answer to the claim made for imported images such as the mandylion, that they were authentic or had originated miraculously. This revaluation of the veronica also attests to the fact that the use of images changed. Images offered a sharing in what was depicted through the fascination of visual presence. They thereby acquired a new or intensified reality (as discussed in Chapter I).

The importation of icons and the institution of a cult of images as described above prove that images found new conditions in the thirteenth century. A thirteenth-century diptych from the school of Lucca, now in the Uffizi, introduces us to a second context of images, the sphere of the mendicant orders (fig. 81).[8] It was painted for a convent of the Poor Clares, as indicated by the choice of saints and pictorial themes. Among the saints shown in the diptych, Francis and Anthony of Padua are conspicuous. Clare, the foundress of the female Minorite order, occupies a place of honor on the left panel, next to the Madonna. The Archangel Michael enjoyed a special veneration in the order. Of crucial importance is the dominance in the diptych of Mary and the crucified Christ, who incorporate both of the central themes of the order's liturgical and extraliturgical piety. The plan of cultic veneration for the entire year was anchored to the two poles of Mariology and the Passion. The relevant texts of Marian mysticism and the mysticism of the Passion attest to this just as much as does Bonaventura's official biography of Saint Francis, which can be read as a manual for the order's program of veneration. The program was transmitted into popular piety through sermons and devotional exercises. Proof of this is furnished by those brotherhoods that received their religious profile from the mendicant orders. Some of these named themselves after Mary and

Fig. 80a Cambridge, Corpus Christi College, Cod. 26, fol. VII. Matthew Paris, Chronicle, ca. 1235

the crucified Christ; many included corresponding devotional practices in their statutes.[9] Some of the statutes directed the members to pray before the images of Mary and the crucified Christ, indeed to venerate just these images through genuflection.[10] In the lauds, regarding which, according to a thirteenth-century text, it was more a matter of tears than of words, dialogues between the *Mamma* and her Son were performed with actors, and in the context of the Passion the two great figures of identification became a pair.[11] There is written evidence that images of Mary and of the crucified Christ were hung in the monastic cells of the Dominicans dating from as early as the thirteenth century.[12] The Lucca diptych summarizes the order's program of veneration.

It does this in a structured way that calls for our attention. The diptych, like the two-sided icon, is, by its origin, an eastern genre, both as a private and as an official image (p. 109). The Lucca diptych is too large and has too official a program to be a private image. In the Poor Clares' convent for which it was intended, it may have stood on an altar or someplace where devotional practices

The Image and Its Public

could be performed in front of it. The function it fulfilled there is expressed in its complex pictorial structure.

The truncated half-length figure of Mary is an image within an image. Whether directly or indirectly, it reproduces an icon, something the diptych as a whole does as well. In the East, a double image showing the Eleousa and the Crucifixion must have been one of the important cult icons of the Passion rite, but the Italian panel radically alters the pictorial schema. The icon of Mary no longer fills the entire frame, but only the upper part of the image. It is enlarged by a kind of predella in which the convent's other recipients of cultic veneration are assembled. Here the multipartite altarpiece with a composite content of meaning is anticipated. The wing with the Crucifixion has little connection with the self-contained Crucifixion image as it was known also in the West (see the *Crucifixion* in S. Domenico in Naples, fig. 38).[13] In fact, nothing remains of the traditional Crucifixion; to put it briefly, it has been replaced by an Italian pictorial creation, the painted cross.[14]

Both the size ratio between the crucified Christ and the other

Fig. 81 Florence, Uffizi. Diptych from Lucca, mid-13th c.

Fig. 82 New Haven, Museum. Crucifixion from Lucca, 13rh c.

figures and the relationship of the main figures to the secondary figures corresponding to a common schema of the *croce depinta* (Jesus'
followers are depicted as if they were supposed to fill the *tabellone*
under the horizontal crossbeam) point to such a model. An example of this model is an early thirteenth-century painted cross in the
Pinacoteca of Lucca.[15] But this description is still incomplete. Here
the treelike cross, a popular motif in the early Gothic period, offers
its own object of contemplation as a reference to the Tree of Life. It
appears again in a panel from Lucca (now in New Haven), which,
incidentally, makes evident the difference between a regular Crucifixion and the pictorial form of the diptych under discussion here
(fig. 82).[16] Moreover, the additional scenes of the Carrying of the

Fig. 83
Bologna, Bibl.
Com. dell'Ar-
chiginnasio,
Fondo
Ospedale 1
(1), fol. 2.
Statutes from
ca. 1285

Cross and the Deposition enclose the crucified Christ between them, as it were, and they place him within a story line from which he nonetheless stands out as a figure of contemplation. A balance is struck between his integration into, and his separation from a narrative context.

Such organization of the picture produced a devotional image intended for the limited public of a convent. The result offers the advantage of proximity, as is suggested by a portrait, as well as the advantage of a richly detailed narrative that the viewer can recreate. The composite structure of the panels presents no obstacle to the dominance in them of the order's two central cult figures. With formal means, but not for reasons of form, the icon of Mary and the crucified Christ were made similar to each other in size and in their positions in the picture to such an extent that they can be seen as a pair.

The Sienese diptych in London and Budapest, which we analyzed earlier (p.12), is another combination of the icon of Mary and the crucified Christ (figs. 2a, 2b). Both versions can be understood as different solutions to a problem that is presented as such only through these images, the problem, namely, of bringing the great subjects of religious meditation affectively closer to the viewer and of making them capable of expressing meaning. The revaluation of the image which we are tracing is implicit in this process. Both diptychs propose different, and still tentative, solutions to the problem of reformulating the Madonna and the crucified Christ as a devotional image. Thus, they become intermediate stages in the development of the diptych showing the Imago Pietatis (p. 32).

The frontispiece miniature of the articles of a Bolognese brotherhood presents us with a third context closely connected with the second. Within the sphere of religious lay confraternities the image cult received new impulses, and from this sphere it was also conveyed into the private sphere.[17] The theme of the Passion was central to the conception of themselves held by the brotherhoods, the members of which reenacted Christ's Passion upon themselves in their self-flagellation, the *disciplina*.

A good example of this are the statutes composed around 1285 for the *devoti battuti di S. Maria della Vita (fig. 83)*, whose founding, according to a text, dates from the year of the foundation of the flagellant movement, 1261, in the "time of general piety" (*generalis devotionis*).[18] This ecstatic mass-movement was triggered in Perugia by Raniero Fasano, and it transformed Italy into a great Passion-play stage on which the imitation of Christ was practiced. The existing Laudesi brotherhoods and the "third order" of Penitentiaries were joined by the Disciplinati and Battuti, whose religious practices emotionally attuned a generation to the theme of the Passion. The political dimension of this development is illuminated by a remark in our statutes that everything was happening "for the good and peaceable order of the commune of Bologna." The "religious revolution" sought to bring about, internally, peace in the society of the city and, externally, reconciliation between the warring cities. The password used when the processions traversed the countryside, *pace*, attests to this.

The Passion theme of the frontispiece miniature of our statutes is expressed through surprisingly complex images that are rich in nuances. They quote the classical devotional images of an icon of Mary and a Passion scene in order to present the brotherhood's guiding models. The cross in the middle displays the instruments of the Passion, the "weapons of Christ"; the nails are on the crossbeam, and the sponge and the lance are at the side of the cross. The Scourging of Christ requires little explanation, since it was not only an image of meditation, but also an image of the confraternity's program. The brotherhood hoped to avert God's punishment by doing penance. We find the scene as the frontispiece of several sets of Venetian statutes, or *mariegole*,[19] and it also became the subject of panel paintings, as is shown by a Venetian diptych from around 1260 (formerly in the Hirsch Collection) and a triptych from Lucca (in Princeton).[20] It is possible that the laud "Davanti a una colonna," which spoke of the Scourging at the Pillar at a quite early date, was sung before such an image.[21]

It is the icon of Mary that is truly surprising, not because it reproduces an eastern icon of the Virgin Eleousa, but because it implies an unexpectedly exact understanding of that icon (fig. 63). For in the present context at Bologna, the maternal happiness, which we see *prima vista*, must be understood of the other depictions in the miniature as a reference to the Lamentation of Mary; the tenderly affectionate Mother of the Child must be seen together with the suffering Mother of the dead Christ. We do not know how this connotation, proper to the eastern image, was transmitted to the West. Those Lamentations of Mary which adopted the sentiment of their eastern sources may have played a role in its transmission.

The emotional actions of Mary toward her Son after he had been taken down from the cross, her kisses and embraces, recall, for example, as they are presented in the pseudo-Bernardine *Planctus* (p. 157), texts such as the homily of George of Nicomedia (p. 98). This applies as well to the use made of Simeon's prophecy, that a sword would pierce Mary's heart. In addition, the lauds adopted by the brotherhoods present similar notions. In Jacopone's play *Donna del Paradiso*, John summons Mary to her Son, who has been scourged so severely that he is in danger of dying.[22] In the lamentation song "Qui per viam pergitis," the loving remonstrance of the Mother to her Son, asking him why he allows her to suffer, she who had once carried him in her arms, reiterates these antitheses of maternal joy and maternal sorrow that color the pathos of mystagogical hymns in the East.[23] There the texts were essentially a function of liturgical piety. In the West, they increasingly become a function of lay piety and religious theater. The white gown that Mary wears under the dark blue cloak is so uncommon in the pictorial tradition that it can perhaps be understood as the mourning dress that Mary put on in the Passion plays when she learned of Christ's arrest, as we are told in a Good Friday laud of a Disciplinati brotherhood from Assisi.[24]

The cross with the instruments of Christ's passion in the center of the image is, on an ideographic reading, a Passion image *sui generis*. In a noniconic, symbolic, and accumulative manner, it offers a serial and at the same time simultaneous contemplation of the Passion that was experienced both as a redemptive sacrifice and as the sum of Christ's different sufferings.[25] In the context we are considering, it is a symbol and a "pictorial motto" of a religious program. Perhaps it quotes an eastern model, as does the Madonna; the cross with *arma*, a relic from Hagia Sophia, came to be depicted on the reverse sides of such famous images of Mary as the *Vladimir Madonna* (fig. 63). But one should not isolate the symbol of the Passion from the neighboring images by understanding it as a mere symbol. The importation of such relics into the West made an enduring mark on the century's religious imagination and blurred the boundaries between image and relic.[26] The nails used in the crucifixion, for example, were as visually perceptible as images themselves. They, too, possessed the authenticity of certain miraculous images. With this our observations have come full circle. The importation of icons and the importation of relics are merely different sides of the same experience of a new physicality and sensible perceptibleness of what faith held to be real, an experience that inspired the religious activity of the age.

In our miniature, images and symbols that are similar in meaning, but genetically and "syntactically" heterogeneous, are placed next to each other. The semantic level is more homogenous than that of the pictorial forms as such, a state of affairs that is characteristic of a transitional period. At first the new functions did not yet change the pictorial structure. We will see that this is also true in regard to the assimilation of eastern Passion portraits.

We have already spoken of the psychological and political significance of cult images in the service of the confraternities (p. 24). In the statutes of lay brotherhoods, we hear time and again of actual painted panels of this kind.[27] In the fourteenth century, cult images of the brotherhoods multiplied. I will mention only the large image of the *Madonna dell'Umiltà* in Palermo, painted by Bartolomeo da Camogli in 1346 for a brotherhood of Disciplinati.[28] While few such images have survived from the thirteenth century, one famous example is Duccio's *Rucellai Madonna* (1285), made for the Laudesi of S. Maria Novella in Florence.[29] A little known thirteenth-century work is the diptych with the membership list of the brotherhood of Notre Dame du Moutement from Rabastens-en-Albigeois, dating from approximately 1286–93 (today in the Museum Périgueux), which is provided with two scenes of the Passion and two showing Mary.[30] Here the panel painting has a function comparable to that of inventories and statutes. The same is true of a fourteenth-century Pisan panel (today in Palermo) with an obituary list and the image of the Imago Pietatis.[31] Naturally, the titulary saint was the main subject of such panels. Mary often appears in the form of the Virgin of Mercy along with a group picture of the brotherhood, and she is encountered in the same form as a miniature in manuscripts of statutes 9 (fig. 18).[32] In the context of the present discussion, this means that we may assume there were connections between the miniatures and the panel paintings in the possession of the brotherhoods, and that from time to time, the ones were copied from the others.

The analysis of three exemplary situations in which we have come to know images under new circumstances requires a few additional reflections on panel painting in the liturgical, corporate, and

Fig. 84 Florence, Bibl. Med. Laurenziana, Plut. XXV.3, fol. 384v (Emilia 2293–1300). Veronica

private spheres of its functioning. In the liturgical sphere, the painted cross precedes the altar retable, which was developed only later. The development of a composite altarpiece, which becomes the norm for the main altar, is a consequence of the spread of the panel painting in the thirteenth century.[33] There is no need to recapitulate the stages of its development here. Only two aspects of it play a role for our argument: the derivation of the altarpiece from the icon and its development as an icon frieze. Early altarpieces such as those showing Saint Francis still maintained their identity as icons, as evidenced by the accompanying biographical scenes common on eastern icons of saints. Thus the dossals and early retables are group icons that were inspired by the icon screen (iconostasis) placed before the sanctuary in eastern churches. The identifying characteristic of Italian composite altarpieces is the sequence of half-length portrait icons in which the cult program (not the cult image program) of a church was summarized. Their difference from thirteenth-century transalpine retables composed of scenes accompanying a central Crucifixion or Coronation of the Virgin is evident. The Italian altarpiece, as it turns into part of the inventory of the liturgical sphere, no longer testifies to the existence of an actual image cult, but, rather proves to be its heir and successor.

Institutionalized image cults were always tied to individual specimens of images, and their veneration was practiced outside the actual liturgy. Miraculous images, which became the goal of pilgrimages, are proof of this. But they are only the tip of the iceberg. Rarely did the image cult of individual panels become obligatory in the Church as a whole. For the most part, the cult remained limited to a

The Image and Its Public

particular locale. From the beginning, the religious confraternities were an important champion of the image cults, which they promoted at the semiprivate, as well as at the official, governmental, and ecclesiastical levels. The boundaries between cult image and devotional image are just as unclear as those between the community and the private sphere of the cult image. The impulses that the latter received in this context can only be demonstrated for the fourteenth century. Indirect, but important, evidence for the wealth of miraculous and devotional images that had gained vogue in the Franciscan milieu as early as the thirteenth century is found in the manuscript of the *Supplicationes variae*, Cod. Plut. XXV.3 of the Laurenziana in Florence, dated to 1293–1300 (fig. 105).[34] In the appendix, which consists of over forty drawings comprising practically the entire repertoire of then-current cult images and *historiae*, the Imago Pietatis and the veronica are represented, as well as Saint Christopher, whom one was supposed to look at once a day, and also the portraits of the great saints (figs. 84, 85). And it is characteristic of the interdependence of the several functional spheres that it is impossible to tell whether this compilation was used by a monastery or convent, a brotherhood, or privately. Perhaps it was used in all three spheres.

Fig. 85 Florence, Bibl. Med. Laurenziana, Plut. XXV.3, fol. 383 (Emilia 1293–1300). St. Christopher

The Cross and the Descent from the Cross in the Context of the Liturgy, the Sermon, and the Theater

When the eastern Passion portrait was accepted into the Italian repertoire, several standard images of the Passion already existed there. I would like to examine two of them more closely: the painted cross and the sculptural group of the Deposition, in their contexts. Both of these Passion images were characteristic for Italy, where they shaped the conception of the suffering Christ. The Imago Pietatis reacted to both, finding in them models of public devotional images that stood at the focus of liturgical and extraliturgical piety.

This no longer needs to be proved for the painted cross (fig. 3). The wealth of material surviving from the thirteenth century that can be consulted in Garrison's index speaks for itself.[35] To be sure, the painted cross was not a creation of the thirteenth century; the oldest dated specimen known to us is a Tuscan work from 1138. In the Veneto and in Lombardy, the history of the painted cross may go back even further.[36] The thirteenth century, however, transformed the painted cross in a significant way that sheds light on the general metamorphosis of images in this period. The facts are known, but they have not always been sufficiently pondered.

Two features of the transformation of the painted cross have significance for our argument (fig. 86). First, the introduction of the dead, in place of the living, crucified Christ altered the conception of Christ, and second, the recasting of the figures of Mary and John into half-length icons at the ends of the cross's arms altered the appearance of the painted panel in its entirety. Both innovations, which immediately became norms, were adopted in Giunta Pisano's version. But it is not sufficient to regard them as an artist's inventions.

The eastern depiction of the dead crucified Christ had gained so little acceptance in Italy that it was perceived by an eleventh-century Roman visitor to Constantinople as heretical.[37] It first appears on the painted cross—preceding Giunta's *oeuvre*—in two Pisan works from the early thirteenth century which doubtless utilized eastern models.[38] But the *"Christus patiens"* is documented in a Latin milieu as early as a half-century before, namely, in the monastery established by the crusaders at the Holy Sepulcher in Jerusalem. If, as we are told, the crucified Christ was painted in such a way that he aroused profound pity (p. 6), then he was depicted as dead. The Latin caption shows that the crusaders adopted the eastern type and employed it as a devotional image. Thus, we see that the new conception of the crucified Christ was recognized earlier in Outremer than in Italy, and it was so, appropriately, in the shadow of the Holy Sepulcher.

Another set of circumstances having just as important consequences occurred when Giunta developed the classic formulation of the *Christus patiens* for the painted cross. It is tempting to suppose that this occurred when Giunta was working for Saint Francis in

The Image and Its Public

Assisi (fig. 86). Admittedly, the cross of the General of the order, Elias, dated to 1236, has been lost, but it probably resembled a second painted cross by Giunta which is preserved in another Franciscan monastery in Assisi, S. Maria degli Angeli, which shows the version which from then on became a norm (fig. 3).[39] A number of reasons arguing for the reformulation of the image of the crucified Christ occurred at the behest of the Franciscans. In any event, it had not been left to the discre-

tion of an artist. And the reformulation's rapid diffusion, especially in Umbria, would scarcely have been possible without a specimen privileged through the commission that had brought it into being. Above all, the new portrayal of Christ symbolizes the Passion meditation of the Franciscans, who contemplated the suffering and death of Christ from the new perspective of their affective experiential replication, from the standpoint of *compassio*.

On the painted panel, the invitation to pity was not entrusted solely to the main figure. It was also expressed by two figures who functioned as mediators for the viewer's empathy (fig. 3). It is, not without reason, Mary and John, who in their dialogue with the dying Christ and in their grief for the dead Christ offered the viewer a model of behavior (figs. 86, 87). Their turning to both Christ and the viewer is expressed through miming and gesture. These are the figures who remain, as it were, on the painted cross from the richness of a colorful pictorial tale often consisting of many scenes. Their scenic connection with the historical event is eliminated through the abandonment of their spatial relationship with the crucified Christ. It is as though two half-length portrait icons were now mounted on the ends of the cross's arms. In this form, the differ-

Fig. 87 Florence, Santa Maria degli Angeli. Painted cross by Giotto

ence in scale between them and the main figure is reduced and the distance of all three figures from the viewer is lessened owing to better visibility. Through their large-scale depiction, in which the secondary figures approach the main one in size, the three figures draw together into a visual unity. The body of Christ was made even more plastic by the background, which is patterned. An emphasis on strongly expressive motifs that are visible at a distance takes the place of the additive accumulation of motifs in earlier examples. The altered form of the image served the function of allowing another reading, or better, another way of experiencing the figures.

The expression "mysticism of the Passion" does not sufficiently describe the new conception of the crucified Christ in the milieu of the mendicant orders. The postulate that required becoming similar to Christ meant doing so with respect to his suffering. When Saint Francis received the stigmata of the crucified Christ, he provided a classic formula expressing this *imitatio*. The saint was transformed into a tangible likeness of Christ, that is, into the image that the believer was supposed to produce within himself as a spiritual image (fig. 41). The physical reproduction of the prototype was no return to the lower level of the material image, but an advance to the highest stage of the mystical program, to becoming one with the partner in the meditation. When Saint Francis became the living, walking image of the crucified Christ, the mimesis program acquired a prototype who was also the guarantor of its success.

The panel painting of the crucified Christ thus offered the viewer a model that he could become like through contemplation. As a consequence, the role of the viewer, with whom the image initiated a dialogue, so to speak, was altered, and once again a legend found

146

The Image and Its Public

a graphically powerful expression for this. It is the legend of the speaking painted cross of S. Damiano that is supposed to have summoned the young Francis to the Imitation of Christ.[40] The choice of a material image as the instrument of God's intervention is noteworthy. The speaking painted cross naturally became a cult image, one which is still venerated today. There were also such cult images in the Dominican milieu, and again it is the crucified Christ who is said to have spoken to Thomas Aquinas. This

Fig. 88
Naples, San
domenico
Maggiore.
Crucifixion
panel from
Campania,
second quar-
ter 13th c.

legend is associated with a Crucifixion panel in the Byzantine style venerated in S. Domenico in Naples (fig. 88). Two kneeling Dominicans indicate that the panel was commissioned by that order, and its style dates its origin to the second quarter of the thirteenth century.[41]

These observations are indicative of a new self-consciousness on the part of the individual, which was completely independent of social position and theological education. In the conception of God as a crucified man, the viewer found the image of his own ideal; he found not a likeness of a triumphant God, but of a suffering God as his model. The idea of a reciprocal similarity between God and man, between the image and its viewer, an idea which became filled with new meaning at that time, changed the pictorial formulation of the crucified Christ. For the following discussion, it is important to keep in mind that this formulation was found in Umbria and Tuscany as early as the 1230s, and that it underwent no basic changes during the thirteenth century, at least not until the young Giotto painted his panel cross for S. Maria Novella in Florence in the last decade of that century (fig. 87). The latter is not only an achieve-

Fig. 89 Tivoli, Cathedral. Descent from the Cross, ca. 1200

ment of anatomical description, but also replaces the "loud" tension of a stridently distorted suffering body with the quiet relaxation of a form reposing in death, which even expresses beauty. Through these features of his work, Giotto establishes a new quality of the devotional image, which now attains its ends with more subtle, even lyrically refined means.[42] A new generation, for which Giotto made himself the spokesman, found a new model in this work.

The Image and Its Public

The second cult image that presented the Passion theme is of an entirely different genre, and since we know less about it, it must be dealt with at greater length. It is a sculptural group consisting of five, mostly life-sized wooden figures portraying the *depositio Christi*.

G. de Francovich listed ten specimens surviving entirely or in part.[43] In a 1957 exhibition, three further specimens were added to his list (figs. 89, 92, 93).[44] Vasari mentions a group in the *pieve*—the parish church—of Arezzo which he attributes to Margaritone.[45] In all, fifteen examples are known to us today, though originally their number must have been much greater. While all the known specimens date from the thirteenth century, more precise dating is just as difficult as the determination of their places of origin.

The Christ figure of a group from S. Maria di Roncione, now in the museum in Perugia, is said to have formerly borne the date 1236.[46] The two groups in the cathedral of Tivoli and in a Parisian collection are stylistically so close to a sculptured Madonna dated 1199 from Borgo San Sepolcro, now in Berlin (fig. 89), that they could have originated in the same workshop at the same time.[47] The provenance of the preserved pieces, whose radius of diffusion reaches as far as Umbria and Latium, justifies Francovich's thesis that production was centered in the area of Arezzo. All the rest is conjecture. If some specimens are correctly dated to the end of the century, then the group was produced for a hundred years.

The difficulty in arranging the material chronologically lies in the astonishing constancy of this Italian creation. It underwent only very subtle modifications, and it is necessary to pay particular attention to these. The ensemble consists of Christ, Mary, and John, and the two assistants, Nicodemus and Joseph of Arimathea. In the group from Tivoli, it is supplemented with two flying angels (fig. 89). Christ is only nailed to the cross by his feet. His wide-open arms angle out from the body in a gesture of embrace. The accompanying figures form two symmetrically arranged pairs. The two assistants are about to free Christ completely from the cross, while the outside pair stands ready to receive the corpse. Their bent arms, making a gesture at once pleading and pointing, both respond to Christ's gesture and indicate the end points of the action of the *depositio*. The physical, practical activity of the assistants is sublimated by the mental, pious activity of Mary and John. Even the angels participate in the rhythm of the receptive gestures, to which the ensemble is attuned, and to which it attunes the viewer. The main figure is not merely the passive object of the gestures, but also, by the fact that its arms are unsupported even though it is dead, expresses an invitation to be received.

The symmetrical arrangement of the stylized gestures transforms the historical action into a ritual act, which suggests that a symbolic interpretation is called for. That this is a formulation full of meaning becomes evident when we compare it to other images of

The Image and Its Public

Fig. 91
Udine, Santa
Maria di
Catello, side
apse. Descent
from the
Cross, 13th c.

the Deposition. One example is the great panel in the Castello Montegalda near Vicenza, whose wooden figures, carved in low relief, are placed before a mosaic background (fig. 90). This panel is a variant of an eastern-western combination of bas-relief and painted panel documented a number of times in the thirteenth century.[48] In contrast to the sculptural group, this panel recreates a particular moment in the Deposition of Christ. His right arm has already been freed and is being kissed by Mary, while the nail is still being removed from his left hand. A scenic action is being described here. Only the central angel does not play a role in the narration: it alludes to an old type of painted cross, in which it crowns the cross's vertical beam. I would like to call the pictorial type of the Montegalda work a *scenic* Deposition and distinguish it from the *ritual* Deposition of the sculptural group.

The scenic Deposition represents one of two variants that were developed in Byzantine art. Evidence for this assertion is provided by an eastern icon from the Stoclet collection[49] and also by a monumental fresco occupying the right apse of the three-naved basilica, S. Maria di Castello in Udine (fig. 91).[50] The second Byzantine variant occurs among the crypt frescoes of the cathedral of Aquileia from the end of the twelfth century.[51] Two other images may be added to the three examples from the Veneto: a mosaic preserved only as a fragment in San Marco in Venice, which is found near the

Fig. 92 Volter-
ra. Descent
from the
Cross, 13th c.
(after Carli)

southern entrance to the choir; and a fresco in SS. Apostoli, also in
Venice.[52]

When we survey the Italian material, the frequent appearance
in the Veneto of individual, and at times monumental, images of
Christ's *depositio* is striking. The panel in Montegalda, the apse in
Udine, and the mosaic in San Marco show a preference for the
Deposition as an independent image of the Passion, and there may
have been special reasons for this. I can offer only two conjectures,
which will later play a role in the discussion of the wooden group.
On the one hand, the Veneto was the gateway for the drama of the
liturgical *depositio* performed on Good Friday, which was introduced
from Bavaria around 1200.[53] On the other, it was, as the *planctus* of
Cividale shows, the home for a richly developed Lamentation of
Mary, which may have given impetus to this kind of image.[54]

The painted images in the Veneto appear to be counterparts of

Fig. 93 San
Miniato al
Tedesco, Arci-
confrat.
Descent from
the Cross,
13th s. (after
Carli)

the sculptured images that had been widespread in Tuscany and
central Italy. The peculiar presentation of the sculptural group,
which I have defined as a ritual Deposition, has been confirmed
through this comparison. Except for a few significant modifications,
this manner of presentation remained constant. Only the group in
Volterra, which is an attempt to set the ensemble in motion through
the interpolation of the scenic Deposition, deviates from the strictly
observed schema (fig. 92).[55] For the understanding of the ensemble, however, two other groups play a greater role. The group in S.
Antonio in Pescia, if we may credit its present-day arrangement,
brings the five figures more closely together and loosens the rigid
schema (fig. 37).[56] Here Mary and John, by touching Christ's hands,

Fig. 94
Groningen
(Lanz be-
quest). The
Lamentation
from the circle
of Ghirlandaio

increase the expressiveness of the previously rigid, ritual poses. A narrative note is also sounded by Christ's lowered head. The rope encircling Christ's chest, which holds his upper body to the cross, supplies a certain motivation for his upright posture. Indeed, we may mentally supply the rope for other such groups.

While the group in Pescia is modernized through a narrative coloration (fig. 37), the group in S. Miniato al Tedesco is modified in an entirely different way.[57] Even the reduction to the "classic" three-figured Crucifixion is noteworthy. It is consonant with a different role of Mary and John, who make here a gesture of display instead of one of reception. Instead of turning toward the crucified Christ, Mary and John turn toward the viewer, to whom they display, for lamentation and veneration, the pierced and bleeding hands of Christ. To characterize the new mise en scène, one could para-

154   *The Image and Its Public*

Fig. 95
Cividale,
Cathedral.
Crucifix,
13th c.

phrase two rubrics found in the Lamentations of Mary from Cividale: John and Mary "turn to the people" and "show them Christ's [wounded] side" and his pierced hands.[58] The change in the sculptural group points to a change in its semantic function. Which role could the life-sized, polychrome group have fulfilled?

It is quite unlikely that a relationship existed between the group and the *depositio* drama.[59] The *depositio* of the cross in an improvised or permanently installed "Holy Sepulcher" within a church must not be confused with the historical Deposition. The latter was a ritual entombment that followed the Adoration of the Cross in the Good

Friday liturgy and commemorated the Entombment with a symbolic procession and deposition of the cross. Its counterpart was the *elevatio* on Easter morning, a Resurrection ceremony culminating in the raising of the previously buried cross. In addition to the cross and/or the Host, we hear now and then of a figure of the crucified Christ as the buried object, for example, in a text from Aquileia (fig. 95). It might have been possible to un-nail and to bury the main figure of the pictorial groups, but then the ritual function of the group as a whole would have been lost. The *Adoratio Crucis*, which also comes to mind as a possible function, probably took place before a crucified Christ, but if we exclude it, then no rite remains that we could reasonably connect to the sculptured Deposition. However, the greatest obstacle to adducing the liturgical drama or the liturgy to explain the group's function lies in the late and only gradual introduction of the transalpine *depositio* drama into Italy. As Corbin has shown, it made its appearance there only around 1200, and at first only in the regions bordering the Alps.[60]

According to Corbin, the liturgical Passion drama became so little established in Italy owing to the fact that in Italy the Passion play passed at an early date from the hands of the clergy into those of the brotherhoods, who made the Passion the object of a popular *devozione;* the liturgical clerical play in Latin was changed into the extraliturgical lay play in *volgare,* the vernacular language.[61] The earliest forms of this lay activity were evidently the Lamentations of Mary and the *laudi,* texts which at first were only sung and not yet staged.[62] When we inspect the meager information on the use of our sculpted groups, two pieces of information acquire significance for our argument: the group of S. Miniato al Tedesco (fig. 93) was once in the possession of the Arciconfraternità of this Tuscan city, and until well into the early eighteenth century, the group in the cathedral of Tivoli (fig. 89) was "taken around in procession on every Friday in March by the members of the brotherhood of the city . . . , while during the procession verses on the Passion of Christ and the 'Miserere' were sung."[63] At that time, the group in Tivoli was a highly venerated cult image that supposedly was made of cedar and had come to the city by itself on driverless camels. These are all late accounts, but they connect the sculpted groups with the brotherhoods, which had, we know, under their care in the thirteenth century the then customary Passion songs and plays.

The career of the group, which had already begun in 1200, may indeed have started in a different context. The *planctus,* or the Latin song of lamentation by Mary beneath the cross, would have been a possible context. As the rubrics explain, it followed the liturgical unveiling and adoration of the cross on Good Friday.[64] The penultimate strophe of the early hymn "Planctus ante nescia," attributed to Godfrey of St. Victor (d. 1194), can be read as an interpretation of the sculpted group, in that it suggests the mutual embrace of the crucified Christ, who stretches out his arms from the cross, and the faithful.[65] In Theo Meier's study on the Lamentations of Mary, this hymn is identified as the earliest example of the change to a realistic presentation of *compassio*.[66] The forceful description of Christ's Passion and Mary's pity complements the lyrical lament. Mary's grief is the consequence of loving pity. The description of Christ's deformed body increases the pathos of the moving song of lamentation.

The sources of the Passion motifs employed lie in the apocryphal and spiritual literature of the East. We have already spoken of the homilies and *staurotheotokia* which played a role in the Byzantine liturgy (p. 104). In addition to the Lamentations of Mary attributed to Ephraim the Syrian, one should also mention the pseudoevangelia, such as the Greek version of the *Gesta Pilati B*.[67] In Latin literature, the early song texts draw on prose tracts treating of Mary's lamentations that are rooted in the same eastern texts as well as in the meditation literature of the great mystics Anselm of Canterbury and Bernard of Clairvaux. Significantly, even if wrongly, the two most influential texts carry the names of these two mystics. In reality the pseudo-Bernardine text was composed shortly before 1205 by Ogier of Locedio.[68] The descriptions he offers of the scene beneath the cross read like accounts of a performance. They are divided into the event's different phases. After Christ's death, Mary embraces and kisses the cross because she cannot reach the body, and then collapses in a faint. One feels reminded of the homily of George of Nicomedia. The Deposition receives special attention. One assistant supports the body while the other pulls the nails out. Mary reaches out to draw Christ's head and hand to her breast. When the body is lying on her lap, she wets his face with kisses and tears, as described in the Threnos of Metaphrastes (p. 103).

The pseudo-Bernardine text represents a new type of Passion literature whose rhetoric took advantage of the then evolving poetry of the Passion. In these literary genres the tension increases between mystical spiritualization and realistic presentification.[69] The vernacular laud, too, which at first had much more modest linguistic means at its disposal, came to draw on this development. The latter's beginnings may date back to the twelfth century. The Laudesi della B. Vergine, which devoted themselves chiefly to praising Mary, were constituted perhaps as early as 1183.[70] The Servite Order, established in 1233, apparently developed out of this brotherhood.[71] Decisive impulses influencing the development of the laud as a particular genre of sung poetry in *volgare* came from the Franciscans and, a generation later, from the flagellant movement. Francis's famous Canticle to the Sun (1224) is a prominent example of vernacular poetry, which in the course of time became ever more dependent on the production of lauds. The hymn "Donna del paradiso" written during the last third of the thirteenth century by the controversial Franciscan Jacopone of Todi, author of the Latin *planctus* "Stabat Mater," is an early high point of the regular composition of lauds, and this hymn was to hold a permanent place in the repertoire of the genre.[72] In some collections of lauds (*laudaria*), the one who sings the laud in the role of Mary is called upon "to sing in an especially deeply moved fashion and with heartfelt tears" ("pietosamente et con cordiali lacreme").[73] As an antiphon, in which, in addition to Mary, Christ and John also take part, it represents a highly evolved stage in the dramatic variety of the laud, as distinguished from the lyrical or monodic laud.[74]

The antiphon, which already makes use of all the resources of drama, begins with John's bringing Mary the horrifying news of Jesus' arrest. The stylistic means of depicting individual stations of the Passion, to which Mary reacts each time with lamentation, combines narrative description with the hymnic tradition. Mary's futile attempt to oppose the *popolo* and thereby prevent Pilate's judgment further intensifies the drama that hurries through its various phases in an accelerated tempo. The climax is reached in the dialogue between Mother and Son after Christ is nailed to the cross. To her Son's command that she remain behind on earth, Mary responds with the cry, "Figlio, questo non dire / Voglio teco morire" (97).[75] The work ends with a heart-rending lamentation by Mary over her dead Son, in which she paints a portrait of his appearance:

Figlio bianco e vermiglio, / Figlio senza simiglio,
Figlio a chi m'apiglio? / Figlio, pur m' hai lassato! (119).[76]

Apparently there were no firm rules for associating the laud with the liturgy of the Passion. The laud could be joined to an ecclesiastical rite, but it could also take place in the oratory of the brotherhood or accompany the brotherhood's Good Friday procession through the city. The statutes of the Disciplinati of, for example, Perugia, Assisi, and Gubbio, furnish evidence for all these alternatives.[77] The brotherhood of S. Stefano in Assisi made its way "in the first hour of Good Friday to the churches of S. Francesco and S. Maria degli Angeli in order to perform [*represententi*] tearful lauds,

The Image and Its Public

songs of lamentation, and the Lamentation of Mary."[78] Inventories of the confraternities of S. Domenico in Perugia (1339) and of S. Maria della Misericordia in Gubbio list theatrical properties and costumes; the lauds had therefore been performed as plays.[79]

In the theatrically staged laud or *repraesentatio*, performed with assigned parts, we become acquainted with a further genre or phase in the development of early sacred theater. The staging instructions: "angel wings to make the *devozione*" in Gubbio, or "a cross and a column for the *devozione*" in Perugia, identify the kind of laud performed: a *devozione*.[80] The name reveals the origin of this form of drama, namely, among the flagellant associations whose expiatory and devotional practices, the *disciplina* and the *devozione*, could also take place in the form of the staged laud. Dates for this are uncertain, but there was a rich spectrum of performance practices as early as the thirteenth century. The last stage of this development, the *sacra rappresentazione*, need not concern us here. It was hardly reached before the fifteenth century and signified sacred theater's becoming definitely independent of the liturgy in time and place of performance, a further loosening of the tie to the liturgy and the liturgical calendar.[81]

The inventory of S. Domenico in Perugia supplies valuable evidence about theatrical practices. The "pillar to which Christ was bound during the Passion" attests that Christ was a part for an actor (fig. 95).[82] On the other hand, in the same context, "a great crucifix suited for the *devozione*," and three individually stored "nails taken from the crucifix" attest to Christ being a role played by a doll.[83] The combination of wooden figures and living actors allows one to make inferences about the nature of the reality ascribed to the surviving sculptures (and painted crosses?). In Siena, a compensation was paid in 1257 to "the boy who is put in the Lord's place" during the Good Friday Passion play.[84] This example shows that Passion plays were not only possible outside the tradition of the *laudi* and the *devozioni*, but are in fact evidenced at an earlier date. And in its precise stage directions for the glances and gestures of the singers, the *planctus* of Cividale, which dates to the thirteenth century, testifies to the early existence of theatrical stagings also in the domain of the clerical play, that is, in the liturgical milieu.[85] Since Christ is silent in this text, he could, indeed must have been a wooden figure. Either a painted or sculptured crucifix was used, like the one preserved in the cathedral of Cividale which was actually included in the cast (fig 95),[86] or else a pictured group portraying the Deposition, which duplicated in the image the actors posing in front of it.

These speculations lead us back to the question of the function in which the sculpted crucifix, the painted cross, and the picture of the Deposition were primarily important. For the crucifix, whether sculpted or painted, the Good Friday rite provided the liturgical function of the Adoration of the Cross. The rite was already an old one. However, the Passion literature of the thirteenth century provided it with a new perspective which made it desirable to depict the suffering and deceased Christ in the most réalistic manner possible. For the sculpted Deposition another context applied. It was better suited to be an "image of reference" of the extraliturgical Lamentation of Mary that was still sung by the clergy in church. Later, it came into the hands of the lay brotherhoods who performed their *devozioni* before it, and here the extraliturgical Lamentation found a new domain in which it had a function and was diffused.

In the deictic gestures of its secondary figures, the group of S. Miniato del Tedesco, at one time in the possession of the Arciconfraternità della Misericordia, makes an appeal to the public, well-suited to such a context (fig. 93). In the *planctus* of Cividale, Mary and John, "with open arms," already show the crucified Christ to the people, while Mary speaks of the "mournful spectacle of cross and lance" or, through the direction of her gaze, draws attention to Christ's wounded side and crown of thorns.[87] It is the dramatic lauds, whose influence is perhaps already noticeable in this *planctus*, that first develop the pictorial *repraesentatio* of suffering and pity into a scenic event whose plastic recounting approximates and soon surpasses the wealth of action in the sculptured Deposition. The narration of the Deposition, which at first had been the concern only of prose literature, was increasingly taken up also by songs and dramatic performances. The meaning of the sculptured group must have changed correspondingly. While in early specimens the symbolic understanding (of the scene as a symbolic situation) stood in the foreground, the coexperiencing of the actual occurrence of the Passion soon became ever more important.

But this change also narrowed the function of the wooden group. Indeed, it jeopardized its production. While the group was at first only a general paradigm of the Passion, just as the Lamentation of Mary embodied the Passion meditation as a whole, it lost this status once the Passion came to be experientially replicated in ever-increasing detail. It then appeared to be tied too much to an individual "station" of the Passion to be able to embody the Passion as a whole. New images emerged that supplanted the wooden group; in the trecento, these new images were those of the Imago Pietatis (fig. 36) or of the Lamentation, for example, that of Giovanni di Milano

The Image and Its Public

Fig. 96 Naples,
San Domenico
Maggiore.
Fresco from
the school of
Cavallini, early
14th c.

(fig. 5). From the sculptural version of the Descent from the Cross only the specific gesture of Christ's wide-open arms continued to be used (fig. 94, see p.74). Nevertheless, the sculptured Deposition made history. In its relationship to songs and plays of the Passion, and in its rhetorical address to its audience, it contributed to a general change in the use of images.

In this survey of thirteenth-century Passion piety, only the sermon remains to be discussed, and to this we now turn our attention. In the hands of the mendicant orders, which devoted themselves to preaching to the common people, the sermon played a decisive role in the diffusion of models of piety and themes of contemplation.[88] Its chief purpose was the popularization of the theological and mystical writings of these orders. The content of these writings was intended to achieve control over the religious life of the people. Although the rest of the clergy was hostile to the mendicant orders' staging of sermons, which used all conceivable means and was

The Icon in the West   161

aimed at exciting emotions, it ultimately imitated them. The significance of the sermon as a medium in which the Church reached the
public sphere cannot be overestimated. It was also employed in the
recruitment and formation of confraternities. Many of their statutes
called for regular attendance at a sermon.[89] The sermon delivered
before confraternities and in monasteries was addressed to an
audience whose communal ideal it was supposed to promote.

Aside from its role in religious training, the sermon was also
suited to the higher education of the laity, who received free instruction through it. The sermon's didactic scheme sometimes served as
instruction in discursive thought, logical reasoning, and, not least of
all, in terminology. Baxandall speaks of a public "training" of the
people.[90]

The sermon on the cross was a central theme of this genre. If we
may believe the inscription of St. Dominic's book that appears in an
early fourteenth-century Neapolitan fresco, it was absolutely *the* sermon (fig. 96).[91] Since the sermon usually took place within the con-
fines of a church, it must have benefited from the images standing
there before the eyes of preacher and audience alike, and it must
have also exercised an influence on these images. Baxandall has
drawn attention to the connection between the topoi of the sermons and those of the images in the quattrocento.[92] For the thirteenth and fourteenth centuries, such an inquiry is yet to be made. I
must limit myself here to a few observations. The sermon on the
cross and the actual painted cross installed on the tramezzo-beam of
the nave referred to each other (fig. 87). The plastic vividness and
detailed description of the suffering Christ on the painted cross
makes this just as clear as does the expression of *compassio* by Mary
and John. The better visibility of the secondary figures was the
result, if not the intention of the structural changes in the *croce dipinta*. Because it required interpretation, the depiction of Saint Francis, who kneels at the feet of Christ on certain painted crosses, is also
evidence for the connection between image and sermon. The special relation between Francis and the crucified Christ was a thesis
that is presented here pictorially. It explained the saint's presence in
the image and, if one argues from a thirteenth-century point of
view, was "confirmed" by an image that the preacher could point to.

In addition, the altar panels showing Francis function as evidence for the postulate of his likeness with Christ by virtue of his
stigmatization, a postulate which promulgated time and again in
texts and sermons. Francis is presented visibly displaying his stigmata to the viewer.[93] In another domain, that of monastic meditation
literature, the wall paintings illustrating Bonaventura's *Lignum Vitae*

Christi attest to the close interdependence of texts and images.[94] Finally, the ambitious theology of Saint Francis, which is expressed in the painted legend of Francis of the Upper Church of S. Francesco of Assisi[95] and determines even the sequence of scenes, would have been wasted on the lay public if it had not been explained through exegeses in sermon form. It must not be forgotten that images, like sermons, served as a medium of religious instruction, above all for the laity.

That images were referred to in sermons is not mere conjecture, but proves to be part of the presentation of the sermon in which prayers, songs, and dramatic performances also played a role. Of course, sermons have been preserved for the most part, if at all, in collections of texts concerned only with the content or the literary form, and ignoring the manner of their presentation as an extraliterary adjunct. Rubrics giving directions for the staging of sermons are rare and of a late date, as in the Franciscan sermon collections from the Abruzzi that de Bartholomaeis has studied.[96] But they are evidence of a tradition dating back to the fourteenth, if not the thirteenth century. The literary development of the sermon shows so little change in this period that its popular staging must also have been an old custom.

For this reason I would like to emphasize the importance of the staging directions for what de Bartholomaeis calls the "semidramatic sermon" of the Franciscans.[97] Its incorporation of Jacopone's laud "Donna del Paradiso," a showpiece of the early performance of the Passion, confirms that this predicant practice began at an early date.[98] Rubrics in the books of sermons from the Abruzzi indicate that the sermon was given a visual and theatrical form, of which I would like to give a few examples. When the preacher speaks of the *crudelissima crucifixione*, "the crucifix is displayed" (*ostenditur*). The preacher was to recite rhymed poems, strikingly reminiscent of the *planctus* and *devozione* before the image. In many lauds and lamentations of Mary, his cry: "Actendete et vedete. Et con dolore et lacrime considerete," is attributed to Mary as a quotation from the Threnos.[99] It appears as if the *exempla*, which were intended to illustrate the sermons' themes, had emancipated themselves as dramatic performances or pictorial *repraesentationes*. Matters could go so far in this regard that it becomes difficult to distinguish the sermon with dramatic interludes from the play accompanied by predicatory commentary.

According to the directions contained in a manuscript from Capestrano, not only are the lauds to be recited and the members of the audience called upon to kneel and sing the hymn on the wood of the cross. In addition, the stations of the Passion are each performed by several persons and linked together by the preacher's commentary.[100] The most copious staging directions are to be found in the *Sermonale*, or sermon book, of Alessandro de Ritiis: with its hymns and lauds, the Good Friday sermon resembles a play with interludes.[101]

In fact, d'Ancona had seen things differently in his standard work on the origins of the Italian theater. He did not consider texts like those just discussed to be sermons, but a form of *devozioni* that audibly and visibly "illustrated" the sermon and the liturgy.[102] In the union of narration and action, of the preacher's meditation and recitation of the drama, he saw sermon and drama as inseparable. He arrives at this thesis by analyzing texts that originated in Umbria and were transmitted to the Veneto in the first half of the fourteenth century. Contained in the *Cod. Palat.* 170, which is dated to 1375, they were recorded earlier than the sermons from the Abruzzi.[103]

In these texts, the preacher is both director and compère. At his command, actors come onto the stage and exit. He describes and comments on the performance. As d'Ancona explains, he usually stood in the pulpit, which thus became a proscenium. The performance itself took place beneath the tramezzo-beam in front of the entrance to the choir, beneath the painted cross affixed there.[104] The actors entered onto the stage, called the *talamo* (*thalamus*), from the aisles on the men's or women's sides of the nave. In the way it was erected on a detached platform with curtains and stage scenery, the stage may have resembled the "doll's house" of trecento painting, in which biblical events were depicted as theatrical scenes.[105]

The *devozione* of Good Friday, which was introduced with a sermon, and enlivened over and over by a question and answer game between the preacher and his audience, shows the close connection among liturgy, sermon, and theater, which were often combined with one another. Naturally, this connection applies to the case of many feasts such as the Annunciation and Easter, to name just two. The boundaries between the various literary genres and between rite, drama, and devotional practices were for a long time so fluid that a painted image of the Passion Christ, which was given current relevance by the Passion piety of the thirteenth century, could not be associated a priori with any definite and delimited context, such as with the liturgy of the Passion, as it was in Byzantium.

To round off the picture we have been drawing, we must closely consider again the prose texts that, as a new literary genre of the thirteenth century, competed with the Bible in narrating the Passion. They reformulated the Bible in an extensive wealth of episodes and an intensive wealth of emotion, so that they could offer the reading public a different, sensible presentation of the Bible and consequently a new way of seeing. Since they were read either as exciting novels or as textbooks on meditation, they functioned as light reading or as an aid to concentration for the purposes of psychological training. Sometimes the biblical content served as raw material that was only made into something by the storyteller. Of course, many of these texts were written for the internal use of the orders, which popularized them by passing them on through sermons and the like, as well as by translating them into the vernacular. When the texts claimed to be visions, they made a claim to authenticity that otherwise only the Bible could make, and did so in the twofold sense of vouchsafed revelation and immediate inner experience. In this way they also illustrate the powerful need for reality, which the public sought in the texts. The revelations of Brigitta of Sweden, a work of the late fourteenth century, is an extreme representative of a drastic realism. In Meier's opinion, they give an almost pathological description of Mary's emotions.[106]

To cite Meier's study once more, two thirteenth-century texts were devoted to the cause of mystical and didactic spiritualization: the *Legenda Aurea*, the compilation of texts of different kinds made by Jacopo de Voragine, and the so-called *Meditationes Vitae Christi*, which Meier describes with some exaggeration as rigid and lacking in action.[107] This one-sided characterization shows that literary scholarship has problems of classification similar to those of art history, when the topic is the devotional image. It is significant that the *Meditationes*, which circulated under Bonaventura's name, divide the narrative of the Passion, for example, into segments that were synchronized with the canonical hours. The division also constitutes instructions for using the *Meditationes* in private devotional practice. They provide—if one may put it that way—a series of "tableaux," before which the reader could concentrate himself emotionally on a situation, or, to express the matter in traditional terminology, "immerse himself" [*sich versenken*] in an event.[108] The "standing images," which were so popular in the late medieval staging of religious feasts and theatrical plays, are a kind of parallel.

The literary schema of the *Meditationes* thus combines the richly detailed narration of the historical drama with the contemplative close-up view of individual events that are "arrested" in such a way that they offer themselves to the reader's empathy. Here comparison with the painted image seems very appropriate, and what literature practiced, for example, in a tract such as the Zardino de Oration, was virtually prescribed for painting as its normal task. For the purposes of our argument, it should be kept in mind that texts such as the Meditationes pass on a wealth of miming, gestures, and speech by the protagonists of the Passion; indeed, they do not stop at the external expression of pain, but describe in vivid detail the inner feelings of the *dramatis personae*. This literary depiction furnished the public with a stock of mental images and provided the basis for an attitude of expectation with regard to the Passion. The painted images reacted to both with a new "pictorial language."

The Importation of an Icon

The long and rich history of the Imago Pietatis in the Veneto has already led us to the assumption stated above that Venice might have been the gateway for the importation of the eastern icon. Let us see what material allows us to verify this assumption.

The Venetian panels in Torcello and in the Stoclet collection both date from as early as the thirteenth century (figs. 101, 103).[109] Miniature painting, which we have not yet consulted, provides further evidence of the early existence of our image in the Veneto. The group of preserved examples begins chronologically with a missal in Cividale that was written for the patriarchate of Aquileia and probably for the cathedral of Cividale itself. Its Easter tables start with the year 1254.[110] The next example is a Viennese psalter that was produced in a Paduan atelier around 1260–1270.[111] This is followed by a Venetian breviary from Spalato, dated 1291 (fig. 97).[112] The Tuscan manuscript Plut. XXV.3 in Florence, in which Venetian influence clearly played a great role, has the same age (fig. 105).[113] In no other geographic area has such a quantity of thirteenth-century examples been observed.

If we include the examples from the fourteenth century, then likewise in no other region is a similar wealth of variants in the reproduction of an eastern icon to be found, whose identity was not to be questioned until well into the fifteenth century, a further peculiarity. Whether as a single panel (for example, that from Torcello, fig. 103), or as part of a diptych (for example, that in the Stoclet collection, fig. 101), in the center of the triptych in Dordrecht, or on the cover of the retable of the Pala d'Oro in San Marco (fig. 11), which in turn refers back to an eastern iconostasis, the "parent form" of the icon always remains recognizable. On the triptych in Trieste (fig 13) and in the above-mentioned manuscript in Florence,

Fig. 97 Venice, Museo Correr. Breviary from Spalato, 1291 (after Pallucchini)

the Christ figure is the companion of the Virgin of Mercy and of the veronica, respectively, and thus is given a status equal to that of these famous icons. In book miniatures it already appeared in a secondary context. It follows that the Imago Pietatis was not invented as the result of a theological notion, as some studies would have us believe, but arrived in the West as an eastern panel painting. This discovery is fundamental for understanding what follows.

The role of Venice does not preclude the existence of other routes for the importation of our image. It is documented, perhaps for the first time, around 1235 in the world chronicle composed by Matthew Paris, again as the companion of the veronica (fig. 80).[114] After the middle of the thirteenth century, it also appears in Tuscany,[115] and the Entombment of Christ, one of the frescoes of the convent of the Poor Clares of S. Pietro in Vineis in Anagni near Rome (ca. 1270), presents the main figure in such an oddly bent-over pose that its upper part can only be understood as an allusion to the icon (fig. 98).[116] In addition, scattered transalpine evidence

Fig. 98 Anagni, San Pietro in Vineis. The Entombment, 13th c.

from the thirteenth century has come down to us, though its dating is unsure, and it has no lasting connection with the later history of the icon, because other ideas gained acceptance there. Only at the Bohemian court of Charles IV (1347-1378), under the massive influence of Italian art and as a result of special interest in panel painting, did Italian panel painting become important, and indeed was even imported in individual specimens such as the diptych of Tommaso da Modena in Karlstein (figs 8, 33).[117] In Paris and at the courts of the dukes of Burgundy and of Berry, the *Pitié-de-Nostre-Seigneur* was a familiar image both as a diptych and as a triptych, as well as on the altar, transmitted probably via the papal court in Avignon (fig. 34).[118] But this did not occur until the second half of the fourteenth century. Let us return to the thirteenth.

The question arises of why the Imago Pietatis spread so rapidly. The answers can only offer a framework for discussing the question. The Passion mysticism that grew to be so peculiarly intense during the thirteenth century must have welcomed every attractive image of the Passion that came into circulation at that time. The other existing images: the painted cross and the sculpted Deposition, were soon outmoded in the form that had been given to them. Their replacement by the Imago Pietatis can be demonstrated in several cases: its three-figured version, with Mary and John, offered itself as an alternative to the painted cross (figs. 86, 93, 94, see p. 180). Last-

The Image and Its Public

ly, the nature of the new image made it attractive to the public. The close-up view of Christ with its clear delineation of his countenance and its expressive depiction of his suffering qualified the portrait to be a functional form symbolizing meditation on the Passion (p. 40) and offering a good many possibilities for identification. In any event, the portrait-schema that it was using became very popular in the thirteenth century.

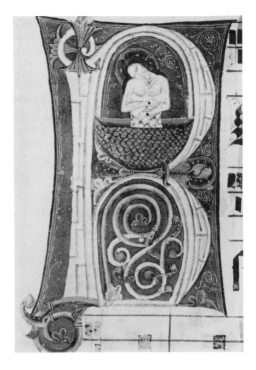

Fig. 99 Formerly in Milan, Hoepli Collection. Folio of a choir book (after Toesca)

But it is still possible to raise the objection that the Imago Pietatis lent itself to a content which still lacked a proper visual symbol in the repertoire of images, for example, the eucharistic Christ. However, the evidence provided by the surviving material argues against that thesis. The miniatures reproducing the Imago Pietatis make it clear that no consensus existed in the understanding of the image. There are as many interpretations of it as there are examples.

In the above-mentioned missal in Cividale, the image is located before the Canon, the truly sacrificial part of the mass. In this liturgical context, it is a symbol of the eucharistic sacrifice.[110] It is such a symbol on the paten of Werben, also.[119] In a book of Gregorian chants from central Italy, from which the Milanese Hoepli collection possesses a single page (fig. 99), it adorns the Introit of the Easter mass: *Resurrexi* . . . (I am risen . . .). The added sarcophagus, clearly an ad hoc expansion of the figure, underscores the intention of depicting the resurrected Christ, who in the burial pose "esce dal munimento."[120] In the Paduan manuscript in Vienna, we find the icon figure, this time with an added cross and bleeding welts from the scourging, in the illuminated capital letter beginning the psalm, "Beatus vir," combined with David, the harp-playing author of the psalms, just as in a psalter originating from Hildesheim, now in Munich, dating from ca. 1270.[121] Its meaning is revealed by Psalm 1, which speaks of the righteous man who walks in the way of the Lord. The figure also replaces the traditional Savior as the frontispiece of the Book of Psalms as a whole, just as, on the painted cross, *Christus patiens* replaces *Christus triumphans*. Perhaps in this "change of paradigms" a preference for a different conception of Christ is being expressed. The Viennese psalter was probably written by a Dominican for a member of the Hallthal community of gentlewomen in Tyrol. As a devotional book, especially in the hands of the laity, the psalter was the locus of the private image's emergence. In the breviary of Spalato mentioned above, we become acquainted with a further context for the image, Easter, and still another in a Breslau codex, in which the image receives the prayer for the mercy of God at the beginning of the All Saints' litany.[122]

In the frequently mentioned Codex Plut. XXV.3 in Florence (1291–1300), the Imago Pietatis illustrates a pseudo-Bernardine text of Passion mysticism (fig. 38) which quotes the legendary embrace of Bernard by the crucified Christ: "With what a strong embrace you have encompassed me, good Jesus, as the blood ran forth from your side. . . . What have you done that you had to suffer so? Surely I am the cause of your suffering. . . ."[123] This is then a locus classicus of Passion meditation, which refers to the icon portrait that serves the dialogical *compassio* as a devotional image. The identification of the figure with the crucified Christ who has been taken from the cross and is ready to embrace, makes it possible at a later date to take over the gesture of embrace from the Deposition (p. 74). In the miniature, the aforementioned interpretation of the figure prepares the way for this modification of the figure. At the end of the manuscript the figure appears again, namely, as an icon on parchment (fig. 105). In the positioning of the arms, which are folded across the chest, it resembles the Venetian panel painting of the Stoclet collection, but the heavily bleeding wounds are an addition that expressly invites the viewer to contemplate Christ's wounds.

With the lectern of Giovanni Pisano in Berlin that was analyzed above, we cross the threshold into the early fourteenth century (fig. 31).[124] Its peculiar feature is that the Imago Pietatis is shown here to the viewer in a shroud displayed by two angels. The contradiction between the display of the winding sheet, which belongs in the context of the Easter play, and the portrayal of the buried Christ, which belongs in the context of the Passion, was, as we saw, transcended perhaps in a "sacramental realism" (to use Schrade's words). The identification of the figure with the Host, which was also raised from

Fig. 100 Pisa, Cathedral. Lectern by Giovanni Pisano

the grave on Easter, prevents a contradiction between death and life which has no place at all in the eucharistic reality. The understanding of the Imago Pietatis as an image of the *Corpus Domini* has been documented so often for the fourteenth century and afterwards, that it would be absurd to deny it for the thirteenth century. But the sacramental interpretation may neither be generalized nor, in our case, isolated. It precludes neither different nor supplementary interpretations.

If one understands, for example, the display of the shroud as proof of the reality of Christ's death, then our figure represents an advance in semantic precision that restrictively defines the cloth as the *burial* cloth. While the mournful expression of the angels would be suited to this advance, the "objective display-gesture" of the angels, as A. Roeder terms it, was primarily at home in the Easter play where it testified to the Resurrection.[125]

Yet another variant is offered on the lectern of the cathedral pulpit in Pisa, a related work produced by the same atelier (fig. 100).[126] Again the Passion Christ is presented in a cloth, but here he is surrounded by figures of the resurrected. The secondary figures also confirm the Resurrection as the symbolic significance of the Christ figure. But if one interprets them in light of two situations in which the New Testament speaks of a resurrection of the dead, then they are united either to Christ's death on the cross or to the Last Judgment. In the one case, they identify the Christ figure as the crucified Christ; in the other case, as a "sign of the Son of Man," which will appear before the Final Judge. Both interpretations probably apply also to the Berlin relief.

It is important to see the polyvalence of the semantic content that is to be found on both lecterns. Comparable motifs on earlier lecterns in the area of Pisa twice show Christ in an aureole borne by angels.[127] Seen against this background, a newer formula of the Epiphany appears to supplant the older. The Passion Christ in his human suffering replaces Christ in his divine splendor. The process recalls the corresponding change in the conception of Christ recorded on the painted cross, which took place even earlier.

Now the Berlin relief attaches very great importance to Christ's half-length depiction, although there would have been room for an entire figure (fig. 31). It thus identifies the icon form as a privileged one, commenting on it, as it were, by means of the motif of the angels with the shroud, as its counterpart in Pisa does through the resurrected.

We can conclude that the importance and prevalence of the icon figure at this time cannot be satisfactorily explained by the then-current interpretations of it, which not only do not preclude one another, but even involve each other. We have already treated the connection between the themes of the Passion and of the Eucharist, as well as the late appearance of the cult of the Corpus Christi in Italy, which, although shaping the history of the image in the North, became important in Italy only in the fourteenth century (p.81).

Since it had no single and exclusive meaning, the Passion figure attracted a good many theological and mystical interpretations, that is, as many as were circulating in that era. Its description as the "mercy of the Lord" or the "form of *pietas*" alludes to two general concepts that were already developed in the *oeuvre* of Bernard of Clairvaux.

For Bernard, *pietas* was first of all piety, for example, what filled

Mary Magdalene when she anointed the feet of the *magister pietatis*.[128] In a speech before the Knights Templar, Bernard calls the tomb of Christ the most holy treasure of Christendom, for "the recollection of his death disposes one more to piety" than does that of his life.[129] The possession of Christ's tomb, the goal of the crusaders, became, after it was lost once more, a demand that was in the mind of Christendom, particularly in the thirteenth century, and that possibly procured a high degree of contemporary relevance and importance for the pictorial figure of the buried Christ. In the fourteenth-century statutes of a brotherhood from Bologna, a standard prayer is still prescribed "for the tomb of the Lord . . . , that God may return it to the Christians."[130]

Further, *pietas* is the term used to describe the nature of Christ's sacrifice as well as the grace which is merited by Christ and gained by men through piety. The sacrificial act of Christ, an act of *pietas*, occurs in accordance with God's will and calls forth the act of mercy that grants redemption to mankind.[131] Bernard puts the death of Christ into a known theological schema when he terms it the "death of my death" which Christ endured "so that I might live."[132] But the death of the guilty has been vanquished through the death of one who is guiltless. How can divine justice permit this? The answer is that the justice of God has been offset here by the positive counter-principle of the compassion of God.[133] In a writing of Jacopo Passavanti from the mid-fourteenth century, the Virgin's speech at the Last Judgment on behalf of mankind contains the plea that the Judge should put mercy before justice or, in Passavanti's words, "temper the terribleness of his justice with the gentleness of his mercy [*pietà*]."[134] Moreover, according to Bernard, man's death is necessary because it, like Dante's hell, was established by God's justice, but can be counterbalanced by God's mercy or pity.[135] In the polarity of the divine world order sketched out here, the Imago Pietatis could be experienced as the figure that vouchsafed pardon, just as the image of the Judge could be experienced as the figure threatening punishment. It is obvious what importance the Imago Pietatis must have acquired when considered from this perspective, which aroused in the faithful the fear of the hereafter. We will pursue this argument further when we treat of the descriptions and classifications of the image (p. 191).

The connection between the Passion and the Sacrament, which the believer is to receive as nourishment, furnishes Bernard a third aspect under which the sacrificial figure of Christ can be contemplated. Daily he descends upon the altar "in humble appearance"; there he humiliates himself anew by becoming the sacrifice that the believer eats as sacrificial bread.[136] This concept fairly cried out for a pictorial symbol. The image made visible the "real presence" of the Christ of the Passion, which, in the form of bread, was deficient in visuality. In turn, it profited from the reality which the bread or Host possessed as a result of the act of transubstantiation.

Bernard's theological theses classify the notions from which the image of *pietas*, given visual form as the image of the sacrificed Christ, acquired its peculiar importance for the period in question. These theses also confirm the complexity of the possibilities of meaning that lay ready for the eastern icon figure in the West.

From Painted Cross to Imago Pietatis: Functional Change and Assimilation

The reception of the Passion icon in Italy had been prepared in the milieu of the mendicant orders. Here the icon found a forerunner that prepared the way for it: the crucified Christ of the painted panel cross. The special relation between the crucified Christ and the Imago Pietatis can be followed on three distinct paths, which we shall pursue in their chronological sequence.

Early diptychs that replace the crucified Christ with the Passion portrait furnish us with the first example to be analyzed. Two works already discussed allow us to recognize the tendency toward the development of a symmetrical double portrait consisting of the icons of Christ and Mary. In both cases, the formal revisions apply to the Crucifixion and not to the portrait of Mary, which kept its form. In the Sienese diptych in London and Budapest, even the picture frame of the Crucifixion is made similar to that of the panel showing Mary, which, however, for reasons of formal and semantic symmetry, repeats the lamenting angels of the Crucifixion and thereby is reinterpreted as the Madonna of the Passion (figs. 2, 4). The protagonist of the Crucifixion is isolated from that scene and transformed into an *imago* resembling the *imago* of Mary.[137] The integration of the narrative of a Crucifixion scene with object-type of a painted cross reveals the tendency to find a new visual structure for the image's new function in a new medium (p.12).

We observe a similar interpolation in the double panel from Lucca in the Uffizi (fig. 81). Here the crucified Christ is isolated through his size and position, which again are borrowed from the painted cross.[138] The partnership of Christ and Mary thereby becomes so evident that it need not be only induced mentally from a Crucifixion scene. But it was still a pair of two formally heteroge-

Fig. 101 Brussels, Stoclet Collection. Venetian diptych half, 13th c.

nous and only functionally homogenous images which expressed this relation. The solution of the problem thus defined could only be found when one set a second portrait depicting the Passion Christ next to the existing portrait of Mary. And this is, of course, what happened.

Fig. 102
Moscow, Tret-
jakov Gallery.
South Slavic
icon, 14th c.

A Sienese diptych from the circle of Barna da Siena in the Museo Horne in Florence establishes an equation between two half-length figures which functions both on the syntactic and semantic level (fig. 10).[139] If we compare it with the London/Budapest diptych, the difference between the two works lies in the fact that in the former the crucified Christ is replaced by the Imago Pietatis, while the Virgin *Eleousa* is retained (fig. 2). There is a new element in that the *Eleousa* gazes beyond the Child, whom she is caressing, toward her dead Son. In this look, she expresses prolepsis of the Passion and establishes an intrinsic relationship between the two panels.

A similar sequence of a diptych with the Crucifixion and a diptych with the Imago Pietatis can be reconstructed for the Venetian antecedents of the Bohemian diptych in Karlsruhe (fig. 8).[140] In this

176   *The Image and Its Public*

Fig. 103 Tor-
cello, Muse-
um. Venetian
Panel, late
13th c.

work, it is the Virgin Pelagonitissa who, as a constant element, indicates the metamorphosis of the double panel. One could, therefore,
describe this process of structural change using the following stages:
The Passion diptych was revised a first time when the Crucifixion
was assimilated to the painted cross, and altered a second time when
the Crucifixion was replaced with the Passion portrait. The Passion
portrait came closest to the ideal that one had in mind. It is first evidenced on a western diptych in the Venetian panel of the Stoclet
collection (fig. 101),[141] which seems to be one half of the replica of
a Byzantine diptych (fig. 102).[142] In replacing the Crucifixion by the
Imago Pietatis, the painter repeated what had happened during the
twelfth century in Byzantium: the emergence of a pair of portraits in
a double panel.

The identification of the crucified Christ and the Imago Pietatis
with respect to their meaning becomes evident in the metamorphoses of the early diptychs. Grasping the allusion of the Imago
Pietatis to the painted cross is essential to understanding its reception. Small-sized painted crosses of the thirteenth century had
already become images of contemplation that had been moved to a

Fig. 104
Assisi, San
Francesco.
Panel by the
Master of the
Blue Cross,
13th c.

side altar or to a private chapel. The long devotional inscription on
the London panel cross by the Umbrian "Master of St. Francis"
(height: ca. 60 cm), which was to be read by a viewer from close up,
confirms the image's function as a devotional image, and it was this
function which the Imago Pietatis could take over.[143]

A second approach to our problem is offered by a thirteenth-

Fig. 105 Florence, Bibl. Med. Laurenziana, MS Plut. XXV.3, fol. 384 (Emilia 1293–1300)

century Venetian panel in Torcello (fig. 103; 41 x 43 cm).[144] It amplifies the iconic portrait of Christ according to the model of the painted cross. The newly introduced figures, taken from the Crucifixion, are adjoined to the portrait of Christ in a spatial relationship and with a relative size similar to what was customary for painted crosses. In Umbria, in particular, it was still the practice in the later thirteenth century to place Mary and John under Christ's arms in side fields enlarging the cross: a specimen in the museum of S. Francesco in Assisi, a work of the "Blue Crucifix Master," may suffice as an example (fig. 104).[145] The schema surely survived in the Veneto as well. The gesture of John on the Torcello panel indicates a Byzantine pictorial tradition. A Venetian retable in Piave di Sacco repeats the Torcello combination on its pediment.[146]

On the panel in Torcello, the imported eastern icon is transposed into a known schema of the painted cross and is presented to the public in this "translation" (fig. 103). It is therefore significant that this painting not only was always a single panel (note the wide, rectangular format), but certainly also had an eastern single panel as a model from which it quotes the lamenting angels. A single panel with this pedigree needed an "explication" through secondary figures more than a diptych did. The colors also depart from the eastern model. The use of black, but especially the red background was unusual in Byzantium for an icon.

Gombrich has reduced a principle in the development of seeing to a simple formula: The unknown is classified using a known schema.[147] This also applies to our case, though in another sense than that intended by Gombrich: The eastern portrait icon was classified using the Italian schema of the painted cross. This procedure was a process of assimilation, an assimilation of the imported image to a new environment. The solution found on the panel in Torcello remained an exception, however.

More successful was the assimilation to another variant of the painted cross invented by Giunta Pisano (fig. 86).[148] This brings us to a third model the investigation of which will advance our inquiry. Through the montage of half-length ancillary icons at the ends of the cross's arms, Giunta had made the unity of the three participants in the Crucifixion visible in an original way (p. 145). In the painted cross with ancillary icons, he had reduced the difference in size between the three figures without detriment to the "soloist" role of the crucified Christ. The path that had to be followed in assimilating the icon is obvious. One needed only to place the Imago Pietatis as the main icon between the two already given ancillary icons in order to obtain a triptych. I would consider the triptych to be the Italian innovation that was of crucial importance in the process of assimilating the eastern Passion portrait.

Of course, this is an induction, and not an account of what actually happened. But the induction explains what the new ensemble was aiming at and what it signified, that is, again an assimilation to a known pictorial schema, that of the painted cross. The result rarely has been preserved directly, as an independent triptych, but has left its traces in other contexts, for example, on a retable. An early example is Simone Martini's polyptych of 1320 which is in Pisa.[149] At the end of the thirteenth century, the triptych was a familiar form

Fig. 106 Mosciano near Florence. Fresco. late 13th c.

taken by the panel painting. It lived on in the private and cult image after the composite altar retable had gained general acceptance. The Venetian triptych in Trieste is a late-comer in the history of the altarpiece (fig. 13).[150] On the retable, the triad with the Imago Pietatis, which in this context refers to the Eucharist, gained a permanent place in the predella (fig. 35). This convention prevented the triad from finding its way into the center of altarpieces.

The limits to the development of the Imago Pietatis were set from the outset by the size that could be attained by the half-length figure. It appears as the subject of large-sized painted panels only after further changes that do not begin before the trecento. In the dugento it was a devotional image, and in the fourteenth century it is also documented as such for monasteries and confraternities. Critical for its history was the constitution of a triad of half-length figures in the center of which it appeared. The ancillary figures flank-

The Icon in the West 181

ing it, as figures mediating between the viewer and the image, also form a commentary, inasmuch as their origins lie in the Crucifixion.

An early example of the Imago Pietatis in the center of the new triad of icons is a Tuscan fresco from ca. 1290 in Mosciano near Florence located on the southern side wall of the single-naved church (fig. 106).[151] The surviving one of the two ancillary figures draws the beholder's attention to Christ in the same way Simone Martini's retable accomplished this for the Madonna a generation later. The fragmentary early fresco can thus be completed in accordance with more recent examples. It was so important to the painter of Mosciano to preserve the identity of the icons as half-length figures, that he introduced a curtain in order to explain the presence of half-length figures between the neighboring full figures. One would think he had seen the triad as a triptych.

H.W. van Os has been able to identify as a triptych the so-called Passion polyptych of Simone Martini, from which comes the panel in Birmingham showing Saint John that has been dated to 1320 (fig. 107).[152] The apostle's gesture of lamentation and his sideward gaze permit no other explanation. As the 34.5 x 24 cm size of this panel indicates, Simone's triptych must have been a private devotional image. But a polyptych of Segna da Buonaventura, which can be datedat around 1315, and in the center of which, between Mary and John, Stubblebine believes there was an Imago Pietatis, was an altarpiece.[153]

The most important new find from the early history of the Imago Pietatis is a triptych that has recently been published by H.W. van Os (fig. 12). For some time it was on loan to the museum of Dordrecht from a private collection in The Hague.[154] We must consider this work carefully because it helps answer the question of the origin of the triptych in Italy. The difficulty in identifying the painter is due to the mixture of Venetian elements with those of eastern icon painting, in both the technical and stylistic senses. The Venetian elements, which may be expected only in the broader area of Venetian influence, perhaps at a site on the Dalmatian coast, seem to me to be of decisive importance.[155] The reverse side of the image, depicting the donor of the panel, a Dominican, in front of the founder of his order, also points to a western center. The central panel shows the eastern Passion portrait with truncated arms, an early variant that was little known in the West (fig. 49). While Mary is depicted as lamenting, she does not represent an appropriation of the type of the eastern diptych (see p. 111), but follows the corresponding figures of Mary in Venetian paintings of the Crucifixion, as is evident from the way she holds her cloak to her cheek. John,

too, is in the Venetian pictorial tradition. He does not appear as the youthful, favorite disciple, but as the aged evangelist, in the same position next to the Imago Pietatis as later on Paolo Veneziano's *Pala Feriale* in San Marco (1343–45). The exchange of the one type for the other is, from a Byzantine point of view, a misunderstanding, for the aged evangelist had his own place in theapostle frieze of an iconostasis—as this frieze became a model for the *Pala Feriale*—but not in a Crucifixion (fig. 11). John's gesture of lamentation, however, is quoted from a Crucifixion.

In my opinion the triptych in The Hague is not in the Byzantine pictorial tradition; rather, it is the replica of a Venetian triptych, even if it was perhaps the work of a painter residing in the East. The gestures of Mary and John function as quotations from the Crucifixion, and this is important for our argument. The triptych with the Imago Pietatis that was developed in Italy put the eastern icon, in the formal and semantic senses, into a context familiar to the Italian public. I speak of a "semantic" sense, because the triptych identifies the Imago Pietatis with the crucified Christ, leaving aside the question of what that might have implied. While on the painted cross the lamenting figures were subordinated to the main figure, they now are coordinated with it. In the triad constituted here, the precondition was created for presenting a group image of the Lamentation as an emotionally moving *historia*. This solution was arrived at only later, in the trecento.

We have examined the reference of the Imago Pietatis to the Crucifixion and painted cross in three different ways. Clearly, through the imported image's connection with a context familiar to the Italian public, and through its introduction into a known pictorial schema, the non-narrative Passion icon could become the companion of the portrait of Mary (fig. 89). The sculpted Deposition also became important for the imported icon. In the gesture of the outspread arms, a gesture of embrace, it provided a motif of which the Imago Pietatis could make full use (p. 74).

Thus, the figure of the icon became integrated into the Italian pictorial tradition in numerous ways. It did not bring a new theme, but a new pictorial form that was by no means made for use as a devotional image in the western sense, but was at once employed in this manner. A free interpretation of the icon's schema was possible only because there existed no authentic "original" of the picture (fig. 14). The miraculous image of S. Croce in Rome is a later and unsuccessful attempt to create such an "original." The Imago Pietatis was an early devotional image of the crucified Christ of the Passion whom it showed *in forma pietatis*. But its pictorial form was taken over from eastern icon painting. The revisions of the icon's form were the means to its semantic appropriation. On the composite altar retable, the icon became a symbol of the Eucharist. But as a devotional image, it was not confined to a single interpretation. The genesis of the devotional image was a complex process. The prerequisites were devotional practices that invited meditations on images "before the inner eye." It was the piety associated with the Passion

The Image and Its Public

that established such self-training as the way to achieve the desired attitude of pity. Material images were supposed to stimulate inner images. Devotion became devotion attached to images. But the images employed were not created to be used as devotional images. Only in the course of their use did the functional change produce a change of form through which the devotional images became such also in a formal sense.

Chapter VII
Summary

Studies such as the present one venture onto terrain that is not yet completely under scholarly control. Art history still possesses no framework for classifying audiences such as modern literary scholarship has worked out for the literary public. Thus no claim is made that the functional model sketched in these pages has achieved its definitive form, let alone that it may be generalized with no problem. Certainly, it is to be regretted that, for the time being, the inquiry only covers the period up to ca. 1300. Our conclusions must still be validated for the fourteenth century, when our image reaches the acme of its diffusion and its highest degree of internal complexity. For the fifteenth century, see the author's study: *Giovanni Bellini. Pietà* (Frankfurt, 1985).

The investigation undertaken here combines a particular way of analyzing images with a historical argument. The historical account is meant to be a case study illuminating the historical transformation of panel painting in the course of the change of its social and cultural environment. The panel painting is represented by the subject matter of the Passion meditation and the basic type of an imported icon.

The terminology is of necessity modern because the questions we are addressing to the historical works under consideration are ultimately modern ones. Indeed, we do not want to provide answers for the Middle Ages, but comprehensively to decode historical images for ourselves, that is, to reconstruct the functional level of their historical form. Questions not contributing to this end have not received the same attention. Thus neither a history of certain iconographical motifs, nor a history of piety as it is reflected in art was planned.

Readers looking for factual information about the history of the Imago Pietatis are most likely to find it in Chapters V and VI. Chapter V deals with the eastern genesis of the icon as an import to the West, with which the history of our image began. The functional model utilized by the investigation proved to be especially fruitful here. In Byzantium, the icon was so intimately connected with the Passion liturgy that the latter explains not only the form, but also the existence of this icon. Such results cannot be expected for the thirteenth century in Italy, if only because there the liturgy and the tasks assigned to images were different. In this milieu, form and function interacted in a more complicated way than earlier in Byzantium. It is the purpose of Chapter VI to reconstruct the introduction of the imported icon in the new Italian context and, at the same time, to elucidate the assimilation which the image now underwent. In this reconstruction, the context of the already existing Passion images in cultic devotion, sermons, and religious theater received special emphasis, because this context sheds light on the new functions that altered the imported image.

Chapters I through IV deal with basic considerations. They construct a framework for the historical presentation. Chapter I sketches the milieu in which occurred the general acceptance and integration of the painted panel and the transformation of its form and cultural task. By "painted panel" we mean the portable depiction of a "cultic person." The relation between official and private cultic practices, between the Church and the lay world, exhibits a complexity that calls into doubt the explanatory clichés advanced heretofore.

Chapter III treats the question of how to understand the concept of functional form. In this discussion, the concept of the devotional image (a historical notion) plays a role. It is shown that the interaction of form and function is more complex and unstable than generally accepted classifications recognize. This is why concepts derived from medieval theological notions of images are not sufficient for describing the diachronic profile of a historical change of images.

Thus the way narrative images recounted their stories altered in accordance with the changing interpretation of the biblical topics that was evident in contemporary texts. The relation between a narrative and a portrait image, both of which deal with the same material provided by the Passion, must be determined anew, as must be also the relation between the cultic practice of "devotion," which was in no way a merely private matter, and the pictorial convention of the devotional image. Different types of functions exercised by images can be distinguished: the cultural function in general, in which the public's attitude toward images is reflected; an "applied" function in the narrow sense, as in the case of a funereal or sacramental image; and the specific relation that elucidates the form of an image as the function of its content or message.

Chapter IV attempts to reconstruct the reality that the rhetoric of the images conveyed to the viewer. Indeed, the image communicated only as much reality as the viewer could recognize within it. Thus the ecclesiastical rite gave quite specific instructions for experiencing the sacramental reality in the image. In the latter the viewer found again the "cultic gestures" of the liturgy, as it were. Like reliquaries, images make a "display gesture" through which their rhetoric reaches its climax. The mediating activity expressed in this "gesture" conforms to the contemporary staging of cultic practices. Between the reception of cultic devotion and the reception of the relevant images there exists a reciprocal relationship that makes the social-psychological dimension of the pictorial rhetoric understandable. The depiction of reality and the reality of the depiction in the images can be reconstructed on the basis of the functional sphere of ecclesiastical cultic practices and the related "cult plays" performed by the laity. The pictorial rhetoric laid the groundwork for a new instrumentalization of the image. The "language of the image" becomes as important as its "content."

Appendix A
Pietas and Imago Pietatis: The Image in Historical Accounts and Inscriptions

The concept of *pietas* (p. 173) occurs in the oldest mention of the image that I know of. In the statutes (dated 1329) of a Bolognese brotherhood, the person portrayed is distinguished from the form in which he is portrayed: *in forma pietatis*.[1] A familiar image type was Thus designated as the "image of *pietas*," a depiction of Jesus in the form of *pietas*.

In the contract for the tomb of Archbishop Scarlatti of Pisa (died 1362) the central figure of Jesus flanked by angels is called simply *pietas*.[2] As a child, Catherine of Genoa (1447–1510) saw "in her bedroom our Lord Jesus. . .in that form which is usually called *pietà*."[3] In the inventories of Jean de Berry there is a reference to "a painted panel of an ancient sort, probably originating in Rome, as is said, and portraying a *Dieu de pitié*" (tableau d'ancienne facon, semblablement venu de Rome, comme on dit, fait d'un Dieu de pitié).[4] In the will of a certain Migliorati from Rimini (1499), an Angel Pietà by Giovanni Bellini, apparently the panel in the museum of Rimini, is described as "imago Domini . . . mortui et sublati de cruce in formam pietatis," whereby the person portrayed (Jesus) is again clearly distinguished from the biographical situation (the Deposition) and from the type of the depiction (the form of *pietà*).[5] With respect to the correspondence of the merchant of Prato (1390–1391), one is guided only by appearances and moreover misinterprets them if one describes the Pietà as "our Lord, as he is rising from the tomb" (quand'esce dal munimento).[6] Examples of the use of *pietà* as the title of an image, still applicable even to a triptych by Gerard David,[7] can be multiplied endlessly.

The situation changes when, toward the end of the fourteenth century, a particular image—the icon of S. Croce in Gerusalemme in Rome—becomes well known, acquiring the status of a miraculous image, and having the claim made for it that it was the archetype of the pictorial convention under consideration.[8] In its reproduction in Israel van Meckenem's engraving, the icon is defined as the *imago pietatis*. The emphasis has shifted from a form of depiction (*forma pietatis*) to a particular image, the panel of the *pietà* (*imago pietatis*) in Rome. Strictly speaking, then, in light of this historical usage, the common practice in art history of calling all the relevant depictions Imago Pietatis, which we too follow, is incorrect. In the legend of the "Mass of St. Gregory," which was immediately linked with the "prototype" venerated in Rome, is made of a vision that Pope Gregory the Great (590–604) had of Christ during the celebration of the mass. It was concluded that the vision was documented in the preserved image.[9] For this reason the appearance of Christ on the icon is considered both specific and authentic because in the vision Christ revealed himself in just this appearance, namely, *sub effigie pietatis*, as a manuscript written in S. Croce in 1475 formulates it.[10] On an Umbrian fresco from 1466, the image of Christ in "St. Gregory's Mass" is described as a manifestation *in specie d'una bellissima pietà.*[11] In the inscription accompanying a fifteenth-century Umbrian indulgence image (today in Cologne), the indulgence connected with the image and its contemplation is legitimized by the very same vision of Gregory: "Our Lord in the form of the *pietà*" (el nostro signore. . .in forma de pietade) appeared to the pope, "whereupon at the sight of him Gregory was moved to *pietà* and pious devotion" (onde vedendo s. Gregorio fo mosso a pietade et devozione).[12]

The twofold employment of the term of *pietas* is evident here. On the one hand, it refers to the sacrifice of the Messiah symbolizing the act of redemption and its repetition in the sacrifice of the mass. On the other hand, it refers to the Passion of Christ the Man, which invites the beholder to pious pity, to feel *pietas*. Under the latter aspect, the image stimulates a deep-lying spiritual mood or state that can also be described with the term *devotio*. By assuming this religious role, the viewer obtains the right to the reward promised by the sacrificial act shown in the image. Here we can see the nexus between two conceptions of *pietas*, two conceptions that also presuppose two actors: the one portrayed and his viewer (see the Introduction, p. 4, where mimesis is discussed).

On a tapestry in Angers, an angel with the instruments of the Passion expresses to the viewer the same invitation with which many Passion plays were begun: "Behold and contemplate this with devotion and piety" (*Regarde en pieté*).[13] When Mary, in the rhymed *Passion* of Niccolo di Mino Cicerchia of Siena (ca. 1364), bids the spectator or reader to "take pity [*pietà vi prenda*] on my sweet love [that is, Jesus] and console me," the devotion is given the tint of pity, that is, of that empathy with the depicted suffering to which the pertinent images also summon their viewers.[14] In the Passion

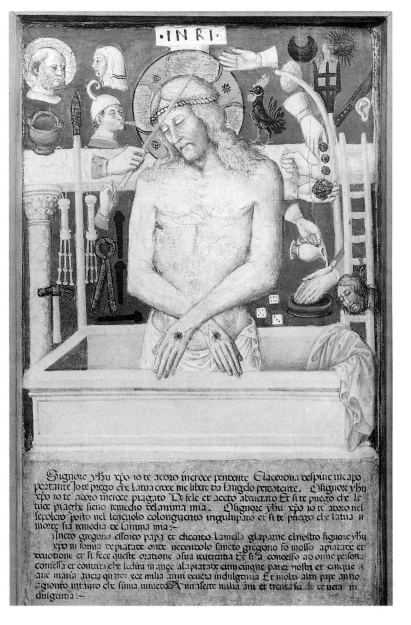

Fig. 108
Cologne,
Wallraf
Richartz
Museum.
Umbrian
indulgenced
panel, 15th c.

Signore yhu xpo io te acozo mercee penoente Elacozona oespine incapo
pertante Jo te prego che latua croce me libere oa langelo percotente. Osignore yhu
xpo io te acozo mercee piagato De fele et aceto abeuerato Et si te prego che le
tuoe piaghe sieno remedio delanima mia. Osignore yhu xpo io te acozo nel
sepolcro posto nel lenzuolo colonguento ingulupato et si te prego che latua ii
morte sia remedia oe lanima mia :–
    sincto gregorio essenco papa et dicenco lamessa glapaune elnostro signore yhu
    xpo in forma oepiatate once necencolo sancto gregorio fo mosso apiatate et
    oeuotione et si fece queste orature asua reuerentia Et si si concesso ao onne persona
    confessa et contrita che ledira manee alapiatare cinncinque pater nostri et cinque a
    aue maria jueta quatez ece mila anni cenesa indulgentia Et molti altri pape anno
    agionto intanto che sima innueto Nui misere mila im et trenta sei oe uera in
    dulgentia :–

rhetoric of the older Marian lamentations, the feeling of *pietà* that
exists between the *Mamma pietosa* and her Son plays a great role.[15] In
a *sacra rappresentazione* of Cast. Castellani, the angel with cross and
chalice proclaims on the Mount of Olives the beginning of the

Pietas and Imago Pietatis   193

Passion, saying that it was now time to open the gates of Hell to God's *pietà*.[16]

In the words of Gerard de Frachet, the significance of the images in the Dominicans' cell lay in the fact that the brothers "looked upon the images and are looked upon by them with the eyes of pity" (*oculis pietatis*).[17] The double meaning of image to be pitied, which applies to the portrayal of Jesus, and image of pity, the pity given to the viewer, could not be better expressed. As a matter of fact, the term *pietas* is often replaced by the notion of the pity shown by God, as on the Bohemian diptych in Karlsruhe ("Misericordia Domini").[18] God's pity for mankind is the motive for the death portrayed so vividly in the images. It is also an indication of the hope promised by the images, the hope, namely, of salvation, which the viewer is supposed to earn through the piety to which the images invite him.[19] What role death and salvation played in the thinking of the time was shown in the discussion of the theological concept of *pietas* (p. 173). There reference was made to a vision of the Last Judgment that, in the account of it given by J. Passavanti, summarizes the understanding, with its full significance, of *pietas* in the context of the Last Judgment.[20] Mary throws herself down at the feet of the Judge and begs him *pietosamente* to "temper the terribleness of his justice with the gentleness of his mercy" (*pietà*). The *pietà* that leads to clemency here is a result of the successful petition by the advocate who is full of *pietà* and *misericordia* for her clients.

The fears, hopes, and desires of the viewers are made explicit by the inscriptions on the images. The text on a panel of Melozzo Marco in the *pinacoteca* of Faenza tells of the promise of a life to come made by the image.[21] On an indulgence panel in Cologne (p. 192), an inscription prescribes saying, as a prayer, that the cross and the tomb should "be the saving cure [*remedio*] of my soul." The eucharistic significance expressed in the notion of salvation through the taking of lifesaving medicine is emphasized in other pictorial inscriptions. Thus, on a Bohemian panel from ca. 1470, the Imago Pietatis is called the "living bread" which "came down from Heaven," and which invites the viewer to eat it.[22] Many depictions were predominantly pictorial symbols of the Eucharist that proclaimed this specialization through appropriate means.

The panel of the Florentine "master of the Straus Madonna" (1405) in Warsaw introduces us to a final group of images with inscriptions.[23] In its quotation of Paul's Letter to the Philippians 2:5ff., the inscription on this panel sounds an exegetical note and speaks of the renunciation and humiliation of the Son of Man who

Fig. 109
Parma,
Baptistery.
Fresco, late
14th c.

was obedient unto death. In a votive fresco from the second half of
the fourteenth century in the baptistry of Parma, the Imago Pietatis,
supported by Mary, holds a scroll bidding the viewer to contemplate
the stigmata or the *arma*: "As you pass by here, always recollect with
reverence the wounds of your King. . ." (Hic semper dum transis,

Pietas and Imago Pietatis   195 recolle Tui vulnera regis. . .).[24] Two prophets with scriptural texts from Zachariah 13:6 and Isaiah 53:5 carry these thoughts further with statements ᐧ about the *plagae* which Jesus's body "received because of our sins." The contemplation of Christ's wounds, a popular theme in the Passion mysticism of the time, is the image's meaning for contemporary viewers, a meaning also given to the image by the positioning of the pierced hand next to the wound in Christ's side. Here the image—its meaning made explicit through textual and visual supplements—is both the recipient and the instrument of a definite, identifiable contemplative practice which the viewer was supposed to recall when he beheld the image.

The descriptions of, and inscriptions on, the image of the Imago Pietatis are corroborating evidence of the complex field of function and meaning in which the image-type had occupied its "locus in life." They permit us to recognize the suitability of the painted figure, and of its variants and transformations, for the multiple semantic tasks with which it was charged. In this connection the ability of the painted figure to be identifiable to everyone matches its other ability to allow the greatest freedom for interpretation of its meaning.

The Image and Its Public

Appendix B
Lament and Accusation: The Verse from
Jeremiah in the Rhetoric of the Middle Ages

In our investigation, the concept of pictorial rhetoric has played a central role (see Chapter IV). The images, we maintained, are painted in such a way that they declaim through visual means and appeal to the emotions of the viewer. They are both a lament and an accusation, a lament over the pain suffered and an accusation of the viewer, that through his guilt he brought about the act of atonement and consequently the suffering of the Messiah. Frequently, the lamentation motifs, which were employed nonspecifically, were channeled into a particular interpretation through their context and precise references made by the image in which they appear. Through a series of visual formulae that were linked with a given image-type, the images express in each different context both pathos and pain, and stimulate both.

These observations on painting can be explained and confirmed by an example from the literature of the Middle Ages from which similar conclusions can be drawn. It is verse 1:12 of the Lamentations of Jeremiah (*Threni* or *lamentationes*) that is quite often added as a caption to the Imago Pietatis as a "devotional legend"[1] addressed to the viewer and that reinforces the *pictorial* rhetoric with a *verbal* rhetoric: "All you who pass by, behold and see if there is any sorrow like my sorrow" (O vos omnes qui transitis per viam, attendite et videte si est dolor sicut dolor meus!). Just as the image was a type, the verse was a topos. It appears as a caption not only on the most varied Passion images (for example, of the Crucifixion and the Lamentation), for which it indicated a unitary perspective, but in addition it was quoted as a formula which could be paraphrased and interpreted as needed in contexts ranging from the liturgy and Passion plays to religious polemics and orations at judicial processes. The relationship between the universal formula and its variable context resembles the relationship between the image-type of the Imago Pietatis and its context which, with its changing function, also determined what the image expressed in a particular instance and concretized its interpretation. The image could be situated in a space or located on an object (an altar or a tomb), or the image-type could be integrated into another Passion image (for example, the Lamentation). It is not the quotation alone, but its application and modification that makes the history of the function of Jeremiah's verse of interest for our investigation.

Even on the images for which the verse was used as a caption, variants and paraphrases were possible. A few examples will suffice. On a predella from the school of Orcagna in S. Croce in Florence (second half of the fourteenth century), the verse, in the vernacular (O voi tutti che passate . . .), is presented as spoken by an Imago Pietatis, with the addition: "and for you have I endured this" (e per voi lo portai).[2] On a Crucifixion panel in the Pinacoteca of Siena[3] the verse is introduced and continued in a way which makes its relation to the Crucifixion specific: "Why are you astonished, O man? I die so that you shall not die. Through death I conquer death so that man need not die" (Cur homo miraris? Morior ne tu moriaris. Mortem morte domo ne moriatur homo). The following quotation of the verse from Jeremiah concludes with verses from Isaiah 53:4: "Surely he has borne our griefs and carried our sorrows. Through the blood of his wounds are we healed" (Vere langores ipse tulit et dolores nostros ipse portavit. Cuius livore sanati sumus). Christological exegesis harmonizes with a moral appeal.

In the passional of Abbess Cunegonde from the convent of St. George in Prague (1320), Jeremiah's verse is placed in the mouth of the "Mother of Sorrow" (*Mater dolorosa*) lamenting under the cross and slightly modified so that it addresses *universi populi* instead of *vos omnes*.[4] Here the image of Mary is placed next to a text of the extraliturgical Good Friday "lamentations of Mary,"[5] as a gloss note, and is accompanied by the inscription: "Behold Mary weeping and suffering bitterly" (Intuemini Mariam amare flentem et amare dolentem). Other images employ the passage from Lamentations in new forms that retain only the motifs of "passing by" and "regarding," but otherwise adopt the exact wording of medieval epigrammatic poetry and thereby refer explicitly to the crucified Christ. Examples are the twelfth-century Latin Crucifixion mosaic in the church of the Holy Sepulcher in Jerusalem[6] and the fourteenth-century votive fresco in the baptistry of Parma.[7]

A final group of images limits itself to simply quoting the verse, but assigns it to very diverse Passion themes. Once again a few examples must suffice. On the so-called Moses Fountain of the Burgundian Carthusian monastery of Champmol, the masterpiece of Claus Sluter from the last years of the fourteenth century, the verse appears, appropriately, on the scroll of the statue of Jeremiah, which thereby comments on the crucified Christ on Mount Calvary, crowning the fountain, like the announcers drawn from the Old

Testament in religious theater.[8]   The verse appears also on Enguerrand Quarton's *Pietà* from Ville-neuve-les-Avignon in the Louvre,[9] on the Lamentation panel of Niccolò di Tommaso in Parma, [10] on a retable of Jacopino di Francesco in Bologna with the Imago Pietatis supported by Mary,[11] and finally in an engraving by Israel van Meckenem depicting the Man of Sorrow.[12]   Of course, while all these depictions share the same Passion material, they display the greatest conceivable diversity in the theme chosen and the type of presentation. Each integrates the verse into a different pictorial context. Only the appellative function remains the same, and it is always the same figures, more frequently Mary than Jesus, who summon the viewer to coexperience the Passion by regarding the image and reading the verse.

In the literature of the Middle Ages, the range of the verse's application is far greater. In the liturgy, the verse found a permanent place at an early date. In the Good Friday antiphons, it is a climax of the intensifying pathos of suffering of the one whose "eyes became blind from weeping," and the *Videte* is taken up in the echo: "Now they saw whom they had pierced" (Viderunt in quem transfixerunt) and recognized in him the Son of God.[13]   In the ritual entombment of the crucified Christ and the Host, the liturgical *depositio* drama,[14] the verse is used to emphasize very sharply various phases of the event. During the symbolic funeral procession to the Holy Sepulcher on Good Friday, not only are the above-mentioned antiphons sung, but new elements and chants are introduced as well.[15]   At the display of the Host, viewed symbolically as the stripping of Christ, two clerics sang the lament of Christ before the "daughters of Zion . . . see my sorrow" (Videte dolorem meum). At the symbolic entombment of Christ, the verse from Jeremiah is used as an outburst of Mary which continues, "I am entirely desolate, because there is no one to console me" (Desolata sum nimis, non est qui consolatur me). The biting lament that life is "dead and has been taken from me," permits a better understanding of the Pietà showing the body of Christ in Mary's lap, the image of which the verse is so frequently a caption.

Proximity to the so-called Lamentations of Mary, the extraliturgical songs based on the Good Friday rituals, is achieved in the entombment phase of the liturgical drama. In the *Planctus* of Cividale, Mary the mother of James, a relative of Mary, puts the audience into the appropriate emotional state for the coexperiencing of Mary's lamentations when in her recitation of Jeremiah's verse she arrives at her climax: "Who would not weep for the Mother of Christ when he sees her in such grief!" (Quis est qui non fleret matrem Christ si videret in tanta tristitia!).[16] And after the verse from Jeremiah, Mary's lamentations end with the cry: "Heu me! misera Maria!" In the lauds, *devozioni,* and *sacre rappresentazioni* of religious theater, this verse became a permanent part of monodic and dramatic performances,[17] and this is true also of the *Passione* of Niccolo di Mino Cicerchia of Siena as well as to the epic recountings of Christ's life.[18]

Homiletic literature also makes frequent use of the verse from Jeremiah precisely because it was familiar to everyone from the liturgy and the stage play. An example of this fact is a sermon on the Assumption from the late thirteenth century by the Franciscan Matteo of Aquasparta, in which the verse is intended to characterize the Mother of Christ.[19] As if this were something taken for granted, she is identified as the one who uttered the verse. In a reference to Matthew 5:4 and the comforting of those who mourn, the sermon says that the greater the sorrow, the greater the happiness will be. And if Mary could lament so, would she not be a model of *compassio,* especially of the *compassio* for the sorrows and sins of her fellow men? She inflicted upon herself the *disciplinas poenitentiales.*

Yet the stimulus effect of the verse from Jeremiah only becomes really clear to the modern historian once it is transferred from the Passion into a different context. Two examples of such a transfer will conclude this survey. In the trial of the assassins of Louis of Orleans, who had performed the deed at the behest of Jean Sanspeur in 1407, the widow's lawyer, Thomas of Cerisi, conjured up in his summation the image of the Imago Pietatis, when he causes the victim to rise from the tomb and cry out to the king: "My lord and my brother, see how I have suffered death on your behalf. Look at my body which was trampled and bruised . . . . All look and see whether any pain is like the pain that has befallen me."[20] There are a number of interesting points to this example. For example, the notion that the dead man rises from the grave and addresses his plaint to the viewer—a notion which perhaps was taken over from the interpretation of the Imago Pietatis and made its understanding recognizable in retrospect.[21] Also revealing is the intent to confer a religious aura on the case and to climax the summation speech with an allusion to an experience familiar to all from liturgy, theater, and art. The political assassination is transformed into the Passion of the innocent divine victim; the judicial proceedings regarding the murder become a reenactment of the Passion. However, what is critically important in this example is the use made of religious rhetoric, the function of which was to cast its spell over the audience of the trial. It shows how great a role the Passion material in its literary and pictorial presentation played in the "emotional economy" and the self-expression of western European man in the late Middle Ages.

The last example also shows a transfer of the verse from Jeremiah into another context, not, however, into the secular sphere, but into the criticism of the Church. In the famous 1405 sermon of Jan Hus, in which the papal Church is criticized by means of rhetorical antitheses between the ideal and the reality of the Church of Christ at that time,[22] a climax is again achieved when the preacher, taking the role of Jeremiah, calls out: "The leaders of the nations . . . have rallied together against the Lord . . . who cries out with a loud voice: All of you who pass by, see whether there is anything like unto this. I weep, clothed in rags, and the clergy takes its pleasure in scarlet robes . . . Exhausted under my cross, I am led to death, while the clergy is led to sleep in drunkenness. Nailed to the cross, I cry out, while they snore in their soft beds." The explosive power of this denunciation of the clergy's lamentation of the Passion must have been enormous, and no less compelling must have been the conclusion implied by it, that this lamentation should be taken out of the clergy's hands and placed in those of the "true Christians." The Passion of Christ becomes an indictment of the Church. Hus's rhetoric confirms the power of ecclesiastical rhetoric, which the reformer was using for his own purposes, to sway an audience even in the antithetical and alienated form he gave it. In the context in which Hus employed it, the verse of Jeremiah acquired a new trenchancy resulting from the disproportion or tension between the verse's familiarity and its unfamiliar function in this sermon. Through its enduring and varied use in the church and on the stage, in images and slogans, this verse became a locus classicus in the rhetoric of the Middle Ages.

Appendix C
Western Art after 1204
The Importation of Relics and Icons

The Orient and Occident After 1204

The plundering of Constantinople by the crusaders, who in 1204 established the Latin kingdom of Romania, belongs among the scandals of medieval history. What the anonymous chronicler from Halberstadt described piously as a *peregrinatio in Greciam*[1] was in reality a crusade by Christians against Christians. So, too, did Pope Innocent III perceive it when he protested in vain after the conquest of Zara. The Doge of Venice was lord of the situation. Economics vanquished religious-political interests. Venice succeeded in vanquishing its rival Constantinople and establishing a powerful trade empire in the Mediterranean.[2] Naturally Rome, too, profited from the coup against Byzantium. The union of the eastern and western Churches was effected by sheer force. But at what price? The defeat of the Greeks created enmity between eastern and western Christianity. The Greek Church went underground. The "wine of Citeaux" which "had been planted in the Greek soil"[3] (as Caesarius of Heisterbach phrased it) was the poison which in fact destroyed missionary hopes. When the Cistercians moved into the monastery at Daphni, the Greeks had to leave.[4]

The conquest of Constantinople appeared to the West as a providential act, and critical voices soon grew silent. This was partly due to the rich booty which the conquerors had hastily sent home. He who brought home a relic could feel himself released from his oath to help conquer Jerusalem.[5] Garnier de Trainel, Bishop of Troyes, as *procurator*, had the duty to oversee the distribution of relics. Naturally he was especially concerned about his episcopal city, but he did not reap the harvest he so desired. Instead his chaplain brought home the *thesaurus* of relics.[6] In a window of the Cathedral of Troyes which shows Hugo with the head of the Apostle Philip,[7] the robbery is represented as a normal transference of relics. This was possible because "the western Church was enlightened by the holy

Fig. 110
Sens,
Cathedral.
Trumeau fig-
ure of St.
Stephen

relics of which they [the Greeks] have proven unworthy."[8] Or so the argument had been formulated by the chronicler Gunther from the Cistercian monastery at Pairis in Alsace. The "enlightenment" also meant the material enrichment of churches and monasteries. Troyes is again a typical example. The relics made it possible to consider rebuilding the cathedral.[9] The holy objects (*sanctuaria*) from the Orient attracted pilgrims, and as publicity spread, the income from the pilgrims' offerings increased, and even became considerable. Thus, in 1205, Nivelon de Chérizy, Bishop of Soissons, pledged that half the future income from certain relics would be devoted to the construction of the cathedral of Chalons-sur-Marne and the other half would be pledged for the construction of a bridge.[10] Relics were an investment. They were also convertible into land and were therefore a kind of currency, which had the character of shares of stock. "Fund-raising tours" served to increase the exchange value of relics. In this sense, in Troyes, the cult of a hitherto unknown, and therefore unrivaled saint, Helen of Athyra, was propagated. An entire window was installed that illustrated the newly created legend of this saint whose protection could be sought against toothache and sexual problems: it repeatedly depicts scenes in which she carries to Troyes wonder-working utensils, the instruments of her thaumaturgic powers. And, in the context of the legend, the church building is significantly represented, accompanied by the architect and watched over by the Bishop.[11]

A similar series of events followed upon the arrival in Chartres of the head of Saint Anne, which was presented as a gift by the Count of Blois in 1205. Building activity was once again set in motion. The trumeau-figure of Saint Anne is a pictorial symbol of the relic, the cult of which was then activated.[12] Indeed, this was nothing new. Some years before in Sens, the Titular Saint Stephen, whose relics drew pilgrims, was represented on the trumeau. It was, in fact, a monumental version of a "speaking reliquary"[13]: Stephen holds the panel reliquary in his hands, which already at the entrance indicated the cult object in Sens (fig. 110). However, the quality and the quantity of the relics *were* new, which in 1204 streamed into the West. The Comte De Riant, whose book is still a fundamental study of this process, compared the cult of relics after 1204 with the "passion des antiquités qui nous a conduits trop souvent au vandalisme; [on] allait demander les corps saints à Byzance comme nous demandons nos marbres aux ruines de Grèce."[14] One could compare the *adventus reliquarum de Grecia,* of which the Chronicler from Halberstadt spoke, with the influx of gold from the New World that the Spanish ships brought home at a later period of history. From this point of view the year 1204 is a key date for the history and financing of architecture in the West.

However, not only building took place. The goldsmiths also profited from the booty from the East, for which they created attractive relic receptacles. Bernard of Clairvaux had bitingly commented upon the relationship between the gold of the reliquaries and the gold which visitors drew from their pockets.[15] Some churches were literally monumental shrines for the relics they had inherited.

The chapel in Kobern (Mosel) with its reference to the centrally planned building of the Holy Sepulcher, is an "architectural reliquary" for the head of the Apostle Matthew which was buried there.[16] More famous is the Ste. Chapelle in Paris, which was built as a "relic treasury" and dedicated in 1248.[17] The great relic collection that had been gathered there transformed France into a kind of facsimile of the Holy Land that, henceforth, no longer lay in the East but rather in the West.

It was in terms of France as the "new Holy Land," by virtue of its possession of eastern relics, that Gauthier Cornut, Archbishop of Sens, writing upon the commission of Louis IX, described the event. He saw the Crown of Thorns, which Louis had purchased for 13,134 gold hyperpera, upon the head of the king; by virtue of possession of the Crown of Thorns, Louis became the incarnation of the true Solomon (Christ), much as the latter on the day of the Last Judgment would place the Crown of Thorns upon his own head. This description was not intended to be audacious, but rather to suggest that Christ and his temporal governor in France could be compared with one another.[18]

It is enlightening that in the representations of the Crucifixion that originated from the Parisian court, special value was laid upon the *corona spinea,* for example, on the covers of the Bibles in Ste Chapelle.[19] The chapel, whose *Grande Chasse* sheltered the Passion

Fig. 111
Vienna,
Nationalbib-
liothek, Cod.
1921, fol. 218.
Book of Hours
of Johanna of
Naples

relics, was built after the Byzantine model from which the new *thesaurus* of relics had been taken, although Gothic forms were adopted; this expressed that the chapel was the successor to its Byzantine antecedent. A generation earlier Robert de Clari had described the model as that church in the Byzantine imperial palace "que on apeloit le Sainte Capele"; the church, he continued, seemed to be filled by heavenly light, so strong was the brilliance of the gold, silver, and jasper columns which blinded the visitor.[20] The imperial relic chapel of Constantinople was now resurrected in the royal relic chapel in Paris.

The Imitation and Assimilation of Imported Reliquaries

However, it was the *idea* and not the *form* that had been imitated. The consequences of the importation of relics were more concrete in the changing forms of reliquaries in the West, which, as Mme Gautier has demonstrated, were the "face" of the relic.[21] The new forms of the receptacle provided a mise-en-scène for the relics, which, it was hoped, would maximize their impression upon the beholder and underline their reality. Unfortunately the treasury of Ste Chapelle, together with the major part of French medieval "treasury" art, was almost completely destroyed during the French revolution.[22] What still remains was impressively documented in the exhibition "Les trésors des églises de France" (Paris, 1965).

The Book of Hours of Johanna of Naples, today in Vienna, remains the oldest pictorial witness of the relic treasury of Ste Chapelle.[23] (fig. 111). One recognizes the great Crown of Thorns reliquary and both relic crosses, which were commissioned by Saint Louis. The royal donation of imperial relics from the East was not the first of this type that occurred after 1204. In 1205 King Philippe Auguste had presented the Abbey of St. Denis with precious relics

Fig. 112 Limburg, Cathedral. Byzantine Staurotheke, 10th c.

Fig. 113
Mettlach,
Staurotheke.
Trier, 1228

"from the Holy Chapel of the emperors which is called the lion's mouth" (*de sancta Capella imperatorum quam Os Leonis vocant*). The relics included a piece of the Holy Wood as wide as a fist and a Thorn from the Crown.[24] The reliquaries that were created for them—the great Cross and the so-called *oratorium* of the king, a panel reliquary of the eastern type with small relic boxes behind "windows"—constituted obvious and influential models for Gothic art, as indeed the reliquaries of the Ste Chapelle were to be later on.

In this context, it is useful to examine some related examples of the metalwork of Trier, which represent a special case since so much is known about them. In 1205, the knight Heinrich von Ulmen brought home the *lignum s. crucis de civitate Constantinopolitana,* and with it acquired fame and riches.[25] Pieces of the "True Cross" were to be found in at least two Byzantine reliquaries. One, the Staurotheke of Limburg (fig. 112), came to be owned by the Augustinian monastery at Stuben, located on the Mosel.[26] In the following years, at least six replicas were produced in Trier, of which only two remain. The triptych reliquary in Mettlach[27] (1228) duplicated the form not only of the Cross-relic, of which it contained a piece, but also of the mother reliquary (fig. 113). A panel reliquary from the booty of 1204 also existed in the monastery at Pairis in Alsace.[28] In 1207 it was successfully given to King Philip von Schwaben. The "panel, most artfully decorated with gold and precious gems . . . contained many kinds of relics, all carefully concealed. . . . The Greek Emperor wore it on a gold chain about his neck as a sign of

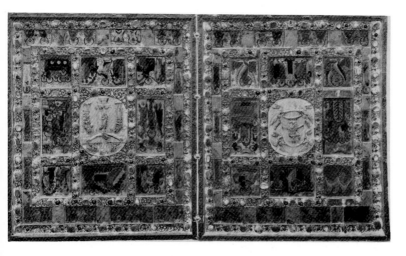

Fig. 114
Bern, His-
torisches
Museum,
"House-altar"
of King
Andrew of
Hungary,
Venice, c.
1290

his dominion." It was a clever compliment to the king to recognize an imperial insigne in the panel. The "jasper of astonishing size" in the center of the panel, upon which the Crucifixion was represented, reminds one of the Venetian "house-altar" of King Andrew of Hungary,[29] today in Bern (fig. 114). Here we find the same theme in the same place in the same material. The Venetian double panel seems to be the western edition of a Byzantine reliquary. The combination of filigree and miniature under crystal paraphrases a technique that had worked with enamel instead of the cheaper miniatures. The comparison of a Venetian diptych in Chilandar with a Byzantine bookcover in Siena confirms this view.[30]

But I would like to go further. Many items of the mixed crystal and gold work of Venice, which were produced in a manufacturelike manner, are imitations of and substitutes for Byzantine prototypes. Prof. Hahnloser has dated them too late, in accordance with the "house-altar" at Bern. A panel in the Athonite monastery of Hagiou Pavlou which combines two different techniques (miniature behind glass and gold glass) must be dated much earlier.[31] The enthroned Christ in the center, in type and style, is reminiscent of an analogous figure on the reliquary at Mettlach[32] (ca. 1228). This comparison also reveals that Venice looked toward the transalpine north. The trade routes between East and West, on which Venice occupied a key position, also shaped Venetian artistic production.[33] As Prof. Laiou has shown, Venetian production of costly vessels was motivated by the desire to supplant Byzantine products in the international market.

From this short discussion, I conclude that the importation of

Fig. 115
Jaucourt.
Staurotheke

Byzantine *relics* entailed the assimilation of the form of Byzantine *reliquaries*. The original reliquary shared, as it were, the aura of the relics and thus remained so vibrant that it, too, was reproduced.

The Reproduction and Mise-en-Scène of the Imported Relics

Of even greater significance than the reliquaries related to Byzantine prototypes were those that constituted new forms. The Staurotheke of Jaucourt (fig. 115) housed in a new setting not only the relics, but also the original Byzantine reliquary so that an "image within an image" was created and the old reliquary itself was transformed into a relic.[34] The new form is thus a functional form. The composite of the old and new parts of the existing reliquary is mounted firmly and thereby enlarged, so that it is suited for permanent public display. Still more important is the realism of the new staging. Two genuflecting angels, who seem to have carried the relics there, reveal them to the viewer and demand his veneration. In the reliquary of Floreffe[35] (made shortly after 1254), two standing angels similarly present a cross with its relics (fig. 116). The aura

210   *The Image and Its Public*

Fig. 116
Paris, The
Louvre. Stau-
rotheke of
Floreffe,
Paris, c.
1254

of the relics of Christ brought from the East was further increased by the new quality of mise-en-scène. The angels introduce the dramatic moment by a ritual *présentation*, as it is known from the arrival of the relics of the Passion in Paris in 1239.[36] Forerunners of such forms are found in the Mosan triptych-reliquaries in the twelfth century. However, our reliquaries differ from the models in that the angels holding the cross stand under a baldachino while using the rhetorical gesture of presentation. I might also add in passing that the tabernacle, which can be closed, anticipates in its open state the structure of an altar retable.

The reliquary of Floreffe is directly linked to the crusade of 1204. Its relic of the cross was given in 1204 as a gift from Balduin I of Constantinople to the Count of Nemours, whose brother Philippe le Noble bequeathed it to the Abbey of Floreffe. Thereafter the relic of the cross began to bleed miraculously. The miracle was repeated fifty years later, as the inscription on the reliquary reports.[37] Clearly, the miracle of the bleeding occasioned the restoration of the reliquary, by which the ritual display received a worthy and functionally proper vessel. In this way the *form* of the representation is the perpetual rhetorical gesture of the *action* of representation of the cult, which is implied here. The *répresentation* of the relics in the image becomes identical to the *présentation* to the viewer, to use two of Mme Gauthier's terms.[38] The *répresentation* of relics is alluding to their organized ritual *présentation* to the public, which was to venerate them. Already in two other types of reliquaries it was *viewing* as an activity by the beholder that was implied: for example, in the so-called "speaking reliquary" whose form repeated the form of the relic, such as a head or an arm, and in the *Ostensorium* made of crystal in which the contents could be seen through a "window."[39] However, I would like to distinguish the reliquaries of Jaucourt and Floreffe from the former by calling them "figural monstrances," because they are composed of carrying figures, that is, angels.

The small statue of Saint Stephen from Les Billanges, who displays his own relic also belongs to this group. Contemporary examples indeed either represent the holy deacon as carrier of his own relic or of the relic of the Holy Cross.[40] Such reliquaries seem to have influenced the statue at the portal of the cathedral of Sens which we have mentioned (fig. 110). The original coloring of the Sens statue must have enforced the analogy of book and reliquary in the hands of the saint. Thus the statue, which is announcing the presence of the relic in the interior of the cathedral, is not only an image but also is the carrier of an image, in other words the monumental version of a reliquary.

A mosaic in Venice (fig. 117), which again refers directly back to the plundering of Constantinople in 1204, fulfills the same function as the trumeau of Sens—the advertisement of the relic treasury—by displaying a reproduction of it over the entrance.[41] This mosaic was made after the fire in the treasury of S. Marco in 1230, when the new *tesoro* with its remaining and replenished relic supply was being decorated. Over the portal two angels display a staurotheke with two hooks for the viewers, and in this way express visually the function of the room as the treasury for the collection of relics. By the reproduction of the cult object, the angels propagandize its cult.

Noteworthy is the formal analogy between the mosaic and the reliquary type of the "figural monstrance" of which I have already spoken (fig. 115). The *formal* analogy is the result of a *functional* analogy. As we have seen, the corresponding reliquary types fulfill the task of making visible, and thus emphasizing the reality of the relic. The gesture of the pointing figure invites the viewer to contemplate the relic and thereby affirms its presence. Official certificates (*passeports* to use the term of De Riant)[42] or biographical legends of the saints, which were translated into Latin, became analogous instruments for cult propaganda. In 1205 bishops gathered at St. Denis to verify the authenticity of the relics from Constantinople by signing a document which proved that the relics had been brought by a "trustworthy ambassador with sealed certificates."[43]

We are here less interested in the cult propaganda as such than in the function that the image had in relation to it. The reliquary became the image of the relic; it gave the relic, which often was only

Fig. 117
Venice, S. Mar-
co. South
Transept, door
to Treasury,
c. 1230

an amorphous fragment, a visual identity that could be understood. Hitherto, the relic was considered *superior* to the image, namely, as objective proof of the existence of the saint. Now the image became its competitor, and the relic had to *adapt* to the image's power of articulation.

The New Function of the Image. Image and Relic

I have now come to the second part of my sketch, to the importation of icons and its relationship to the importation of relics. Mme Gauthier compared reliquaries and images and pointed out that the same term *icona* has been used for both.[44] I would like to go a step further. The pointing gesture in the figurative reliquaries soon appears in *images*, properly speaking, which have in their center a *picture* and not a *relic*. Examples are to be found in Giovanni Pisano's lectern in Pistoia and in the mass-produced *vernacles*. In the first example two angels display the Imago Pietatis;[45] in the second, the legendary Saint Veronica presents the Vera Icon, the portrait of Christ from St. Peter's in Rome.[46] Both images distinguish the figures who *display* from those who *are displayed*. The attending figures are subsidiary to the main figure just as the reliquary is to the relic, the frame to the contents.

The comparison between reliquaries and images suggests two conclusions which I will try to prove:

1. Privileged images could become equivalent to relics and were identified as relics. The Vera Icon as an "authentic" original automatically acquired the status of a relic.[47] Its frame with the enormous "window" made of rock crystal[48] (about 60.5 cm x 56.5 cm) makes it a panel reliquary, consisting of cover and a part which is contained in it. [In Venice crystal glass was earlier used interchangeably as the fastening for relics and images (miniatures).] The indulgence, which since 1216 was linked to the prayer, to be said before the Vera Icon, corresponded to the indulgence that could be gained by a visit to a *relic*. It is obvious that the privileged image in St. Peter's *was* a relic, or rather occupied a position that only a relic could occupy.

2. The observation that *images* could become relics and relics were displayed as images, introduces us into a historical process which can be understood as a general reevaluation of images. The reality that was sought in them was made *visible* by them. But how? Eastern legends which had become familiar explained that images could speak and work miracles.[49] Naturally that meant only *special* images, which were distinguished by their form and thereby individualized. Consequently, what distingished one image from another depended upon this form. A new aesthetic of the image was initiated. The image was expected to reproduce the person represented in an authentic manner and to become sufficiently alive to speak. A new attitude toward the image caused an aesthetic change in the latter. At first this just amounted to a selective attitude. Not every image was thought to be able to receive a cult.

Testimonials as to the authenticity of the eastern icons increased their aura. One had always heard about the portraits of the Virgin which Saint Luke was supposed to have painted in front of the living model. Now these actually could be seen. The aura of authenticity was even more plausible since the eastern icons came from the homeland of the Bible. In 1306, in when Fra Giordano da Rivalto in S. Maria Novella preached upon the origin of the Magi in the East, he said: "The first pictures to testify the appearance of the Magi came from Greece. . . . Originally, they were painted by saints so one could better imagine everything—how they really appeared and what they were like. Thus, Nicodemus first painted Christ in a beautiful panel painting, showing him as he hung upon the Cross. . . . Nicodemus was with Christ when he was crucified. . . . We also know that Luke make an authentic portrait of Christ's Mother on a panel which is highly venerated in Rome. These paintings command the highest authority, especially those that were imported from Greece. And likewise they carry as much weight as the Scriptures."

Outside the walls of Constantinople in 1203, the crusaders captured the icon of the Virgin (*ansconne*), "which the emperors carried with them whenever they went to war, along with their *capel imperial* and the general's coach, which the Greeks have abandoned" (Robert de Clari).[50] Probably the icon, "which was made entirely of gold and precious stones and was so beautiful and rich that one has never again seen the likes of it," was identical with the victory-bringing Nikopoia, which the Venetians later on venerated as an image made by Saint Luke and used as the official cult image of their republic(fig. 118).[51] Inside the walls of Constantinople an even more famous icon was awaiting them, the Hodegetria, "which the Greeks held to be the oldest picture of all, upon which Notre Dame is portrayed" (Robert de Clari).[52] The crusaders almost came to war among themselves when the possession of the icon was at stake. The coronation of Henry of Flanders in 1206 was only possible when the icon was conceded to the Venetians.[53] Obviously, the Latins very much cared for icons and also accepted them as palladia. The Hodegetria did not come to the West. But the multiplication of its replicas in Italy bears witness to the fame of the original. Previously in the twelfth century, a replica was made in Palermo.[54] The "Madonna Strauss" in Lucca from the hand of Berlinghiero (ca. 1230), by meticulously reproducing the figure type, shows the limits of artistic freedom, when the identity of the original was at stake.[55]

The Expansion of the Panel Painting and the Role of Imported Images

The multiplication of eastern icons in the West was accomplished by the proliferation of independent and transportable panel paintings. The history of easel painting had begun. *Garrison's Index* records for the Dugento roughly. 250 extant panels of the Virgin in Italy.[56] Legends spread the fame of the *Madonna di Constantinopoli*. The Madonna of Mercy or *Madonna della Misercordia* was first of all a Constantinopolitan icon, which was linked to the relic of the Virgin's Mantle in the church dedicated to her in the Blachernes district of the city.[57] In the West, as the image of the protection of many religious confraternities, it received not only a new function, but expressed this function through a motive which visually clarified the new semantic content: the Virgin's Mantle was now spread over clients, who were gathered under it.

The Imago Pietatis is another imported icon which soon came to have a career in the West(fig. 31).[58] At the latest, in the first half of the twelfth century, it was formulated for the Byzantine liturgy as a Passion portrait of the sacrificed Christ. Again Venice took a key position in its dissemination in the West. The majority of extant examples (such as the two panels in Torcello and in the Stoclet Collection)[59] came from the area around Venice. Still in the early work of Giovanni Bellini, as in the panel in the Museo-Pezzoli in Milan, the old type of the icon was respected. The supposed original of the Imago Pietatis, which since the late fourteenth century was housed ·and venerated in S. Croce in Gerusalemme in Rome (fig. 14), is nothing other than a Constantinopolitan mosaic icon from the period around 1300, which was usurped first in Rome as the venerable miraculous image of Gregory the Great.[60]

Such statements do not simply concern iconographical matters, but rather introduce us into the early history of panel painting, which had begun with the importation of eastern models. The realism of the representation was attributed not so much to the style of the artists as it was to the authority of a privileged form (that is, that of the model). The existence of "originals" meant that each newly produced panel was to be compared with them and judged accordingly. The multiplication of "original" *panels* occurred by way of *repetition*, the multiplication of relics by way of their *division*. However, the tendencies were similar.

Only in the generation of the Sienese painter Duccio did the originality of the picture begin to rival, as a postulate, the authenticity of its artistic form, just as the newly important social position of the artist had begun to rival the importance of the patron. Duccio's *Maestà* had two predecessors as an image of the Virgin, but it adopted their function without repeating their type of image.[61] Duccio belongs to the third generation of painters to work under the impact of Byzantine models. What interests us here is the early period of the importation of icons and its consequences.

To describe all this under the heading "Byzantine influence" would would be understatement. I am referring not so much to the influence of Byzantine *style*, which could only be the concern of the *artist*, as to the introduction of panel painting which had to be the concern of *all.* Whether or in what way a painting seemed really similar to its eastern model is secondary to the fact that it was *meant* to be similar. Many art historians are not at all interested in this primary aspect which is my subject, properly speaking.

Also most important are the social functions of the panel painting in Italy (for devotion, propaganda, protection, or another specif-

The Image and Its Public

ic purpose) which in turn reflect the complexity of western society, specifically that of Italy. In 1285, the published statutes of a Bolognese confraternity show the representation of a Madonna Eleousa next to an arma-cross, which was venerated in the Hagia Sophia.[62] In my opinion the miniature reproduces a bilateral icon in which the two subjects were combined. The role of the image as a symbol of confraternities and civic communities is well known. It symbolizes the bilateral relationship to divine authority, which materializes in the image and replaces temporal authorities. More important in our case is that the Bolognese miniature obviously embodied the reference to the Passion which the Eleousa, the Byzantine forerunner of the Pietà group, expressed in the East. The affective relationship between Mother and Child is symptomatic of a new, vital pictorial language, which satisfied the wishes of western meditations on the Passion. It was from *imported* images that the viewer began to expect *liveliness* and therefore *reality* for the represented person.

Fig. 118
Venice, S. Marco. Nikopoia Icon

More famous is the image of the Dead Christ on the Cross. This type first appears on the Italian painted cross in the Dugento, to be sure, as a replica of eastern models.[63] The crusaders already knew it at Jerusalem in the twelfth century. Theodoricus describes around 1175 a mosaic of the crucified Christ in the Latin convent near the church of the Holy Sepulcher. It was represented such that it moved every spectator to a deep compassion.[64] The Byzantine image must have acted in the sense of a western image of devotion. An inscription, in addition, qualified the image as a "speaking image."

The fruits of the new expansion of panel painting, however, were not limited to Italy. I would like to illustrate this point with two examples. The first is the giant Cross of Wimpassing (destroyed 1945), which was commissioned in 1250 from a Salzburg workshop by the Viennese Minorites.[65] It repeated not only the Italian *Croce dipinta*, but also in its style reflected models from the Veneto which again stemmed from eastern crusader art. The painted cross as

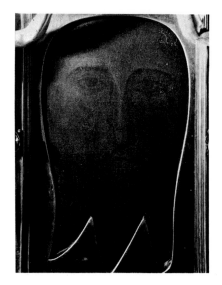

Fig. 119
Rome,
Pal. Vaticani,
Cap. Matilde.
Icon from S.
Silvestro in
Capite

image carrier, which in the twelfth century had been encouraged by the constitutions of the Cistercians,[66] was not such a rarity in the North, as it appears from the extant examples.

The other example, a fresco from St. Johann zu Taufers (southern Tyrol), quotes a tripartite Deesis panel, which could be imagined to have been situated on the templon of an iconostasis.[67] The three half-figures appear in the form of a panel, which could be interpreted as a triptych or as the center of a frieze of icons with round arches. (Perhaps this quotation of an icon relates to the fact that the building, which stood on a mountain pass and was supposedly founded in 1218, belonged to a hospice of the order of the hospitallers which could have become acquainted with such icons from the East.) Eastern imported panels and local panel paintings are also well represented: the former, directly through examples such as an icon in Freising or in Burscheid,[68] the latter through examples which Stange has already studied.[69] Panel painting was no longer a rare curiosity in the thirteenth century.

The Vera Icon as Paradigm of the New Authenticity of the Image

In the following section I would like to illustrate my thoughts on the icon in the West with the description of a famous example: the image relic of the true portrait of Christ. The oldest known "original," the image on cloth (Mandylion), which puportedly was commissioned by King Abgar of Edessa, was located in Constantinople since the tenth century.[70] Robert de Clari saw the image (*touaille*) still in Ste Chapelle, together with its duplicate, the miraculously derived impression upon a tile (*tuile*).[71] Later, in 1237, Balduin of Constantinople, Louis IX, and others testified to the ownership of the image on cloth (*sanctum toellam tabulae insertam*), which in 1239 was due to come to Paris.[72] But it seems to have landed in Rome, where today, the extant Abgar image (fig. 119) is still venerated in S. Silvestro in Capite, (it seems to be a late-antique product).[73]

An equally Byzantine Abgar image, the one presented to the republic of Genoa by the Byzantine emperor John V Palaeologos (1341–1391), matches exactly the length of the image of S. Silvestro (21 cm) and thus testifies to the eastern origin of this very type, if not of this very example.[74] Therefore it makes sense when Vincent of Beauvais reports that the holy *sindon* came to Rome but the image on the tile remained in Byzantium.[75]

In Rome everything possible was done to eliminate the Abgar image as a rival of the Veronica. Even as late as 1517 the Clarissas were forbidden to officially display their image *ob confusionem vitandam*, in order to avoid confusion, namely, with the St. Peter's image.[76] It now seems that the canons of St. Peter themselves had actually created this confusion much earlier. In the twelfth century the Veronica may have been just a handkerchief without bearing an image at all. Gervase of Tilbury (ca. 1211) is the first to testify to the existence of an image on the relic.[77]

In 1216 Matthew Paris, the chronicler from St. Albans, reports a miracle by which the cloth won fame and confirmed itself as a relic. He also reproduces the image without ever having seen it, in the form of an icon of the Pantocrator.[78] It must have been the years between the late twelfth century and 1216, when, in my opinion, the cloth received an image or became one itself. The face of Christ then became identified with the relic of the Veronica. The Veronica was the Roman answer to the claim of the newly imported images to be originals, and finally won over all its eastern rivals which had created interest in the true appearance of Christ. Also the golden *arma*-cross in the Hagia Sophia was recognized as having been fashioned "according to the size of Christ's body."[79] A Tuscan manuscript from ca. 1300 referred to this; if one multiplies by twelve the figure of Christ as it is drawn here, so it says, then one has the measurements of Christ's body as given by the cross in Constantinople.[80] The imagination becomes inspired by material proofs which existed in the East linking the reality of the *relic* with the evidence of the *photograph*. This is not surprising to us who have understood that photographs are the relics of our time.

A document for the fame of portrait originals is the *Ste Face* of Laon (fig. 120). In 1249, Jaques Pantaléon, archdeacon of Laon and head of the Treasury of St. Peter's, sent his sister Sibyl, abbess of Montreuil-les-Dames, a portrait of Christ which "shows Him as He

Fig. 120
Laon,
Cathedral.
Sainte Face,
Slavic, c. 1200

had been seen on earth and which I have in my keeping."[81] The abbess was to "accept" the image "as the Veronica"—a remark which, though unclear regarding any relationship to the Roman original, can only be understood if there *was* an original to be referred to. The Ste Face, soon a great pilgrimage attraction, was copied in the Book of Hours of Yolande of Soissons,[82] written between 1275 and 1285, and here is in fact identified with the Veronica. In fact, it is a slavonic replica of a Byzantine Abgar image, the dark face of which was explained by the sender as the deep suntanning that Christ received during his wanderings through Palestine.

Epilogue

Curiosities like the Ste Face not only have anecdotal value but also are witnesses to the cult of visual documents which materialized in image relics. The visual arts, in general, henceforth were looked at with different eyes: one expected a new mimetic standard of the image. The image is no longer restricted to the function of a silent symbol which merely means or takes the place of reality. Instead it became capable of portraying reality as the beholder knew it and, by showing it, of proving the very existence of such reality. It begins to *speak*. It can be said that the world, above all the world of faith, allowed itself to be experienced by each individual beholder, by way of the material image and its convincing visual likeness of reality. This applies especially to lay viewers, who expected to participate more in the life of the Church, and by nonliterary means.

Panel paintings had existed prior to 1204. However, after 1204, they were given a new use and function in the life of the cult. Panel

The Image and Its Public

paintings were endowed with the power of relics, while relics by virtue of the reliquaries in which they were enshrined, adopted the outspoken visual fascination of images. The inspiration from objects imported from the East (relics as well as images) contributed much to this change in the function of art. This is attested by the new articulation and vivacity of the independent panel painting. The original image with which the West had become acquainted stimulated the imagination of the beholder and changed his experience of art as such. The Veronica can be cited in this context. It possessed first the status of a relic, and only after 1204 assumed the status of an image (that is, an image relic). The later veronicas and the Christ portrait by Jan van Eyck, which can also be understood as a modern icon, prove the new importance of the mimetic achievement of the image. The detailed physiognomic and lively description of the human face, which was thought to be the true likeness of the historical Jesus, was an important contribution to the rise of portraiture in Europe.

Literature Cited in Abbreviated Form

d'Ancona

d'Ancona, A. *Origini del teatro italiano.* 2nd ed. Turin, 1891.

Bartholomaeis

Bartholomaeis, V. de. *Origini della poesia drammatica italiana.* Bologna, 1924, 2nd ed. Turin, 1952.

Baxandall

Baxandall, M. *Painting and Experience in Fifteenth-Century Italy. A Primer in the Social History of Pictorial Style.* Oxford, 1972.

Belting

Belting, H. "Die Reaktion der Kunst des 13. Jahrhunderts auf den Import von Reliquien und Ikonen." In *Il Medio Oriente e l'Occidente nell' Arte del XIII secolo,* ed. H. Belting. In Atti XXIV. Congr. Internaz. Storia dell'Arte. Bologna, 1979. II, 1982, 35–53.

Belting, *Bellini*

Belting, H. *Giovanni Bellini, Pietà. Ikone und Bilderzählung in der venezianischen Malerei.* Frankfurt a.M., 1985.

Berliner

Berliner, R. "Bemerkungen zu einigen Darstellungen des Erlösers als Schmerzensmann." *Das Münster,* 9 (1956), 97ff.

Berliner, "Arma"

Berliner, R. "Arma Christi." *Münchner Jahrbuch der Bildenden Kunst,* 6 (1955), 35ff.

Berliner, "Freedom"

Berliner, R. "The Freedom of Medieval Art." *Gazette des Beaux-Arts,* 28 (November 1945), 263ff.

Corbin

Corbin, S. *La déposition liturgie du Christ au Vendredi Saint. Sa place dans l'histoire des rites et du théâtre religieux.* Paris, 1960.

Dobrzeniecki

Dobrzeniecki, T. "Niektore zagadnienia ikonografii meza bolesci." *Rocznik Muz. Narodowego w Warszawie,* XVI, 1 (1971), 7ff.

Dobschütz

Dobschütz, E. von. *Christusbilder. Untersuchungen zur christlichen Legende.* Texte und Untersuchungen zur Geschichte der altchristlichen Literatur, N.F. 3. Leipzig, 1899.

Francovich   Francovich, G. de. "A Romanesque School of Wood
                      Carvers." *Art Bulletin,* 19 (1937), 5ff.

Garrison   Garrison, E.B. *Italian Romanesque Panel Painting. An
                      Illustrated Index.* Florence, 1949.

Hager   Hager, H. *Die Anfänge des italienischen Altarbildes.*
                      Veröffentlichungen der Bibl. Hertziana. Munich,
                      1962.

Hamann-Hallensleben   Hamann-MacLean, R., and Hallensleben, H. *Die
                      Monumentalmalerei in Serbien und Makedonien vom 11.
                      bis zum frühen 14. Jh.* Giessen, 1963.

Kermer   Kermer, W. *Studien zum Diptychon in der sakralen
                      Malerei.* Düsseldorf, 1967.

Kitzinger   Kitzinger, E. "The Cult of Images before Iconoclasm."
                      Dumbarton Oaks Papers, 8 (1954), 83ff.

Larner   Larner, J. *Culture and Society in Italy, 1290–1420.*
                      London, 1971.

Meersseman   Meersseman, G.G. *Ordo Fraternitatis: confraternità e
                      pietà dei laici nel medioevo,* 3 vols. Rome, 1977.

Meier   Meier, T. *Die Gestalt Mariens im geistlichen Schauspiel des
                      deutschen Mittelalters.* Berlin, 1959.

Meiss   Meiss, M. *Painting in Florence and Siena after the Black
                      Death.* Princeton, 1951.

Millet, *Broderies*   Millet, G. *Broderies religieuses de style byzantin.* Paris,
                      1939–1947.

Pallas   Pallas, D.I. *Passion und Bestattung Christi in Byzanz. Der
                      Ritus—das Bild.* Miscellanea. Byzantina Monacensia 2.
                      Munich, 1965.

Pallucchini   Pallucchini, R. *La pittura veneziana del Trecento.* Venice,
                      1964.

Panofsky   Panofsky, E. "Imago Pietatis." In *Festschrift für M.J.
                      Friedländer zum 60. Geburtstag.* Leipzig, 1927, pp. 261ff.

Parker   Parker, E.C. *The Descent from the Cross: Its Relation to the
                      Extraliturgical Depositio Drama.* Dissertation, New York,
                      1975.

PG   *Patrologia graeca cursus completas,* ed. J.P. Migne.

PL   *Patrologia latina cursus completus,* ed. J.P. Migne.

Pilz   Pilz, W. *Das Triptychon als Kompositions- und Erzählform in der deutschen Tafelmalerei von den Anfängen bis zur Dürerzeit.* Munich, 1970.

Ragusa–Green   Ragusa, I., and Green, R.B. *Meditations on the Life of Christ. An Illustrated Manuscript of the Fourteenth Century.* Princeton, 1961.

Ringbom   Ringbom, S. *Icon to Narrative. The Rise of the Dramatic Close-up in Fifteenth Century Devotional Painting.* Abo, 1965.

Schmidt   Schmidt, G. "Patrozinium und Andachtsbild." *Mitteilungen des Instituts für österreichische Geschichtsforschung,* 64 (1956), 227ff.

von Simson   Simson, O. von. "Über die Bedeutung von Masaccios Trinitätsfresko in S. Maria Novella." *Jahrbuch der Berliner Museen,* N.F. 7 (1965), 119ff.

Sotiriou   Sotiriou, G. and M. *Icones du Mont Sinai.* I. Athens, 1956.

Suckale   Suckale, R. "Arma Christi. Überlegungen zur Zeichenhaftigkeit mittelalterlicher Andachtsbilder." *Städel-Jahrbuch,* 6 (1977), 177ff.

Taft   Taft, R. *The Great Entrance: A History of the Transfer of Gifts and Other Preanaphoral Rites.* Orientalia Christiana Analecta 200. Rome, 1975.

Van Os   Van Os, H. "The Discovery of an Early Man of Sorrows on a Dominican Triptych." *Journal of the Warburg and Courtauld Institutes,* 41 (1978), 65ff.

Vetter   Vetter, E.M. *Die Kupferstiche zur Psalmodia Eucaristica des Melchior Prieto von 1622.* Münster, 1972.

Vetter, "Iconografia"   Vetter, E.M. "Iconografia del 'Varon de Dolores.' Su significado y origen." *Archivo espanol de Arte,* 36 (1963), 197ff.

Young, *Drama*   Young, K. *The Drama of the Medieval Church,* 2 vols. Oxford, 1933.

Notes

Introduction

[1]See Belting and Ihm's *Sub Matris tutela. Untersuchungen zur Vorgeschichte der Schutzmantelmadonna,* Heidelberger Akademie der Wissenschaftten, Abhandlungen (1976).

[2]For the Bibliography for literature on the devotional image. On devotion, a concept with many meanings, see J. Grotz in *Lexikon für Theologie und Kirche,* 2nd ed. I (1957), 502 f., and E. Bertaud and A. Rayez in *Dict. Spiritualité,* III (1957), 747 ff. H. Seuse owned a devotional image on parchment that he contemplated "andaht nah bildricher wise" (H. Seuse, *Deutsche Schriften,* ed. K. Bihlmeyer [Stuttgart, 1907], 103). Charles Sanspeur owned "un petit tableau de dévocion, où est la passion" (L. de Laborde, *Les ducs de Bourgogne,* II, 2 [Paris, 1851], no. 3844). We learn from the *Decor puellarum* Venice, 1471), fol. 8^r f. (see Ringbom, 26, note 21), that prayers of indulgence were said before such images.

[3]W. Dürig, *Pietas liturgica* (Regensburg, 1958); Vetter, 191f., 222 and 227, and esp. (also for what follows) H. Friedrich, *Die Rechtsmetaphysik der Göttlichen Komödie* (Frankfurt, 1942), 144ff. Cf. esp. our discussion of the significance of the concept in the writings of Bernard of Clairvaux (Chapter VI below) and the application of the concept to characterize our image (Appendix A).

[4]Meiss, *Black Death,* 123f.

[5] See p. 14.

[6]W. Benjamin, "Lehre vom Ähnlichen" in *Ges. Schriften,* II, 1, ed. R. Tiedemann and H. Schweppenhäuser (Frankfurt, 1977), 204ff. On motion as a sign of life and in the context of perception, C.F. von Weizäcker, *Der Garten des Menschlichen* (1977), 169ff., 206ff. The connection between mimesis and the sight of God is expressed in a mystical formulation by Bernard of Clairvaux: after exposure to the sight of God, man becomes "in eandem imaginem transformabitur, et similis erit illi, videns eum sicut est." The controversy over the preferential, direct sight of God enjoyed by the saints, even prior to the Last Judgment, was part of the great theological polemics of the fourteenth century.

[7]See Panofsky, 261ff. Cf. on the concepts, J. Kollwitz, "Bild und Bildertheologie im Mittelalter" in W. Schöne, ed., *Das Gottesbild im Abendland* (Witten, 1957), and on the interpretation of the *imago,* K. Bauch, "Imago" in *idem, Studien zur Kunstgeschichte* (Berlin, 1967), 1ff.

[8]This is how the image is described in the regulations of a Bolognese confraternity from 1329 (C. Mesini in *Archivum Franciscan. Historicum,* 52 [1959], 388f.) and in the 1499 will of the Migliatori in Rimini (A. Campana in *Scritti di storia dell arte in onore M. Salmi,* II [Rome, 1962], 405ff.). See also p. 191.

[9]On this definition, see K. Bauch "Bildnisse des Jan van Eyck" in *idem, Studien zur*

Kunstgeschichte (Berlin, 1967), 79 ff. and esp. 117.

[10]Siccard of Cremonas, *Mitrale Liber III* (*PL* 213, 124 C).

[11]Theodoricus, *Libellus de Locis Sanctis (1164–74)*, ed. M.L. and W. Bulst (Editiones Heidelbergenses XVIII: Heidelberg, 1976), 18. Cf. now, M.L. Bulst, "Die Mosaiken der 'Auferstehungskirche' in Jerusalem und die Bauten der 'Franken' im 12. Jh." *Frühmittelalterlichen Studien*, 13 (1979), 442ff. and esp. 461f.

[12]O. Demus, *Byzantine Art and the West* (New York, 1970), 218, and Hager, 75ff.

[13]Cf. note 10. The speech reads as follows: "Aspice qui transis quia tu mihi causa doloris. / Pro te passus ita, pro me noxia vita."

Chapter I
New Forms of Existence of Images in the Middle Ages

[1] Not many studies have dealt explicitly with this question, which has again become a matter of interest since the "easel picture" has been called into question as a norm of artistic production (cf. W. Hofmann, *Von der Nachahmung zur Erfindung der Wirklichkeit* [Cologne, 1970], 7ff.). On the history of the medieval panel painting, see, among others, the works by Hager, Ringbom, Kermer, and Pilz, as well as the scholarly literature on early Dutch painting and on the early altarpiece.

[2] Practices in Rome are especially informative in this regard (see Hager, passim). Not only processions (e.g., the *Assuntà* procession in the early hours of August 15, in which the Savior icon of Sancta Sanctorum "visited" the icon of *Salus Populi Romani* in S. Maria Maggiore) are attested there, but also ciborium shrines for images (in S. Maria Maggiore) and for relics (veronica in St. Peter's): cf. Hager, illus. 41–43. On images of Christ, see Dobschütz, passim. On the early Byzantine cult of images, see Kitzinger, passim; and notes 13 and 14 of the present work; and M. Dejonghe, *Roma Santuario Mariano*, Roma Christiana, VI (Bologna, 1969).

[3] Of course, we are speaking of an ideal type. Examples from monumental painting are the nave cycles of the Roman basilicas, and from book illumination, textual illustrations in the strict sense.

[4] An example is the stigmatization of Francis as found in the altarpiece signed by Giotto in the Louvre. This structural change is particularly characteristic of the so-called devotional images with themes from the Passion that have come down from the trecento: cf. Panofsky; Meiss, *Black Death.*

[5] Kermer, no. 16, illus. 22, 23, with bibliography (both panels 36 x 32 cm), and Garrison, nos. 272–73.

[6] See Garrison, 174ff. and nos. 447–605 for the twelfth and thirteenth centuries, as well as Hager, 75ff.

[7] Examples in Sotiriou, passim, and K. Weitzmann, *Die Ikone* (Munich, 1978).

[8] Berliner, 104.

[9] List of Art Works, no. 13.

[10] On the devotional image, see the Bibliography, and the Introduction, note 1.

[11] I am thinking especially of books; for example, books of hours with full-page miniatures or the Franciscan MS Plut. XXV.3 with its appendix of more than forty full-page illustrations for pious contemplation. In wall painting, too, the single image that

needs to be viewed separately was coming to occupy more and more space at this time.

[12] On this point, see especially Ringbom, 30ff., who cites abundant evidence.

[13] For example, consider the multiplication of the miraculous image of S. Croce in fifteenth-century panel painting, miniatures, and printing (for literature on this subject, see the "List of Art Works," no. 31), as well as the corresponding popularization of the image of the veronica, for example, as a pilgrimage souvenir (see the study by A. Chastel, "La Veronique," *Revue de l'Art* [1978], 71ff.: Chastel refers to parchment copies of the image that functioned as "wall icons" in the bedchamber). An especially interesting example of the relationship between the publicly venerated miraculous image and replicas commissioned privately is reported for the "picture of St. Luke" of the *Notre Dame des Graces* in the cathedral of Cambrai ("miraculous image" is even part of the panel's title) and for the copies produced soon after the establishment of her cult: see P. Rolland in *Revue belge d'archéologie et d'histoire de l'art*, 17 (1947/1948), 97ff., and E. Panofsky, *Early Netherlandish Painting* (Cambridge, Mass., 1953), 297f.

On the image cult of an eleventh-century Greek lay brotherhood in Naupaktos, see Meersseman, 85ff., and J. Nesbitt–J. Wiita, "A Confraternity of the Comnenian Era," *Byzantinische Zeitschrift*, 86 (1975), 360ff. These authors also cite documentary evidence of an institutionalized image cult of thirteenth-century Italian brotherhoods (esp. the Laudesi and Disciplinati): Meersseman, 480 (Statutes of the Battuti of Bologna from 1286, 8: "Quod homines dicte congregationis debeant revereri picturas sanctorum cum fuerint coram eis . . . et sibi inclinare," esp. before panels of the Virgin and the crucifix), 951 and 1041 (contract of the Laudesi with Duccio).

[14] Cf. note 2. The Greek brotherhood of Naupaktos (see note 13) carried its cult image successively to all the members' homes. On special occasions, the miraculous image of the "Rainmaker Madonna" of Impruneta was "activated," indeed was made at all visible, as the Madonna herself, as it were, coming to Florence: see R.C. Trexler, "Florentine Religious Experience: The Sacred Image," *Studies in the Renaissance*, 19 (1972), 7-40.

[15] Cf. Introduction, note 11. See, however, Berliner, "Freedom," passim, as well as Baxandall, 41ff., who treat, among other matters, the anagogical and stimulating function of images which was considered to lie chiefly in the possibilities of the pictorial medium and its effect, via the eye, on the soul.

[16] See Chapter III, note 55, and esp. Chapter IV, note 3.

[17] Ringbom, 23ff.; N. Paulus, *Geschichte des Ablasses im Mittelalter* (Paderborn, 1923). See, especially, the literature on the miraculous images of the veronica, the Imago Pietatis, and the *arma Christi* (on the latter, see Suckale, passim).

[18] See Ringbom, 30. On the importation of icons and the instrumentalization of the image, see Belting, passim.

[19] Of the many relevant interpretations, I shall cite only two: E. Panofsky, *Gothic Architecture and Scholasticism* (Latrobe, 1951), and A. Katzenellenbogen, *The Sculptural Programs of Chartres Cathedral* (Baltimore, 1959).

[20] The interpretations of Giotto's use of perspective and of his interpretation of the world are legion: see D. Gioseffi, *Giotto architetto* (Milan, 1963), and my own remarks in *Die Oberkirche von S. Francesco in Assisi* (Berlin, 1977) (listed under "Padua" in the index), as well as "L'arte come testimone della società bizantina alla Fine del medioevo," in *La civiltà bizantina dal XII al XV secolo*, Università degli Studi di Bari, Centro di studi bizanti-

ni, Corsi di studi III (Bari, 1979).

[21] J. Szöverffy, "Bruch mit der Tradition: Subjektivist. Tendenzen in der Epik des 13. Jahrhunderts," in *Geschichtliche Schriften* (Leyden, 1977), 5ff., and H.B. Wilson in *Modern Language Review*, 58 (1963), 364ff. On the literature of the thirteenth century, see the fundamental investigation by H. Kuhn, *Entwürfe zu einer Literatursystematik des Spätmittelalters* (Stuttgart, 1980), 1ff. and 19ff., as well as R.J. Jauss, "Theorie der Gattungen und Literatur des Mittelalters," in his *Alterität und Modernität der mittelalterlichen Literatur* (Munich, 1977), 327ff.

[22] G. de Lagarde, *Bilan du XIIIe siècle*, vol. 1 of *La naissance de l'esprit laïque au declin du moyen age*, 3rd ed. (Louvain-Paris, 1956), esp. 31ff., 158ff., and 175f. The brotherhoods (on their lay character, see Meersseman, passim, and 428ff. and 509ff.) contested the Church's monopoly of "vertu" (89). The economic development in the city-states created additional barriers, primarily by means of the money economy and the jurisdiction over the clergy, who nevertheless enjoyed tax immunity, but also by means of the growing autonomy and "immanence" of the worldly authority of the city-states, which limited the influence of the Church. See also H. Schüppert, "Kirchenkritik in der lateinischen Lyrik des 12. und 13. Jahrhunderts," *Medium Aevum* 23 (Munich, 1972), and Larner, passim, on the "secularization" of art in the domain of the city-states.

[23] R. Seeberg, *Lehrbuch der Dogmengeschichte*, III (1930), 675.

[24] H.A. Oberman, *The Harvest of Medieval Theology: Gabriel Biel and Late Medieval Nominalism* (Cambridge, Mass., 1963), 323ff. The criticism of William of Ockham's writings, which were rejected in 1326, was directed in part against their skepticism and separation of faith and knowledge. For the literature on nominalism, see the literature on Ockham.

[25] M. Grabmann, *Mittelalterliches Geistesleben* (Munich, 1926ff.); H. Grundmann, *Religiöse Bewegungen im Mittelalter*, Historische Studien 267 (1935); R.C. Petry, *Late Medieval Mysticism* (Philadelphia, 1957), 17ff.; see the entry "Contemplation" in *Dictionnaire de spiritualité*, II (1953), 1643ff., esp. 1966ff. (twelfth century) and 1991 (Dominican mysticism of the fourteenth century); H. Denifle, *Die deutschen Mystiker des 14. Jahrhunderts*, ed. O. Speiss (Fribourg, 1951).

[26] Moreover, objects, such as relics (*arma*) and the Host, as well as ideas, such as the liturgical sacrifice and the real presence of Christ in the Sacrament, were not sharply demarcated from one another. Metaphors, such as Christ in the winepress, could be experienced in visions, and much theological dispute was devoted to the delimitation of metaphors and directly, concretely perceptible reality. Schmidt, 282f., speaks of "contemplation of the mysteries of faith in the sense of a popularized mysticism" that was made possible through the representation of an "abstract" doctrine such as that of the Eucharist by the "concrete" image of the "Man of Sorrows." The boundaries between symbol and depiction are fluid: see Suckale, 179, who speaks of the "conversion of dogma into images," so that images stand for ideas; the *arma*, as an image symbol, were a "product of theological thought," according to Suckale (183), but could be directly viewed and experienced in their physical existence, insofar as they had, as it were, the status of relics, as in the case of the Crown of Thorns.

[27] Address delivered in New York in November 1977 at a symposium held on the occasion of the exhibition "The Age of Spirituality." See also Kitzinger, passim.

[28] W. Durandus, *Rationale Divinorum Officiorum* 3.1 (ed. *Prochiron, vulgo Rationale*

divinorum officiorum auctore G. Durando [Madrid, 1775], 12ff.).

[29] On this topic, see Chapter V, as well as Belting, *passim.*

[30] H. van Os, "The Madonna and the Mystery Play," *Simiolus,* 5 (1971), 5ff.

[31] See Hager, *passim.*

[32] See the example of the *Nikopoia* or *The Madonna of St. Luke* of S. Marco in Venice, which the Venetians carried off from Constantinople in 1203: H.R. Hahnloser, ed., *Il tesoro di San Marco,* II (Florence, 1971), catalog no. 15 and pl. XIV; G. Tiepolo, *Trattato dell'Imagine della Glor. Vergine dipinta da S. Luca* (Venice, 1618), *passim*; and R. Gallo, *Il tesoro di S. Marco e la sua storia* (Venice, 1967), 133ff. On the legends surrounding images generally, see Dobschütz, *passim*; the literature on *The Madonna of St. Luke* and on the later period, L. Kretzenbacher, *Bilder und Legenden* (Klagenfurt, 1971).

[33] R. Davidsohn, *Geschichte von Florenz* (Berlin, 1927), IV.3, 214. The sermon was held in S. Maria Novella in Florence.

[34] But see the remarks in Chapter V distinguishing between the semantic and functional relationships of the icon and the cultic object (e.g., the relic).

[35] See the recent study by Meersseman, *passim.*

[36] Cf. notes 13 and 14. See also the literature on the cult image of Or San Michele in Florence (see note 40).

[37] One of many examples is the consecration of Siena to the Virgin after the battle of Montaperti in 1260. On the corresponding cult images commissioned by the town, of which Duccio's *Maestà* was the latest, see Hager, 105ff. (*Madonna degli occhi grossi*), 134ff. (*Madonna del Voto*), 146ff. (*Maestà*), as well as J. White, *Duccio. Tuscan Art and the Medieval Workshop* (London, 1979), 80ff. On the cultural and political milieu and on the governmental commissioning of art works, see Larner, *passim.*

[38] On the "cult center" of the brotherhoods, see Meersseman, esp. 466ff., 512. Sometimes such a "center" consisted of a brotherhood's own chapel or even church, for example, one connected with a hospital. But most often we may understand it to be a room, in a monastic church of a religious order, for example, in which a brotherhood enjoyed the right to hospitality.

[39] Hager, *passim.* Cf. also J. Braun, *Der christliche Altar in seiner geschichtlichen Entwicklung* (Munich, 1923), II, 277ff. (the retable), and E.F. Werner, *Das italienische Altarbild vom Trecento bis zum Cinquecento,* Dissertation, Munich, 1971. On the structure of the composite altarpiece (polyptychon) and its development in Tuscany, see White, *op. cit.* (note 37 above), 64ff., whose research has yielded new results.

[40] The latter is the case, for example, when AN INDIVIDUAL person demonstrates his adherence to, and his participation in a cult through a donation of an image. On the other kinds of agent, see notes 13, 14, and 37.

[41] Panofsky, for one, makes this error. See also Chapter III.

[42] Hager, 144ff. and illus. 214, 215; R. Davidsohn, *Forschungen zur Geschichte von Florenz* (Berlin, 1908), IV, 435ff., with sources.

[43] One such product of regressive development that is pertinent to our inquiry is the mosaic icon of S. Croce in Gerusalemme in Rome, which, although of eastern origin, was transformed in that city ex post facto into an ancient miraculous image and exemplar, into the Imago Pietatis pure and simple (List of Art Works, no. 31).

[44] J. Habermas, *Strukturwandel der öffentlichkeit* (Neuwied, 1971), *passim.* On the relation of art and the public sphere in the trecento, see G. Antal, *Florentine Painting*

and its Social Background (London, 1948), and Larner, passim.

[45] Ringbom, 11ff. and 30ff. See the recommendations of the preacher Giovanni Dominici (end of the fourteenth century) for private devotional images and their use (*Regola del governo di cura familiare*, ed. D. Salvi [Florence, 1860], 131ff., and Larner, 310f.) or the correspondence between Domenico di Cambio and the merchant Francesco di Marco Datini of Prato (end of the fourteenth century), who procured "appropriate" devotional images for bedchambers, etc. (R. Piatolloi, "Un mercante del Trecento e gli artisti del tempo suo," *Rivista d'Arte*, 11 [1930], 228ff.; I. Origo, *The Merchant of Prato, F. di Marco Datini* [London, 1957], 257ff.; and Larner, 314ff.). The correspondence of the merchant of Prato from 1390 to 1391 was concerned with the commission for an Imago Pietatis. After much negotiation, in which the choice of subject and the price of the image (which represented a not very large, and therefore not very attractive commission) played a role, the merchant and the artist agreed on a diptych that would show, on one side, "una Pietà, cioè Nostre Signore quand' escie del monimento" ("a Pietà, that is, our Lord as He comes out of the grave"), with Mary and John, and, on the other, the intercessors ("prochuratori") of the family. Among Florentine artists the Pietà was considered the "più divota chosa" that could be found in painting.

[46] Most recently, White, *op. cit.* (see note 37 above), 25ff. on Coppo and the artist of the *S. Bernardino Madonna*, whom White does not identify with Guido of Siena, as well as on the dimensions of the S. Bernardino Madonna; ibid., 32ff. on the *Rucellai Madonna* (with the text of the contract, 185ff.).

[47] S. Orlandi, "Il VII centenario della predicazione di S. Petro Martire a Firenze: I ricordi di S. Pietro M.," in *Memorie Domenicane*, 64, n.s. 22 (1967), 111.

[48] G. Milanesi, *Documenti per la storia dell'arte senese* (Siena, 1854), I, no. 60, 258f. G. Gaye, *Carteggio inedito d'artisti dei sec. XIV, XV, XVI* (Florence, 1839), 258f., no. 60. Partial English trans. in Larner, 76.

[49] On the various Franciscan devotional forms, see Bonaventura, *De Sex Alis Seraphim Cap. VII* (ed. Quaracchi), 333f., 336; for a devotion before the crucifix, see his *De perfectione Vitae Cap. VI* (*ibid.*), 265. Cf. also note 13, and Bonaventura's *Lignum Vitae* or Ubertino de Casali's *Arbor vitae Crucifixi Jesu*, or, finally, the *Meditationes vitae Christi* as instructions for contemplation from which the reception of images was able to profit. On the connection between the sermon as training and the image as an object of contemplation, see Baxandall, 48ff. For a general study of the influence of the mendicant orders, see H. Hefele, *Die Bettelorden und das religiöse Volksleben Ober- und Mittelitaliens im 13. Jahrhundert* (Leipzig-Berlin, 1910), as well as Meersseman, passim, esp. 950 (on the guidance of the confraternities by such sermons). Offensively, the secular clergy at once made fun of the mendicant sermons: see Schüppert, *op. cit.* (note 22 above), 137: "Predicant clamose / tractim et morose / sed dicunt jocose: / 'Date tabulariis, / Qui nostra ferunt tabulas.' / Inducunt fictas fabulas / loquendo parabolas"; or: "Jacobite [Dominicans] predicant multaque loquuntur / De multis que scripta sunt nec intelliguntur."

[50] Cf. note 13. This assessment can also be drawn from the material. In their predominance, the cultic images of the crucified Christ and the Mother of God corresponded to these as cultic persons. See Hager, and Meersseman, 480f. (cf. note 13). In addition, the names of the confraternities testify to the existence of both of these cults.

[51] Hager, 79, 160 and pl. 90, 91. According to the legend of Saint Francis, it is the

Cross that spoke to the saint.

[52] Cf. the panel of the cathedral of Orte (second half of the thirteenth century) on which, amid the four accompanying scenes showing Saint Francis, a miraculous healing before a waist-length portrait icon is shown. See C. Brandi, "Il maestro del paliotto di S. Giovanni a Siena," in *Scritti di storia dell'arte in onore di M. Salmi*, I (Rome, 1961), 351ff., illus. 4 and 9. On the altarpieces showing Saint Francis, see Hager, 94ff.

[53] Hager, 80, 100, 110, and pl. 141.

[54] Cf. Chapter III, note 50.

[55] Most recent is White, *op. cit.* (note 37 above), 46ff. On the iconographic scheme, see Belting-Ihm (see Chapter II, note 23), passim.

[56] See the correspondence of Francesco di Marco Datini (see note 45 above).

Chapter II
The Portrait of the Dead God (Imago Pietatis)

[1] List of Art Works, no. 18.

[2] N. Beljaev, "L'image de la Ste Vierge Pelagonitissa," *Byzantinoslavica*, 2 (1930), 386ff.; V. Lasareff, "Studies in the Iconography of the Virgin," *Art Bulletin* (1938), 42ff. with illus. 17–22; *idem*, in *Arte Veneta*, 8 (1954), 80, illus. 75–76; P. Milkovic-Pepek, in *Recueil des Travaux*, 2, Mus. Archéol. (Skopje, 1958), 1ff.

[3] Pallucchini, illus. 231 and 233.

[4] L. Coletti, *Tomaso da Modena* (Venice, 1963), 122, no. 12, and illus. 102–03; catalogue for Tomaso da Modena, edited by L. Menegazzi (Treviso, 1979), no. 9.

[5] List of Art Works, no. 14.

[6] List of Art Works, no. 1.

[7] List of Art Works, no. 30.

[8] Cf. the *pala feriale* in S. Marco or the triptych in Trieste and subsequent works (Pallucchini, illus. 39, 101, 193). List of Art Works, nos. 35, 34.

[9] On the transalpine conception, see G.V.D. Osten, *Der Schmerzensmann* (Berlin, 1935); W. Mersmann, *Der Schmerzensmann* (Düsseldorf, 1952); Vetter, 182–242, and Berliner, esp. 108: "The simplest...solution to the problem of representing the Divinity in the humanly suffering Christ...consisted in depicting Christ's body as dead, while nevertheless permitting it to be capable of doing something, a state of affairs that runs contrary to the natural laws governing men." But this formula of the "living dead man" appears to me to ignore the expression of the motif, which determines the nature of the contact with the viewer.

[10] Cf. notes 1–6, above.

[11] List of Art Works, no. 6.

[12] List of Art Works, no. 30, for Simone Martini; no. 5 for Giotto.

[13] M. Meiss, "Alesso di Andrea," in *Giotto e il suo tempo*, Atti Congr. Internaz. VII Centen. Giotto (Rome, 1971), 415ff. and illus. 30.

[14] List of Art Works, no. 23.

[15] List of Art Works, no. 35.

[16] A. Xyngopoulos, "Byzantinai eikones en Meteorois," *Archaiol. Deltion*, 10 (1926

[1929]), 37ff.

17 List of Art Works, no. 16.

18 Plut. XXV.3, the so-called "Supplicationes Variae" of 1291 (see List of Art Works, no. 12).

19 See p.75.

20 List of Art Works, no. 2.

21 List of Art Works, no. 33.

22 List of Art Works, no. 34.

23 See C. Belting-Ihm, *Sub Matris Tutela. Untersuchungen zur Vorgeschichte der Schutzmantelmadonna,* Abh. Heidelberger Akad. der Wiss., Phil.-Hist. Kl. (1976).

24 List of Art Works, no. 31; and Chapter I, note 43.

25 This term has been generally adopted since the fundamental study by Panofsky (1927).

26 This conclusion was drawn, for example, by J. Stubblebine, "Segna di Buonaventura and the Image of the Man of Sorrows," *Gesta,* (February 8, 1969), 3ff.

27 Ringbom, 39ff

Chapter III
Functions of Medieval Images

1 See the Bibliography in this volume for the Devotional Image.

2 Panofsky, 264f. Panofsky distinguishes here the devotional image from the scenic "narrative image" and from the hieratic or cultic "representational image." The devotional image resulted in either the transformation of the narrative image into a situation or the conferring of movement on the timeless representational image. See the criticism by Berliner, 97ff., directed against the postulation of firm "compositional types" and corresponding meanings and his warning against a linking or mixing of formal and functional conditions. In the image theory of the Church (cf. Introduction, note 6), *imago* is used at times simply as a general term for the image, and at other times, in contrast to , for a certain type of image that did not narrate but representationally depicted persons. In his handbook, W. Durandus (1230–1296) summarizes the current state of the doctrine: see his *Rationale* (cited in Chapter I, note 28), 12ff. and esp. 14. Admittedly, he imputes to the various "imagines Christi," among which he includes the crucified Christ, corresponding "significationes" in the biographical, hence narrative sense. However, he not only maintains the distinction between the "imagines Christi" and the "historiae tam novi quam veteris testamenti," but also establishes it qualitatively in that he grants artistic freedom to the creators of the latter on a par with that of the "poetae." Cf. Berliner, "Freedom," passim.

3 List of Art Works, no. 13.

4 List of Art Works, no. 11.

5 *Summary Catalogue of European Paintings* (National Gallery of Art: Washington D.C., 1975), 214, nos. 232 and 807, no. 11. On Margaritone, see F.R. Shapley, *Paintings from the S.H. Kress Collection. Italian Schools XIII–XV Centuries* (London, 1966), 3f. and illus. 1.

6 Durandus, *Rationale,* 12f. (see Chapter I, note 28), cf. also Ringbom, 40 and note 9: "Graeci etiam utuntur imaginibus, pingentes illas, ut dicitur, solum ab umbilico supra,

et non inferius, ut omnis stultae cogitationis occasio tollatur."

7 List of Art Works, no. 34.

8 List of Art Works, no. 4. Bologna, Archiginnasio MS 52 (Fondo Ospedale 3), fol. 1. The title page with the Virgin of Mercy and Imago Pietatis is described in the text: "...cum Virgine matre omnium, sub manto eius...homines societatis prefate sunt inclusi et cum Domino Yhesu Christo in forma pietatis...." (C. Mesini, "La compagnia di S. Maria delle Laudi e di S. Francesco di Bologna," *Archivum Franciscanum Historicum*, 52 [1959], 361ff., esp. 388). Cf. also Belting-Ihm, *Sub Matris Tutela*, illus. 1; and M. Fanti, "Il 'Fondo Ospedale'," *L'Archiginnasio*, 58 (1963), 1ff.

9 Ringbom, 39.

10 Ringbom, 48. See also Suckale, 185 and 187, on the detailed and simultaneous depiction of the *arma* and of images showing the Five Wounds. It is his opinion that in their detailed rendering they are presented in a manner suitable to an "ideographic mode of perception" (194).

11 Berliner, 100ff., include criticism of Panofsky. See also E.B. Garrison, "A New Devotional Panel Type in Fourteenth-Century Italy," *Marsyas*, 3 (1946), 54ff.; Garrison correctly observes that the and icon first functioned as devotional images.

12 If it were not so, art history would be reduced to a history of style that moreover would not know how to interpret the changes it observed. However, the difference between a twelfth-century representation of the Crucifixion and one from the fourteenth century cannot be understood by means of a history of style.

13 Cf. Ragusa-Green, passim; this work gives an English translation of the text in question. The projection of historical events into the present, in which they can be experienced "first-hand," is just as characteristic as their dramatization, which emphasizes the course of the action, and their stationary treatment, which serves psychological empathy or visual perception and contemplation of the events. Narratives and "portraits" alternate in counterpoint. The detailed rendering of the events both serves the chronicle and gives a close-up of the heroes of the action and their emotional status.

14 L.B. Alberti, *Kleinere Kunsttheoretische Schriften*, ed. H. Janitschek (Vienna, 1877): "A narrative picture *Historia* will move the feelings when the people presented in these images themselves show strong emotions. For the fact that we weep with those who weep, and mourn with those who mourn, is grounded in nature, in which nothing attracts more strongly than what is similar." On this point and the double meaning of *mostrare* as "to depict" and "to express," as well as on the meaning of *esprimere* as "to express," see M. Barasch, "Der Ausdruck in der italienischen Kunsttheorie der Renaissance," *Zeitschrift für Ästhetik und allgemeine Kunstwissenschaft*, 12 (1967), 33ff., and esp. 34, 39, and 42.

15 Florence, Bibl. Laurenziana, Plut. XXV.3 (1291). See List of Art Works, no. 12. It is a question of fol. 366 (the Enthroned Virgin) and fol. 373 v. (the Crucifixion). See also Durandus, *Rationale*, 14, where the observation can be found that the "Salvatoris imago...depicta in matris gremio (rememorat) puerilem aetatem" (a contemporary testimony) (see Chapter I, note 28).

16 Hager, passim. Similar stylistic forms and motifs are found in the frescoes added about 1300 to the baptistery of Parma, among which an Enthroned Virgin also appears.

17 Ragusa-Green, 31f. and 55 (where the viewer is included in the affection between Mother and Child), as well as 68f., 75, and 94.

[18] Cf. note 15.

[19] Rome, Bib. Vaticana, Cod. Reg. lat. 2048, fol. 129 v. Regarding similar depictions, including those in miniatures, see F. Bologna, *I pittori alla corte angioina di Napoli 1266–1414* (Rome, 1969), 82ff. and pl. II.16–22.

[20] From the translation in Baxandall, 46. Representation, as commemoration, is a typical contemplative act which also embodies a function according to the current doctrines of images.

[21] Ringbom, 56.

[22] Schmidt, passim.

[23] Ringbom, 57.

[24] If this term is used to refer to those symbolic images that embody religious concepts (see Ringbom, 57), then the question arises of how they do it.

[25] Ringbom, 39.

[26] Ringbom, 72ff. and illus. 26ff. On Mantegna's Berlin panel, see E. Tietze-Conrat, *Mantegna* (London, 1956), 179, pl. 30, and the catalogue for *A. Mantegna* (Venice, 1961), no. 18, illus. 26.

[27] Ringbom, 82, and esp. 108f. and illus. 61, 62. On Bellini's panels in Berlin and in the Brera, see List of Art Works, nos. 3 and 20, and also H. Belting, *Giovanni Bellini. Pietà* (Frankfurt, 1985).

[28] Here I have in mind Giusto da Menabuoi's predella of the polyptychs in the baptistery of Padua, a work that is a good hundred years older than Bellini's (Pallucchini, illus. 400), and also Antonio Vivarini's polyptychs from the 1440s in Parenzo and in the Brera in Milan (R. Pallucchini, *I Vivarini* [Venice, 1961]), illus. 3, 77, and 85).

[29] Ringbom, 108.

[30] Ringbom, 118 and 141.

[31] Ringbom, 141.

[32] There are pertinent brief discussions of the medieval understanding of symbols and images in Berliner and Suckale. The *arma Christi* call for reformulation of the relationship between symbol and image in the Middle Ages (Suckale, 188f.), which was not stable. Suckale speaks of a diminishing of the symbol's "power," as the culture made even greater use of texts, and with the "development of an art that was becoming increasingly visual" (190). But the latter occurrence is less an explanation than a symptom of an increasing importance of images that must be understood and interpreted as a historically ascertainable factor that changed images. As for the polyvalent *arma*, one must also reckon with growing contradictions between symbol and image, which increased with qualitative change of both categories. Cf. note 52.

[33] List of Art Works, no. 8.

[34] Cf. note 14.

[35] Joh. Balbus (John of Genoa, end of the thirteenth century), *Catholicon* (Venice, 1497), speaks of the threefold reason (*triplex ratio*) for the introduction of images into the Church: (1) for the instruction of the uneducated (*instructionem rudium*); (2) for the visual commemoration of the Mysteries of the Faith and the lives of the saints (*dum cotidie oculis nostris repraesententur*); and (3) for the stimulation of emotional piety (*ad excitandum devotionis affectum*), which takes place more easily through the eye than through the ear. On this point and on the assessment of the anagogical function of images in general, see Baxandall, 41ff.; Berliner, "Freedom," 273ff. (Berliner draws inferences

about the structure of "pictorial language," in contrast to written language, and about the varieties of its reception); and Ringbom, 11f.

Durandus (see Chapter I, note 28) speaks in Chapter III (12f.) of his *Rationale*—faithful to Gregory—of images as "laicorum lectiones et scripturae," of their suitability "ad memoriam" of religious matters, and finally, again in agreement with Gregory, of the fact that "the image moves the spirit more than writing does" *(pictura namque plus videtur movere animum quam scriptura)*. In this connection, he also invokes the authority of Gregory's *Regula Pastoralis* with a passage asserting that the form of visible things "quasi in corde depingitur," and that one thinks "in fictis imaginibus."

Finally, cf. Fra Michele da Carcano *(Sermones quadragesimales fratris Michaelis de Mediolano de decem preceptis* [Venice, 1492], 48 v.; partial English trans. in Baxandall, 41): "Sciendo sunt imagines introducte propter tarditatem et affectivam: ut homines qui non excitantur ad devotionem: cum aliqua audiunt de sanctorum memoria: saltem moveantur, dum ea in picturis quasi praesentia cernunt. Plus non excitatur affectus noster per ea, quae videt, quam per ea, quae audit."

[36] Cf. the Bibliography in this volume on the devotional image, and the Introduction, note 2.

[37] See Schmidt, Berliner, "Arma," and Suckale, passim; see esp. Suckale on the cognitive "reading" of images as symbols in the case of the *arma*.

[38] See A. Wilmart, *Auteurs spirituels et textes dévots du Moyen Age latin* (Paris, 1932), on the texts and forms of lay devotion, and Lagarde, *Bilan du XIIIe siècle*, on the social background. Cf. also von Simson, 131ff., where he gives evidence. See also the obligation to observe the canonical hours in the statutes of lay confraternities during the thirteenth century (e.g., Meersseman, 391: "Omnes dicant quotidie septem horas canonicas [for the penitents]"), and the manifest evidence for lay devotion given by breviaries for the laity. Cf. O. Clemen, *Die Volksfrömmigkeit des ausgehenden Mittelalters* (1937).

[39] Ringbom, 30ff., and V. Leroquais, *Les livres d'heures manuscrits de la Bibliothèque Nationale I–III* (Paris, 1927), as well as Chastel (see Chapter I, note 13). On the private devotional image (*icona* or *cona di cammara...,cone ad modum grecorum*), see the material and the commentary in G. Bresc-Bautier, *Artistes, Patriciens et Confréries* (Rome, 1979), 29ff.

[40] For a comprehensive treatment of this topic, see E. Benz, *Die Vision. Erfahrungsformen und Bilderwelt* (Stuttgart, 1969), passim. Cf. also Ringbom, 18ff.

[41] Cf. Introduction, note 2.

[42] Cf. Chapter I, note 50, and Origo, *The Merchant of Prato*, 257f., Larner, 310ff., as well as R. Piattoli in *Riv. d'Arte*, 11 (1929), 221ff., and 12 (1930), 97ff. In addition to a fresco of Christopher over his threshold, Datini commissioned three devotional images for his bedchamber as well as several for guestrooms and his office (Origo, *loc. cit.*). In response to the merchant's inquiry, the spiritual advisor Domenico di Cambio asked whether Datini wanted Christ to be painted on the Cross or in another way, and he recommended that Datini choose "a Pietà, that is, our Lord as he is rising from the grave" *(quand' esce dal munimento)*. Such images were supposed "to move man's spirit to devotion," and the "pious stories" were particularly important for men who had grown unfeeling in worldly pursuits. Cf. also p. 24.

[43] Cf. Introduction, note 2.

[44] A. Neumeyer, *Der Blick aus dem Bilde* (Berlin, 1964), 29ff.

[45] Von Simson, 144f.; Gerardus de Frachet, *Vitae patrum IV* (ed. B.M. Reichert, *Monumenta ordinis fratrum praedicatorum historica* [1847], 149): "In cellis habebant eius [of Mary] et filii crucifixi imaginem ante oculos suos, ut legentes et orantes et dormientes ipsas respicerent et ab ipsis respicerentur, oculis pietatis."

[46] G. Troescher, *Burgundische Malerei* (Berlin, 1966), 48 and 52f., and illus. 8–9, and H.S. Francis, "Jean de Beaumetz. Calvary with a Carthusian Monk," *Bull. Cleveland Museum of Art* (1966), 329ff., as well as *Cleveland Museum of Art: Catalogue of Paintings* (Cleveland, 1974), no. 5. The duke of Burgundy commissioned twenty-six panel paintings from Jean de Beaumetz in 1388 for the Carthusian monastery of Champmol.

[47] Meersseman, 476. See also note 48.

[48] Bologna, Archiginnasio MS ex-Fondo Batutti 42: Fondo Ospedale 1, fol. 1. See *Catalogo: Mostra storica Nazionale della miniatura* (Rome) (Florence, 1954), no. 169. On the dating of these statutes from 1286, see Meersseman, 468ff., and M. Fanti, "Gli inizi del movimento dei disciplinati a Bologna e la confraternitá di S. Maria della Vita," *Bollettino Deputaz. storia patria per l'Umbria*, 66/1 (Perugia, 1969), 181ff., esp. 185f. Cf. also Belting, as well as Chapter VI, p.139.

[49] M. Horster, "'Mantuae sanguis preciosus'," *Wallraf-Richartz-Jahrbuch*, 25 (1963), 151ff., and C. Eisler, "The Golden Christ of Cortona and the Man of Sorrows in Italy," *Art Bulletin*, 51 (1969), 233ff.

[50] See the fundamental study by Berliner, "Arma," and Suckale, passim.

[51] List of Art Works, no. 9.

[52] On the problem of "reading" such images, in the literal and metaphorical senses, see the observations of Suckale, passim. It is certainly not possible, in the analysis of our images, to ignore the problem of the medieval viewer's reception of images, and it belongs to the images' semantic function to correspond to a particular "reading" of them, to make the "reading" possible. To expand and supplement the viewpoint worked out by Suckale for understanding images as symbols and agents of certain meditation practices (in which cognitive and affective experiences often became inseparable), reference must be made to the accepted reality or presence of figures and objects (relics of the Passion, etc.) which guaranteed a pure pictorial experience with a concomitant possibility of the identification of object and image.

[53] Baxandall, 46ff.

[54] New York, Pierpont Morgan Library M. 729 (ca. 1275–1285), fol. 15; K. Gould, *The Psalter and Hours of Yolande of Soissons*, Speculum Anniversary Monographs 4 (Mediaeval Academy of America: 1978), pl. 7.

[55] For literature on the veronica, see Dobschütz, 158*ff.; 29*ff.; 102ff., S.K. Pearson, *Die Fronica* (Strassburg, 1887); C. Bertelli, "Storia e vicende dell'immagine edissena di S. Silvestro in Capite a Roma," *Paragone*, 217 (1968), 3ff.; Gould, *The Psalter and Hours*, 81ff., and Belting. Cf. also Chapter VI, note 3.

Chapter IV
Realism and Pictorial Rhetoric

[1] Cf. p. 35, and List of Art Works, no. 2.

[2] Staatliche Museen, Skulpturenabt. Inv. 8477 (Upper Rhine, ca. 1420; height: 44 cm; material: linden wood). See *Berlin, Staatliche Museen. Bildwerke der christlichen Epochen*

von der Spätantike bis zum Klassizismus (Munich, 1966), no. 239 and pl. 45. Cf. G. Swarzenski, "Insinuationes divinae pietatis," in *Festschrift A. Goldschmidt* (Leipzig, 1923), 65ff., on the type.

³ Young, *Drama*, I, 112ff. and esp. 122–144, and Corbin, passim, on what follows. On the Passion play, cf. also Bartholomaeis, 112ff., and Meier, 145ff. and 179ff. The *depositio* and *elevatio* (of the Host and the crucifix) are documented from the tenth century onward; however, the texts and performance practices of the plays developed only gradually, principally after the thirteenth century, as the plays increasingly passed from the hands of the Church into those of the religious brotherhoods and were also translated from Latin into the vernacular languages. Independent Lamentation plays developed from paraliturgical actions interpolated into the liturgy, such as the burial of the Cross and the Host, and from dramatized songs of lamentation, for example, those performed during or after the adoration of the Cross that was uncovered on Good Friday. The *officium Sepulchri* as *repraesentatio* of a liturgically staged station of the cross becomes a self-contained *rappresentazione* or *devozione*, the Passion play (Young, I, 503ff.). A *rappresentazione* published by A. Castellani contains a rubric stating that *stanze* should follow that were to accompany the display of the crucifix (A. d'Ancona, *Sacre Rappresentazioni dei secoli XIV, XV e XVI* [Florence, 1872], I, 325ff.). While the reproaches attributed to Christ were dominant during the veneration of the Cross, Mary's *planctus* or lament, the germ cell of the Passion play, was dominant before and afterward. On the burial of the Host and/or the crucifix in a *sepulcrum* prepared for that purpose and "depicting" the historical tomb of Christ, cf. the documentary evidence given in Young, *Drama*, I, 112ff. and 122ff., as well as in Bartholomaeis, 461f. (*Officium Sepulchri* from Aquileia). On the entire subject, cf. Chapter VI below.

⁴ Young, *Drama*, 132: Such a ceremony has the effect of making the Eucharist represent the living body of Christ as "mortuum . . . quod est . . . absurdum." However, this fixation on dogma overlooks the implied simultaneity of Christ's human death and divine life, which plays such a role in the relevant images.

⁵ On this topic, see H. de Lubac, *Corpus mysticum*, 2nd ed. (Paris, 1949). Among the important views on this matter, see the formulations of Innocent III's *De sacro altaris mysterio* IV.19 (PL 217, 869), which were formally approved at the 1215 Lateran Council. Invoking the authority of John VI, Innocent II wrote: "panis sicut vere mutatur in carnem ipsius [that is, of Christ], ita vere mutatur in ipsum." The concept of transubstantiation played a great role in the development of the notion of the "real presence" of Christ, which made mystics, and others also, capable of the experience of the Host that was transferred to the experience of the Imago Pietatis. For the official doctrinal opinion of the Church, cf. the relevant *quaestiones* in the *Summa theologica* of Aquinas, Part III, Quaestiones LXXIII–LXXXIII (e.g., LXXV.1, where it is stated that "in hoc sacramento . . . sit corpus Christi secundum veritatem," not only "secundum figuram" or "sicut in signo," which is not to be experienced with the senses, but only in faith, that is, as the presence of the flesh of Christ; LXXV.4, on the "conversio substantialis" of the bread into the "totam substantiam corporis" of Christ; LXXVI.2; LXXVIII.2 and LXXXII.1, on the fact that "celebratio . . . huius sacramenti . . . imago . . . est repraesentativa passionis Christi quae est vera eius immolatio," and consequently, "ita altare est repraesentativum crucis ipsius, in qua Christus in propria specie immolatus est").

⁶ See E. Dumoutet, *Le désir de voir l'hostie* (Paris, 1926); P. Browe, S.J., "Die Elevation

in der Messe," *Jahrbuch für Liturgiewiss.*, 9 (1929), 20–66, and *idem, Die Verehrung der Eucharistie im Mittelalter*, 2nd ed. (Munich, 1967), 26ff. The earliest documentary evidence is a decree of the bishop of Paris Odo of Sully (1196–1208). Among the Cistercians, the elevation became the rule beginning in 1210. Soon it was adopted generally. On the prayers and devotional practices of the common people, which make it clear that the elevation was the culmination of participation in the mass, see Browe, *Verehrung*, 51 ff. Indulgences and the ringing of bells promoted the practice of going into a church several times a day just to see the consecrated Host "uncovered." "To look at it became one of the most popular acts of piety" (*ibid.*, 55). The view of the Host, enjoyed through the act of seeing, was as it were an anticipation of the future beatific vision. Especially revealing are the legends about the unworthy who were not able to see the Host (*ibid.*, 60), and the cult practices employing bleeding Hosts that multiplied from the thirteenth century onward. According to a fourteenth-century chronicler, "maxime dependet devocio modernorum" of the Eucharist, and Margarete Ebner was summoned "to the coffin" in the choir in order to find there the "Body" of Christ in the tabernacle (*ibid.*, 22f.). On the cult and image of the eucharistic Christ and the bleeding Host, see R. Bauerreiss, *Pie Jesu. Das Schmerzensmannbild und sein Einflub auf die mittelalterliche Frömmigkeit* (Munich, 1931).

[7] Berliner, "Freedom," *passim.*

[8] Cf. the evidence cited in the article by G. v.d. Osten, "Engelpietà," in *RDK* V (1967), 602ff.

[9] Ludolph of Saxony, *Vita Jesu Christi redemptoris nostri* (Lyon, 1519), f. Vli: "perinde enim est immo plus Christi sumere de ara altaris quam de ara crucis. Illi enim acceperant eum in brachiis et manibus, sed isti sumunt eum in ore et cordibus." Cf. also f. CCXIu, a passage on the Holy Sacrament as *memoriale* of the Passion of Christ's human nature, in which it is said that at the ostension one ought to say "ecce homo," because "homo patens fuit in illa ostensione et deus latens." Cf. also, Parker, 73ff.

[10] See the *Vita* of Angela of Foligno written, by the Franciscan Arnaldus (*AASS*, January 1, 186ff., esp. 202). At the elevation of the Host (see note 6 above) "apparuit mihi effigies illius benedicti Dei et hominis crucifixi, quasi tunc noviter de cruce depositi: cujus sanguis apparebat sic recens . . . et per vulnera effluens," that the saint was "tanta compassione transfixa" at this sight. She then heard "crucifixum super devotis . . . et . . . sibi compatientibus" say the words of the Judge at the Last Judgment that are intended for the blessed. Cf. the vision of Douceline (d. 1274) in Marseilles, who saw Christ emerge from the tabernacle, bleeding from all his wounds, "as if He were just descending from the Cross" (Browe, *Verehrung* [see note 6 above], 21).

[11] Vetter, 215ff.

[12] Chapter I, note 42, and List of Art Works, no. 31.

[13] On this type, see G. Swarzenski, *op. cit.* (see note 2 above), 69f. and illus. 2, as well as Eisler, *op. cit.* (see Chapter III, note 49), 115 and illus. 17, and v.d. Osten, *op. cit.* (note 8 above). On art-historical evaluation, see Th. Müller, E. Steingräber, "Die französische Goldemailplastik um 1400," *Münchner Jahrb. Bild. Kunst*, 5 (1954), 38f. and 68f. (catal. no. 5) and illus. 10. In 1457, the large 70 x 45 cm panel was in the possession of the Venetian Cardinal P. Balbo in Rome, who had its frame reshaped between 1457 and 1461. In 1586 it was donated by Sixtus V to Montalto.

[14] See P. Balbo's (later Paul II) inventory of his collection in the Palazzo Venezia:

"Item una tabula argentea deaurata magna pro·altari in qua est crucifixus depositus in cruce manibus unius angeli magni . . . sub pedibus etiam ipsius crucifixi est sepulcrum in quo deponitur ipse crucifixus...."

[15] Amsterdam, Rijksmuseum. Size: 12.7 x 12.5 cm. Cf. Müller–Steingräber, *op. cit.* (note 13), 48, 72 with no. 11 and illus. 25–27; M. Meiss, *French Painting in the Time of Jean de Berry. The Late Fourteenth Century and the Patronage of the Duke* (London, 1967), illus. 572.

[16] Paris, Bibliothèque Nationale, Nouv. acq. lat. 3093, p. 155. Cf. Meiss, *op. cit.,* illus. 15.

[17] J. Braun, S.J., *Der christliche Altar in seiner geschichtlichen Entwicklung,* II (Munich, 1923), 310, 468, and pl. 212.

[18] On the reconstruction of this image in its original form, see J. White, "Donatello's High Altar in the Santo in Padua," *Art Bulletin,* 51 (1969), 1ff. and 119ff., esp. 125 and illus. 34e.

[19] Francovich, 5–57, with illus. 61 (shows the group after the restoration and reconstruction of its original state: *Burlington Magazine,* 89 [1947], opp. p. 55). Francovich establishes the existence of ten groups of monumental Depositions, preserved in their entirety or in part. For three further groups, preserved or inferable, see the catalogue of the exhibition, *Sculture lignee medioevali* (Museo Poldi Pezzoli: Milan, 1957), nos. 15, 17, and 18. Other literature: G. de Francovich, *Scultura medioevale in legno* (Rome, 1934); G. de Francovich, F. de Maffei, *Scultura lignea medioevale* (Milan, 1957); E. Carli, *La scultura lignea italiana dal XII al XVI secolo* (Milan, 1960); E. Panofsky, *Early Netherlandish Painting* (Cambridge, Mass., 1953), 273f.; and Parker, 180ff. Cf. also Chapter VI, Section "The Cross and the Descent from the Cross...."

[20] Cf. the information about the group of the Tivoli cathedral (thirteenth century) in G.C. Crocchiante, *L'istoria delle chiese della città di Tivoli* (Rome, 1726), 42ff. The group was locked inside the altar of SS. Crocifisso and was displayed to the whole people and addressed by a confraternity with "versi esprimenti la passione di Cristo e il Misere" only on the highest feast days and on Fridays in March. According to the local legend, it was supposed to have miraculously come to Tivoli from the mountains of Lebanon.

[21] See the *Vita prima* of Bernard (PL 185, 420). The miracle occurred as Bernard "devotissime adorabat" the crucifix. Christ, "separatis bracchiis a cornibus crucis, videbatur eundem Dei famulum [Bernard] amplectantem ac astringere sibi." On this and the corresponding pictorial formulations, see Vetter, "Iconografia," 212ff., and Vetter, 197ff.

[22] On this famous twelfth-century hymn, which maintained a prominent place in the paraliturgical Lamentations of Mary and the Passion plays (on the plays, see note 3 above, and Chapter VI, Section "The Cross and the Descent from the Cross . . . "); see Young, *Drama,* I, 496–98 (with a copy of the text and the attribution to Godfrey of St. Victor); G.M. Dreves, *Analecta hymnica medii aevi,* vol. 20 (1895), 156ff.; and esp. Meier, 153ff. The formulation of the metaphor that we quote occurs in strophe 13b (Young, 498): "In amplexus ruite, / dum pendet in stipite, / mutuis amplexibus / parat se amantibus / manibus extensis." Cf. also p. 157.

[23] H.W. van Os, M. Prakken, *The Florentine Paintings in Holland, 1300–1500* (Amsterdam, 1974), 49f., no. 20, and the plate.

[24] Cf. pp. 75, and 130, and List of Art Works, no. 12.

[25] U. Middeldorf, "Three Sculptors of the Veneto Represented at Fenway Court," in

Fenway Court 1973 (1974), 6ff., and the catalog, *Sculpture in the Isabella Stewart Gardner Museum* (Boston, 1977), 128f., no. 159.

[26] Copies of the plaque (10.3 x 7.7 cm) are in Berlin, Staatliche Museen, and in Cleveland. See M. Tripps, *Hans Multscher. Seine Ulmer Schaffenszeit, 1427–67* (1969), 66, 269f. and illus. 252.

[27] List of Art Works, no. 26. 54.9 x 38.8 cm (47 x 31.1 cm). The blood and the Crown of Thorns are in relief; the wounds are incised. Perhaps this is the panel that Giambono sent to Treviso in 1431. Literature: F. Zeri, E.E. Gardner, *Catalogue of the Metropolitan Museum. Venetian School* (New York, 1973), 26 and pl. 23; N. Land, *Michele Giambono*, Dissertation, University of Virginia, 1974, 24ff. and 151ff.

[28] Cf. London, BL 17047, fol. 1v (*Mariegola del Corpo di Cristo*) (H. Schrade in *Deutschkundliches, F. Panzer z. 60. Geburtstag* [Heidelberg, 1930], 176ff.) and Princeton, Art Museum, no. [40–401], fol. 13v (*Mariegola d. Scuola del . . . corpo di Christo . . . in la giesia di S. Maria Mater Domini* [Venice, 1512]). Cf. also H. Belting, *Giovanni Bellini's Pietà* (Frankfurt, 1985).

[29] G.v.d. Osten, "Engelpietà" (note 8 above), 603.

[30] M. Weinberger, "Nino Pisano," *Art Bulletin* (1937), 85 and illus. 36.

[31] M. Meiss, *French Painting in the Time of Jean de Berry. The Late Fourteenth Century and the Patronage of the Duke* (London, 1967), 62, and illus. 433; T. Müller, *Sculpture in the Netherlands, Germany, France and Spain, 1400–1500,* Pelican History of Art (1966), pl. 25B.

[32] On what follows, see E. Meyer, "Reliquie und Reliquiar im Mittelalter," in *Festschrift C.G. Heise* (Berlin, 1950), 55ff. Cf. also Belting.

[33] Cf. note 6.

[34] Young, *Drama*, 122ff. and 128. Even before the *elevatio* of the Easter rituals, the Host was on occasion raised during the procession to the grave (*idem*, 128).

[35] Browe, *Verehrung* (note 6 above), 141ff., on the exposure of the Holy Sacrament within and then chiefly outside the mass, accompanied by devotions from the fourteenth century onward.

[36] Browe, *op. cit.*, 71ff., on the feast of Corpus Christi, and 89ff., on processions with the Holy Sacrament.

[37] See Gauthier de Cornut, archbishop of Sens, *Acta translationis* (Comte de Riant, *Exuviae sacrae Constantinopolitanae* [Geneva, 1877], 55) on the "great display stand" (*eminens pulpitum*) that was built before the walls of Paris so that the *loculus* with the newly arrived relics could be displayed from its platform. On the custom of such exhibitions in general, see G.F. Koch, *Die Kunstausstellung. Ihre Geschichte von den Anfängen bis zum Ausgang des 18. Jahrhunderts* (Berlin, 1967), 30ff.; and Belting.

[38] See Chapter III, note 55.

[39] Koch, *op. cit.*, 143.

[40] J. Braun, *Die Reliquiare des christlichen Kults und ihre Entwicklung* (Freiburg i. Br., 1940), 301ff. and 380ff., as well as Meyer, *op. cit.* (note 32 above), 58ff. Cf. also Belting, and M.M. Gauthier in her contribution to vol. II of the *Atti del XXIV. Congr. Internaz. Storia dell'Arte in Bologna, 1978* (Milan, 1980).

[41] Braun, *op. cit.*, 55ff. (on the designation of relic ostensories as *monstrantia* since the fourteenth century), 301ff. and 377ff.; as well as Meyer, *op. cit.* (note 32 above), 61 ff., and Belting.

[42] Braun, *op. cit.*, illus. 237 and 238, as well as the exhibition catalog, *"Rhein und Maas." Kunst und Kultur 800–1400* (Cologne, 1972), no. G5.

[43] Braun, *op. cit.*, illus. 104 and 224. In all probability, the statuette reliquary (e.g.,

242

Stephen displaying his own relic) preceded the type with exhibitory angels. Cf. Belting.

[44] W. Wolters, *La scultura veneziana gotica (1300–1460)* (Venice, 1976), 157, no. 20, and illus. 57.

[45] There is a long history of research dealing with the interpretation of the Pietà. It begins with W. Pinder, "Die dichterische Wurzel der Pietà," *Repertorium für Kunstwiss.*, 42 (1920), 146–63. Cf. the survey of the discussion by W. Krönig, "Rheinische Vesperbilder aus Leder und ihr Umkreis," *Wallraf-Richartz-Jahrb.*, 24 (1962), 98ff.; and J.H. Emminghaus, "Vesperbild," in *Lexikon der christlichen Ikonographie*, 4 (1972), 450ff. Particular attention should be paid to the studies by E. Reiners-Ernst, *Das freudvolle Vesperbild und die Anfänge der Pietà-Vorstellung* (Munich, 1939); Berliner, 112ff.; T. Dobrzeniecki, "Medieval Sources of the Pietà," *Bull. Musée National de Varsovie*, 8 (1967), 5ff.; and Suckale, 194f. (Suckale emphasizes the presentational function as well as the mediating role of the figure of the Virgin, who invites the beholder to venerate Christ's wounds—thus Suckale's view is one that approaches ours.)

[46] H. Seuse (Suso), *Büchlein der ewigen Weisheit*, Deutsche Schriften, ed. K. Bihlmeyer (Stuttgart, 1907), 276: "Owe, reinu zartu frouwe, nu beger ich, daz du mir din zartes kind in der toetlichen angesiht bietest / uf die schoze miner sele, daz mir nach minem vermuggene geistlich und in betrahtunge werde, daz / dir do wart liplich."

[47] S. Waetzoldt, *Die Kopien des 17. Jahrhunderts nach Mosaiken und Wandmalereien in Rom* (1964), no. 583 and illus. 322: the fresco is located on the inner wall of the entrance to St. Paul Outside the Walls in Rome, and was dated by Waetzoldt to the pontificate of John XXII; and P. Hetherington, *Pietro Cavallini: A Study in the Art of Late Medieval Rome* (London, 1979), 97ff. and illus. 135.

[48] W. Körte, "Deutsche Vesperbilder in Italien," *Röm. Jahrb. für Kunstgeschichte*, 1 (1937), 1–138 (fundamental) and the complementary study by Wolters, *op. cit.* (note 44 above), 262 and illus. 732–38, as well as 263 and illus. 749. It is often a question of imports or works commissioned by Germans, at least in the beginning. In Padua, the order was for "unam ymaginem b. Virginis cum crucifisso in brachiis" (Wolters, 263). Cf. also Meiss, *op. cit.* (note 31 above), 182ff. with illus. 635, 638–42, 645, 647. In contrast, G. Swarzenski ("Italienische Quellen der deutschen Pietà," in *Festschrift H. Wölfflin* [Munich, 1924], 127ff.) had emphasized motifs from Italy as stimuli in the development of the Pietà.[49] In this Chapel of S. Felice of the Santo in Padua. Cf. Meiss, *op. cit.* (Chapter V, note 15), illus. 547; G.L. Mellini, *Altichiero e Jacopo Avanzi* (Milan, 1965), pls. 117–18; and H.W. Kruft, *Altichiero und Avanzo*, Dissertation, Bonn, 1966, 13ff. and 43ff.

[49] In this Chapel of S. Felice of the Santo in Padua. Cf. Meiss, *op. cit.* (Chapter V, note 15), illus. 547; G.L. Mellini, *Altichiero e Jacopo Avanzi* (Milan, 1965), pls. 117–18; and H.W. Kruft, *Altichiero und Avanzo*, Dissertation, Bonn, 1966, 13ff. and 43ff.

[50] In the Pinacoteca Nazionale in Bologna. The work is a polyptych, one part of which shows the Presentation in the Temple (inv. 159). It was painted ca. 1365, and perhaps came from S. Maria Nuova. See A. Emiliani, *La Pinacoteca Nazionale di Bologna* (Bologna, 1967), 141ff., no. 41; and F. Arcangeli, *Pittura bolognese del '300*, ed. C. Gnudi (Bologna, 1978), 128ff. and pl. XX.

[51] See the discussion, p. 115, with evidence of the use of the threnos in literature, religious drama, and the plastic and graphic arts.

[52] Cf. note 3, as well as A.M. Lépicier, *Mater Dolorosa* (Paris, 1948), and Meier, 145ff. Cf. also Chapter VI, Section "The Cross and the Descent from the Cross...."

[53] Young, *Drama*, I, 698: "Ita Planctus dicitur in cathedra predicatorii, et debet esse

coperta . . . de cortinis . . . ad finem quod . . . cantantes . . . . Planctum non possint videri a gentibus nec ipsi videant gentes, ut securius possint cantare sine timore, quia forte videndo gentes turbarentur."

[54] A detailed description is given in a fifteenth-century Regensburg codex (Young, *Drama*, I, 504ff.): "veniant duo scolares, indutis vestibus lamentabilibus, sub typus b. Virginis et s. Johannis, et plangant ante Crucifixum alternatim planctum: Planctus ante nescia [cf. note 22 above] et alium: Hew, hew! Virgineus flos" [after which the solemn adoration of the Cross and the burial of the crucifix took place].

[55] Young, *Drama*, I, 507ff. The stage directions read, for example: "hic percutiat manus, hic ostendat Christum apertis manibus [for Mary], Hic demonstret populum proiiciendo se, Hic vertat se ad Mariam, suas lacrimas ostendendo [for John], Hic amplectet unam Mariam ad collum, Hic ostendat latus Christi [i.e., the wounds in His side], Hic ostendat angelum [of the Annunciation, which is also identified with the prophecy of Simeon about the pain Mary would suffer], Hic amplectet Johannem [for Mary], Hic se flexis genibus ante crucem [for Mary Magdalene], Hic volvet ad aliam partem amplectendo Magdalenam [for Mary], Hic terget sibi lacrimas, Hic se percutiat ad pectus [for Magdalene], Hic se vertat ad homines manibus apertis, Hic ostendat Christum, Hic ad oculos suos ponat manus, Hic ostendat crucem,... Coronam spineam,... latus [for Mary]." Cf. also Chapter VI, Section "The Cross and the Descent from the Cross...."

[56] Young, *loc. cit.*, lines 90 and 93.

[57] L. Razzolini, ed., *Scelta di curiosità letterarie inedite o rare dal sec. XIII al XVII: Dispensa CLXII: La passione del NS Gesù Cristo, poema attributo a G. Bocaccio* (Bologna, 1878), 11ff. (on the attribution to Niccolò Cicerchia of Siena, see N. Sapegno, *Storia letteraria d'Italia: Il Trecento*, 2nd ed., I [Milan, 1942], 542), esp. 68. no. CXCV: "O tutti voi che passate per via / Attendete e videte, se dolore / Simil si trova a la gran doglia mia. / Pietà vi prenda del mio dolce amore [Christ] / per consolare me triste Maria...."

[58] Cf. note 55.

[59] List of Art Works, no. 13.

[60] Von Simson, 131.

Chapter V
The Icon of the Passion in Byzantium

[1] See the Bibliography, p. 267.

[2] Recently, the historical priority of the East has been denied, chiefly by Stubblebine, *op. cit.* (Chapter II, note 26), 3ff. But it had always at least been called into question, at least for certain pictorial variants (e.g., the folded arms).

[3] List of Art Works, no. 19.

[4] Pallas, 76ff. (on the use of the Cross in Passion rites first in the narthex), 87ff. (on the image of the Crucifixion as a Good Friday feast icon). In Hagia Sophia in the tenth century, according to a typikon, the relic of the holy lance that pierced Christ's side was venerated on Holy Thursday and Good Friday (J. Mateos, *Le Typicon de la Grande Eglise*, II [Rome, 1963], 72ff. and 78ff.).

[5] Pallas, 67.

[6] K. Weitzmann, "The Painted Crosses at Sinai," in *Kunsthistorische Forschungen O.*

Pächt, zu seinem 70. Geburtstag (Salzburg, 1972), 23ff.

[7] Constantine VII Porphyrogenitus, *De cerimoniis aulae byzantinae* I.1.1 (ed. J. Reiske, I [Bonn, 1829], 15f.). See Pallas, 69f. and 74f., where further evidence is given for the placing of the second cross at the entrance to the *skeuophylakion.*

[8] Pallas, 88; Pallas cites Leo the Deacon, *Historia* X.4f.

[9] R. Cormack, "Painting after Iconoclasm," in *Iconoclasm*, ed. A. Bryer and J. Herrin (Birmingham, 1977), 151ff. For the homily of George of Nikomedia (one of the partisans of Photios and bishop before 867 and after 877), see *PG* 101, no. VIII, cols. 1457ff., esp. 1488 and 1489.

[10] See the Georgian *vita* of Saints John and Euthymios composed by George the Presbyter (Latin trans. by P. Peeters, in *Analecta Bollandiana*, 36/37 [1917–19], 13ff. and esp. 26). On the Deposition, see also Pallas, 105ff.

[11] In the church of Lagurka in Kala, Georgia (48.5 x 49 cm); G.V. Alibegashvili, in *Srednevekovoe Iskusstvo Rus i Grusija* (Moscow, 1978), 158ff. and esp. 160ff.

[12] V. Lasareff, "Duccio and Thirteenth-Century Greek Icons," *Burlington Magazine*, 59 (1931), 154ff. and pl. III.

[13] A. Goldschmidt and K. Weitzmann, *Die byzantinischen Elfenbeinskulpturen des X.–XIII. Jahrhunderts*, II (Berlin, 1934), no. 40, and cf. also nos. 23 and 71.

[14] E.g., Oxford, Magdalen College, Cod. 3, fol. 104v; T. Velmans, "Le dessin à Byzance," *Fondation E. Piot, Monuments et Mémoires*, 59 (1974), 137ff., esp. 164 and illus. 25.

[15] K. Weitzmann, "The Origin of the Threnos," in *De artibus opuscula XL. Essays in Honor of E. Panofsky*, ed. M. Meiss (New York, 1961), 476ff. Important examples of the Threnos, aside from those Weitzmann discusses and the frequently reproduced fresco in the church of St. Pantelemon in Nerezi (1164) (on the latter, see Hamann and Hallensleben, 17f. and illus. 39) are: a miniature in the lectionary Vat. Gr. 1156, fol. 194v; a fresco in Kastoria, Hagioi Anargyroi (end of the twelfth century); a fresco in Koutsovendis, Cyprus (mid-twelfth century) (cf. A. Papageorgiou, *Masterpieces of the Byzantine Art of Cyprus* [Nikosia, 1965], pl. XV.1). Cf. also the examples cited by Maguire (note 16 below) as well as by G. Millet, *Recherches sur l'iconographie de l'évangile. . .* (Paris, 1916), 489–513 (Le Thrène).

[16] H. Maguire, "The Depiction of Sorrow in Middle Byzantine Art," *Dumbarton Oaks Papers*, 31 (1977), 125ff. and esp. 161ff.

[17] Cf. p. 100.

[18] Cf. p. 101.

[19] Robert de Clari, *La conquête de Constantinople*, ed. Ph. Lauer (Paris, 1924), 90. The chronicler speaks of the "tavle de marbre ou Nostre Sires fu estendus quant il fut despendus de le crois, et si i paroient encore les lermes que Notre Dame avoit plouré deseure." Cf. also C. Mango, in *Dumbarton Oaks Papers*, 23/24 (1969–1970), 373ff. On Christ's lying in state on a stone, cf. also the poem of Manuel Philes, *Carmina*, ed. E. Miller, I (Paris, 1855), 8, no. 17.

[20] This name begins to play a role only from around 1300. Cf. also the poem of Manuel Philes "on the epitaphios of Tetragonites," *op. cit.*, no. 69. The equation of the *aer* and the *epitaphios*, which makes explicit the Passion symbolism of the *aer* or *katapetasma* in the image, is first a matter of course for Symeon of Thessaloniki, i.e., around 1400 (cf. *De sacra ordine, PG* 155, col. 385, where the same image-bearing cloth is called a

"lamb" [*amnos*], and *De sacra liturgia, PG* 155, col. 288, as well as *De Divino Templo, PG* 155, col. 729, where the form of the cloth embroidered with the image of the dead Christ and the fact that it was carried in the Great Entrance of the bread and wine in the context of the eucharistic mass are mentioned, to wit, that deacons held the cloth above their heads). For literature on the *aer-epitaphios*, see G. Millet, in *Comptes rendus de l'Académie des Inscriptions* (1942), 408ff., as well as Millet, *Broderies*, 72ff., 86ff.; P. Johnstone, *The Byzantine Tradition in Church Embroidery* (London, 1967), passim; and Taft, 216ff.

[21] On the history of the Byzantine liturgy, see the good introduction by H.-J. Schulz, *Die byzantinische Liturgie. Vom Werden ihrer Symbolgestalt* (Freiburg, 1964). On the liturgy of the Passion, see J.B. Thibaut, *Ordre des Offices de la Semaine Sainte à Jerusalem du IVe au Xe siècle* (Paris, 1926); A. Schmeman, *Great Lent* (New York, 1969); and G. Bertonière, *The Historical Development of the Easter Vigil ...*, Orientalia Christiana Analecta 193 (Rome, 1972). On the Lamentation of Mary, see M. Alexiou, *The Ritual Lament in Greek Tradition* (Cambridge, England, 1974), 62ff., and her article in *Byzantine and Modern Greek Studies*, 1 (1975), 111–40.

[22] Mateos, *op. cit.* (note 4 above), passim (for the liturgy of the Passion, see vol. II, 72–82). Cf. also Pallas, 22ff.

[23] Pallas, 29ff. and 34ff. (transitional phase of the Constantinopolitan liturgy). Cf. also Thibaut, *op. cit.* (note 21 above) on the Palestinian tradition.

[24] The history of the institution of family-owned monasteries has not yet been written. But cf. the following works on monasticism in the tenth through twelfth centuries (for these references I am indebted to Prof. A.P. Kazhdan): N. Skabalanovic, *Vizantijskoe Gosudarstvo i Cerkov* (St. Petersburg, 1884), esp. 425ff. and 433 for relevant passages on personal monasteries, namely those of Basil II and Psellos; H. Delehaye, *Deux typica byzantins de l'époque des Paléologues* (Brussels, 1921), giving the first list of those typika which, in addition to being liturgical rules, were also wills and property regulations of the founders (*ktetores*); R. Janin, "Le monachisme byzantin au moyen âge," *Revue des Etudes Byzantines*, 22 (1964), 29ff. (specifically on the typika); and A.P. Kazhdan, "Vizantijskij monastyr' XI–XII vv. kak socialnaja gruppa," *Vizantijskij Vremennik*, 31 (1971), 48ff. (see 51f. for a survey of the typika and the number of monks in monasteries). The 1059 testament of Eustathios Boilas (P. Lemerle, ed., *Cinq études sur le XIe siècle byzantin* [Paris, 1977], 24) bequeaths the movable and immovable property of the church of Boilas's personal monastery, and the same holds true for a division of property among three brothers dating from 1110 (*Actes de Lavra I*, ed. P. Lemerle et al. [Paris, 1970], 305ff.). On typika in general, see the edition prepared by Dmitrievskij (note 25 below).

[25] A. Dmitrievskij, *Opisanie liturgicheskich rukopisej*, I (Kiev, 1895), 550ff., and Pallas, 30ff.

[26] M. Arranz, *Le Typicon du Monastère du St. Sauveur à Messine. Cod. Messinesis Gr. 115 A.D. 1131*, Orientalia Christiana Analecta 185 (Rome, 1969), 236ff. and esp. 239 (the homily is referred to here as: "*Logos . . . eis ton stauron*" and the Holy Theotokos), as well as Dmitrievskij, *op. cit.*, 550. On this sermon, see note 9 above.

[27] Ed. J. Grosdidier de Matons, *Romanos le Melode, Hymnes*, IV (Paris, 1967), 160; as well as P. Maas and C.A. Trypanis, *Romanos Melodos, Cantica* (Oxford, 1963), 142ff. Cf. E. Follieri, *Initia hymnorum ecclesiae graecae*, Studi e Testi 211ff., IV (Vatican City, 1963), 195.

[28] Dmitrievskij, *op. cit.* 553f. (on the other hand, cf. Arranz, *op. cit.*, 343, where the hymn "Noble Joseph" is also mentioned). Cf. Pallas, 32, and Alexiou (note 21 above).

[29] W. Christ and M. Paranikas, *Anthologia graeca carminum Christianorum* (Leipzig, 1871), 88, and Follieri, *op. cit.* (note 27 above), III (1962), 31.

[30] *Roma e l'Oriente*, 5 (1913), 302ff. and esp. 307f. Cf. also *Epeteris Hetaireias Byzantinon Spoudon*, 8 (1931), 63v*; Pallas, 33f.; and Follieri, *op. cit.*, II (1961), 116.

[31] Pallas, 38ff.; Taft, 245ff.; and Alexiou (note 21 above).

[32] Dmitrievskij, *op. cit.*, 554.

[33] Cf. note 35, and Pallas, 42f. and 50f.

[34] Cf. the homily on the Interment of the Lord: *PG* 98, 244ff. (the pertinent passage is at the beginning).

[35] A.-M. Maffry Talbot, ed., *The Correspondence of Athanasius I, Patriarch of Constantinople*, Dumbarton Oaks Texts III (Washington, D.C., 1975), no. 52, p. 116f. Cf. the interpretation in Pallas, 38 and 230, with which I do not agree.

[36] Talbot, *op. cit.*, no. 71, p. 178f.

[37] Pallas, 42f. and 231. Cf. also the encomia to the epitaphios published by E.G. Pantelakis, *Theologia*, 14 (1936), 225ff. and 310ff.; the third encomium mentions in strophe 6 (p. 311) the image of Christ, who, alive in death, is stretched out upon the tomb and receives a dirge (*epitaphios ode*): "ἐν εἰκόνι, Σωτῆρ, σὲ τὸν ζῶντα νεκρὸν / ὡζὲν τάφῳ νῦν ὁρῶντες προκείμενον."

[38] Pallas, 226ff. and esp. 231f. Cf. also Dobrzeniecki, 210ff.

[39] See Canon 82 of the Quinisextum (J.D. Mansi, *Sacrorum conciliorum nova et amplissima collectio* [Florence, 1765; 2nd ed., Paris, 1901], XI, 977ff. See also J.D. Breckenridge, *The Numismatic Iconography of Justinian II* (New York, 1959), 83f.

[40] Pallas, 226ff. There is an extensive bibliography on the phrase *Basileus tes doxes*. See Taft, 84f., on the discussion about this notion in the sixth century, as it related to the entrance into the church of the unconsecrated offerings. The notion is found in a hymn utilizing the Twenty-third Psalm that replaces, in the presanctified liturgy on Good Friday, the Cherubicon during the Great Entrance: "Now the powers of heaven worship with us unseen, for behold the King of Glory enters, behold the mystical sacrifice, already accomplished, comes escorted" (Taft, 53ff.; and F. Brightman, *Liturgies Eastern and Western* [Oxford, 1896], 348). Cf. also the hymn sung on Good Friday: "Let all mortal flesh be silent . . . for the King of Kings . . . comes forth to be slain and given as food to the faithful" (Brightman, *op. cit.*, 41f.). The contrast is always emphasized between the earthly evidence of the Passion and the heavenly might of God, as in connection with the Descent into Hell and the redemptive power of the human death of God. It is in this context that the notion receives a sharpening of its semantic focus.

[41] Symeon Metaphrastes, "Λόγος εἰς τὸν θρῆνον τῆς ὑπεραγίας θεοτόκου" (Sermon on the threnos of the Holy Theotokos as she embraced the venerable body of Christ our Lord). See *PG* 114, 209–217, esp. 212f. and 217. In some MSS this homily is attributed to Nikephoros Bailakes; see A. Pignani, in *Boll. Commiss. per la prepar. dell'edizione nazionale dei classici greci a latini*, Acad. Lincei, 19 (1971), 131–46 (this reference was kindly provided by H. Maguire). On the homily's relation to the Threnos scene, see Maguire, *op. cit.* (note 16 above), 161ff.

[42] *PG* 140, 644f. (citing Song of Solomon 3:7, he calls the Cross, "on which [Christ] slept the life-bringing sleep and bent His head of His own free will," the bed of

Solomon). Cf. also the Holy Saturday homily of the same Germanos (*PG* 89, 269) on the metaphor of the *anapeson*: the resting lion that sleeps with open eyes (cf. note 44 below).

[43] Depositum of Queen Beloslava (G. Cremosnik, "Kancelariski i Notariski Spisi 1278–1301," *Monumenta Historica Archivi Ragusini*, Srpska kraljevska akademija, ser. 3, 1 [Beograd, 1932], 53). Cf. S. Radojcic, in *Jahrbuch der österreichischen byzantinischen Gesellschaft*, 5 (1956), 69, and Djordjevic (note 58 above), 83 (for evidence of the reproduction of our icon in an early thirteenth-century church in Tirnovo, in the calendar image of Chrysostom).

[44] Pallas, 181ff. and 194f., where reference is made to the liturgical use of Genesis 49:1ff. (*anapeson leon*) and to the use of the image (e.g., in *Cod. Stauronikita* 45). Cf. also Hamann–MacLean, *Grundlegung* (note 58 below), 58ff.

[45] Cf. the writings of M. Alexiou, *op. cit.* (note 21 above).

[46] R. de Clari, *op. cit.* (note 19 above), 90.

[47] A. Heisenberg, *Die Palastrevolution des Johannes Komnenos* (1907), 30. Cf. C. de Riant, *Exuviae sacrae constantinopolitanae*, II (Geneva, 1878), 213f. and 216f., where further evidence is given for the *syndone* and the *sudarium*, or the *fasciae* or *linteamina*.

[48] P. Vignon, *Le Sainte Suaire de Turin* ..., 2nd ed. (Paris, 1939), 100ff. Cf. the recent attempt to reconstruct the period between 1204 and 1353 by J. Wilson, *The Turin Shroud* (London, 1978) and, especially, Averil Cameron, *The Sceptic and the Shroud* (London, 1980).

[49] List of Art Works, no. 31.

[50] H. Wentzel, in *Aachener Kunstblätter*, 44 (1973), no. 24, illus. 16b. On the type of the reliquary and an attempt at a derivation of the figure of the saint, see A. Grabar, in *Dumbarton Oaks Papers*, 5 (1950), 1ff., 6, and 12ff.; and D. Pallas, "Le ciborium hexagonal de H. Demetrios de Thessalonique," *Zograph*, 10 (1979), 44.

[51] List of Art Works, no. 25.

[52] Leningrad, Public Library, Cod. Gr. 105, fol. 65v and 167v; H.R. Willoughby, *The Four Gospels of Karahissar* (Chicago, 1936), pl. 34 and 106; Pallas, 208; on the twelfth-century date, see A. Cutler and A. Weyl Carr, "The Psalter Benaki 34.3 . . . . ," *Revue des Etudes Byzantines*, 34 (1976), 281ff. and esp. 304ff.

[53] List of Art Works, no. 27. Cf. also a later Cypriot icon with this formulation in Ktima, Paphos, reproduced in C. Walter, *Icons* (Paris, 1976), 39, no. 29.

[54] Cf. note 14.

[55] List of Art Works, no. 22. For the inscriptions, see Xyngopoulos, *op. cit.* (Chapter II, note 16), 42. See also Pallas, 197ff.

[56] On the two icons, see List of Art Works, nos. 31 and 32. For one example of the parchment copies, see Ringbom, illus. 16–17.

[57] C. Amiranachvili, *Les émaux de Géorgie* (Paris, 1962), 55; Kermer, no. 6, illus. 10, 11.

[58] R. Hamann-MacLean, *Grundlegung zu einer Geschichte der mittelalterlichen Monumentalmalerei in Serbien und Makedonien* (Giessen, 1976), 63 and pl. 6a; W.F. Volbach and J. Lafontaine-Dosogne, *Byzanz und der christliche Osten*, Propyl. Kunstgesch. 3 (Berlin, 1968), illus. 248; G. Subotic, *Crkva Sv. Dimitrija u Peckoj Patrijarsiji* (Belgrade, 1964), 46f.; and I.M. Djordjevic, in *Sbornik za likovne umetnosti*, 14 (1978), 83.

[59] Cf. icons depicting the burial of Ephraim the Syrian and the remarks of Symeon

of Thessaloniki (*PG* 155, 676); Pallas, 202.

[60] P. de Lagarde, ed., "Johannis Euchaitarum metropolitae quae in codice Vaticano graeco 676 supersunt," *Abhandlungen der hist.-philol. Klasse der königl. Gesellschaft der Wissenschaften in Göttingen*, 28 (1881), 10, no. 20: "Σὶς τὴν θεοτόκον δακρύουσαν. Ὦ τοῦ πάθους δέσποινα, καὶ σὺ δακρύεις."

[61] List of Art Works, no. 24.

[62] Pallas, 167ff. On the Eleousa, cf. also v. Lasareff in *Art Bulletin*, 20 (1938), 36ff.; K. Kolb, *Eleusa. 2000 Jahre Maddonenbild* (1968); v. Lazareff, *Vizantijskaja Zivopis* (Moscow, 1971), 275ff.; and H. Hallensleben, in *Lexikon christl. Ikonographie*, III (1971), 170ff.

[63] K. Onasch, *Icons* (London, 1963), pls. 1, 2, and 102 (a reverse that was painted over later), as well as p. 341f., 387; and V. Lazarev, *Storia della pittura bizantina* (Turin, 1967), illus. 326.

[64] Pallas, 168f. On the homily, which H. Maguire also related to the Threnos scene (cf. note 16 above), see note 41.

[65] Pallas, 170ff.

[66] Maguire, *op. cit.* (note 16 above), 126.

[67] Pallas, 91ff. and, on the activity of Symeon Metaphrastes in the Hodegon monastery, 94f. On the history of the monastery and the icon, see R. Janin, *Les églises et les monastères*, vol. III of *La Géographie ecclésiastique de l'empire byzantin* (Paris, 1953), 212ff.; as well as Hallensleben, *op. cit.* (note 62 above), 168ff.; and R.L. Wolff, in *Traditio*, 6 (1948), 319ff.

[68] Sotiriou, pl. 234, and Kermer, no. 12, illus. 18. Cf. H. Belting, "Manouel Eugenikos: un peintre de Constantinople en Géorgie," *Cahiers Archéologiques*, 28 (1979), 103ff.

[69] Messina, Bibl. Univ. F.S. Salvatore 51, fol. 9v; see G. Musolino, *Calabria bizantina* (Venice, 1967), illus. 82 (showing John Chrysostom as the celebrant). Cf. Octoechos, *Tomus* 2 (London, 1898), 21; C. Diehl, in *Mélanges d'histoire et d'archéologie*, 8 (1888), 312ff.; and R. Mancini, *Codices graeci monast. Messinensis S. Salvatoris* (Messina, 1907), 99f.

[70] Cf. note 67.

[71] Pallas, 173ff. Hamann–MacLean, *Grundlegung* (note 58 above), 60ff. and pl. 5b. Reproduction of the inscriptions and analysis in G. Soteriou, *Archaiologike Ephemeris* (1953–1954), 87ff., esp. 88, and the plate. On the frescoes generally, A. Stylianou, in *Actes (Pepragmena) du IXe Congrès international des études byzantines*, Thessaloniki, 1953 (Athens, 1955), I, 459ff.; and A.H.S. Megaw and A. Stylianou, *Cyprus. Byzantine Mosaics and Frescoes* (New York, 1963), 16, pl. 18. On the subsequent history of the Madonna of the Passion as an icon, see M.G. Sotiriou, "Παναγία τοῦ Πάθους," in the 1400th anniversary volume on the foundation of the Sinai Monastery (Athens, 1969), 27ff.

[72] Janin, *op. cit.* (note 67 above), 196ff.; and Pallas, 178.

[73] *PG* 18, 364. Cf. Pallas, 176f.

[74] Cf. note 44.

[75] Onasch, *op. cit.* (note 63 above), 374f. and pls. 10–11. V.N. Lazarev, *Novgorodian Icon Painting* (Moscow, 1969), pls. 8, 9 (77 x 71 cm; dated 1130–1200).

[76] A. Grabar, *La Sainte Face de Laon* (Prague, 1931), passim. K. Weitzmann, "The Mandylion and Constantine Porphyrogennetos," *Cahiers Archéologiques*, 11 (1960), 166ff.; and Pallas, 134ff.

[77] See Pallas, 137f., for documentary evidence, especially regarding the role of Leo of Chalcedon.

[78] I.N. Sola, "De codice Laur. X Plut. V," *Byzantinische Zeitschrift*, 20 (1911), 376. Cf. Pallas, 233f.

[79] List of Art Works, no. 17.

[80] H.R. Hahnloser, ed., *Il Tesoro e il Museo*, vol. II of *Il Tesoro di S. Marco* (Florence, 1971), 22f., no. 15, pls. XIII–XIV. Cf. also R. Gallo, *Il tesoro di S. Marco e la sua storia* (1967), 133–55.

[81] M.V. Sedova, in *Sovetskaja Archeologia*, 3 (1965), 264, illus. I.3; and A. Bank, in *L'Art Byzantin du XIIIe siècle. Symposium de Sopočani* (Filozofski Fakultet: Belgrade, 1967), 93, illus. 5.

[82] To my knowledge, no photograph of the icon has yet been published (Inv. 458; ex. Inv. 987–88: Michigan-Princeton negative no. 2511; size: 13 x 8.5 cm; canvas with green priming, on the right there is a red spot).

[83] List of Art Works, no. 32.

[84] List of Art Works, no. 31.

[85] List of Art Works, no. 15. Cf. especially the program-schema in Hamann–MacLean, *Grundlegung* (note 58 above), illus. on p. 340.

[86] Millet, *op. cit.* (note 15 above), 483ff., and S. Dufrenne, "Images du décor de la Prothèse," *Revue des Etudes Byzantines*, 26 (1968), 297ff. See also the polemic in Pallas, 236ff. Both sides seem not to have noticed that they have forgotten the historical development in which the image was first used in the Passion liturgy and then in the eucharistic liturgy.

An important example is the Georgian church of Savane near Sacheri (first half of the thirteenth century), in which the Passion icon (instead of the Melismos) appears under the central window of the main apse; see Pallas, 207. In the church of the Peribleptos at Mistra (second half of the fourteenth century) and in the church of the Assumption in Volotovo near Novgorod (1363), it appears in the apse of the prothesis; see Dufrenne, *op. cit.*, passim, and Pallas, 211, 213, and 215f.

[87] Taft, 418ff. and 216f., for a detailed and fundamental treatment from the point of view of liturgical history.

[88] Taft, passim, esp. 3ff., 53ff. (*cherubikon hymnos*), 178ff. (procession of the offerings as a true "Great Entrance"), 217ff. (funerary symbolism of the Great Entrance).

[89] On the enamel, see G. Schlumberger, in *Monuments et mémoires de la Fondation E. Piot*, 1 (1894), 99ff.; A. Bank, *Byzantine Art in the Collections of the USSR* (Moscow, 1966), 364f. and pls. 186–89 (dated to the eleventh to twelfth centuries). I am obliged to Dr. L. Bouras for the reading of the inscription.

On the fresco, see H. Grigoriadou-Cabagnols, "Le décor peint de l'église de Samari en Méssenie," *Cahiers Archéologiques*, 20 (1970), 177ff., esp. 182, 184f., and illus. 4, 5.

[90] G. Millet, "La vision de Pierre d'Alexandre," in *Mélanges Ch. Diehl*, II (Paris, 1930), 107ff. (here the image is based on a prior literary model). G. Babic, "Les discussions christologiques et le décor des églises byzantines au XIIe s.," *Frühmittelalterliche Studien*, 2 (1968), 368ff. Hamann–MacLean, *Grundlegung* (note 58 above), 147ff. and 279f., giving a comparison of Nerezi (1164), where the Etoimasia still appears, and Kurbinovo (1192), where we already find the Melismos. G. Babic's suggestion that the controversies about the Eucharist that took place in the local synods from 1156 to 1157

might provide an explanation of the Melismos, does not seem to have met with much acceptance. Perhaps the image originally referred to the epiklesis or transubstantiation, as the location of this scene is the main altar (see the example in the north chapel of Studenica; G. Babic, *Les chapelles annexes des églises byzantines* [Paris, 1969], illus. 112). In the fourteenth century, for example, in an image in the prothesis of the church of Sv. Nikola near Ljuboten (1337), the two celebrants cut the child in the chalice into pieces, and the location of the image in the prothesis chamber indicates the shift of emphasis to the liturgy of the prothesis.

[91] Hamann–MacLean, *Grundlegung* (note 58 above), pl. 18. Cf. a similar example in the narthex of Decani (ca. 1340); V.R. Petkovíc and D. Boskovic, *Decani* (Belgrade, 1941), pl. 95.1.

[92] Millet, *Broderies*, 89 and pl. CLXXVIII; Johnstone, *op. cit.* (note 20), illus. 93. The inscription reads: "Μέμνησο ποιμὴν Βουλγάρων ἐν θυσίαις ἄνακτος ᾿Ανδρονίκου Παλαιολόγου."

The inscription alludes to the fact that "le titulaire grec d'Ochrida se nommait archevêque des Bulgares" (Millet, 90). It must refer to Gregorios I, friend of Andronikos II and archbishop of Ohrid from 1313 to 1328. On this topic, see I. Shevchenko and J. Featherstone, "Two Poems by Theodore Metochites," *Greek Orthodox Theological Review*, 26 (1981), 1–46. I thank I. Sevcenko for this information.

[93] In the Muzej Srpske pravoslavne crkve in Belgrade. Cloth from Fruska Gora. Cf. Millet, *Broderies*, 87, and Pallas, 251ff.

[94] Cf. notes 46–48. The cloth was not used in the Great Entrance in Hagia Sophia, as Pallas believes (p. 254). The "radiant Jerusalem" mentioned by Anton of Novgorod around 1200 (ed. C. Loparev, in *Pravoslavn. Palestinskij Sbornik*, 5 [1899], 12f.) was a metal pyx (reference kindly provided by F. Kämpfer).

[95] Pallas, 251ff.

[96] Cf. notes 46 and 90.

[97] Millet, *Broderies*, 87ff., passim, for a wealth of examples (e.g., the epitaphios of Bachkovo: Matthew and Anna; the one in London, Nicholas Eudaimonoiannes; and those already mentioned). The liturgical inscriptions referring to the Eucharist corroborate this evidence.

[98] Taft, 227ff.

[99] Millet, *Broderies*, 89ff. and pl. CLXXX. Johnstone, *op. cit.* (note 20 above), illus. 98. *Il tesoro di S. Marco* (note 80 above), no. 116 (with a too-early date) and pl. LXXXIV.

Chapter VI
The Icon in the West
Its Reception during the Thirteeenth Century in Italy

[1] See Chapter I, note 50.

[2] See Chapter I, note 42.

[3] List of Art Works, no. 7. Cambridge, Corpus Christi College, MS 26 (vol. I of the *Historia Maior* of Matthew Paris of St. Albans), fol. VII. On the drawing at the end of the text, see M.R. James, *The Drawings of Matthew Paris*, The Walpole Society, vol. 14 (Oxford, 1926), no. 25, pl. IV. In vol. II of the *Historia Maior*, which carries the history of the world up to 1233 (*ibid.*, MS 16, fol. 49v; James, *ibid.*, pl. XXIX and nos. 140 and 141) the

head of the living Jesus (Pantokrator) recurs as a "veronica." It is reported (fol. 221v) how the pictorial relic performed a miracle during Innocent III's procession in 1216; the indulgence prayer composed at that time is then given. See also Dobschütz, 294* and 297*; and Gould, *op. cit.* (Chapter III, note 54), 81ff. On Matthew Paris, see R. Yaughan, *Matthew Paris* (Cambridge, England, 1958), passim.

4 See note 3.

5 See note 3 and Chapter III, note 55.

6 See Belting. Cf. also Chapter I, note 17.

7 See Belting. For the literature on this topic, see Chapter III, note 55.

8 Garrison, no. 243; see Hager, 86f. and 132, and illus. 108.

9 See Chapter I, note 56. See especially, G.M. Monti, *La confraternità medievali dell'alta e media Italia* (Venice, 1927), I, 149ff., 230ff. and 254ff., on the brotherhoods and Disciplinati in Florence and Siena, as well as Meersseman, 453ff. (on the Disciplinati in the dugento) and 922ff. (on the Marian brotherhoods).

10 See Chapter I, note 13. The image cult of the Confraternità of the Madonna of Or San Michele in Florence (see Chapter I, note 44) and that of the Disciplinati del Salvatore in Rome (the Achiropite of Sancta Sanctorum) are two well-known, though dissimilar examples. See also Chapter IV, note 20.

11 Bartholomaeis, 227ff. on the Disciplinati (especially those of the "Crocefisso" and the "Madonna della Misericordia") in Gubbio. The latter were said to gather in church on Good Friday and "to present in front of the people the tearful lauds and lamentations of Mary [*lacrimosas laudes et cantus dolorosas*] with respect, and in doing so to pay more attention to tears than to the words [*representent magis ad lacrimas attendentes quam ad verba*]." This example is one of many stagings either of the dialogue between the crucified Christ and Mary, or of a dialogue of both with the cult community. See also Chapter VI, Section "The Cross and the Descent from the Cross...."

12 See Chapter III, note 45.

13 Garrison, no. 611.

14 See Garrison, 174ff. and nos. 447–605; E. Sandberg-Vavalà, *La croce dipinta italiena e l'iconografia della passione* (Verona, 1929); and Hager, 75ff. On the sequel in the trecento, see M. Lisner, *Holzkruzifixe in Florenz und Toskana* (Munich, 1970), 9ff.

15 Garrison, no. 476, signed by Berlinghiero.

16 Garrison, no. 501.

17 See note 10.

18 See Chapter III, note 48.

19 See, for example, Pallucchini, illus. 271 and 679.

20 Garrison, nos. 320 and 303. Cf. also Antonio Veneziano's obituary panel in Palermo, which was donated in 1388, certainly by the Compagnia di S. Niccolo Reale; for a recent source, see G. Bresc-Bautier, *Artistes, Patriciens et Confréries*, Ecole Française de Rome, vol. 40 (1979), 75f. and illus. 2 and 3.

21 See Bartholomaeis, 328; and Corbin, 213f. There are early forms of the laud in *volgare*, the popular language, in which the theme appears. They still resemble the *planctus* songs. Edition of the laud referred to: F. Liuzzi, *La lauda e i primordi della melo-*

dia italiana (Rome, 1935), II, 79.

[22] The most recent edition, with a bibliography, is in E. Faccioli, *Il teatro italiano I.1: Dalle origini al Quattrocento* (Turin, 1975), 121ff. See also d'Ancona, 156ff.; E. Auerbach, *Mimesis* (Bern, 1946), 165ff.; F. Mancini, *Jacopone da Todi, Laude* (Bari, 1974); and A. Monteverdi, "Jacopone poeta," in *Jacopone e il suo tempo* (Todi, 1959), 37ff. The Franciscan Jacopone (ca. 1236–1306) belonged to the party of the spirituals in his order. On the laud, see Chapter VI, Section "The Cross and the Descent from the Cross...."

[23] Young, *Drama*, I, 500–502 (on these Lamentations of Mary, see, among others, Meier, 153ff. and 173ff.). Cf. also the hymn *Planctus ante nescia* (Young, *Drama*, I, 496–98).

[24] Bartholomaeis, 274f. The statutes of the Disciplinati of S. Stefano in Assisi are preserved in a version from 1327. In the *Inventario nuovo* (1339) of the Confraternità of S. Domenico in Perugia, a white and a black "mantello da devozione" for the singers and actors of the Passion laud are mentioned (d'Ancona, I, 164).

[25] On the *arma* cross in Constantinople, see Chapter V, notes 7 and 75; on the *arma* in general, Chapter III, notes 10, 32, and 52.

[26] Belting, passim.

[27] Chapter I, notes 13, 44, and 56. The inventory of the Società delle Laudi di Noxadella in Bologna (1329) mentions banners with pictures (e.g., a *pannus* showing the Virgin of Mercy), as well as painted panels (e.g., a "venerabilis tabula deaurata sive tabernaculum" with the image of Mary, and two crucifixes). On this inventory, see Chapter III, note 8.

[28] The panel comes from the Franciscan brotherhood of S. Nicolo close to S. Francesco in Palermo and was obviously commissioned in Genoa. The most recent study is by Bresc–Bautier (see note 20, above), 78 and illus. 1.

[29] The most recent study of this painter is J. White, *Duccio* (London, 1975), 32ff. and 185f., which reproduces the contract and gives an English translation of it. Cf. also p. 24 above.

[30] See Kermer, 121f. and illus. 165–66. The diptych, produced in memory of the first mass celebrated for the brotherhood in 1286 and inscribed with a membership list, contains the images of Christ's Scourging and Crucifixion on the left and images of Mary's death and Assumption into Heaven on the right. The protagonists are the same as on Italian counterparts, but the depictions are more scenically specific and placed next to each other.

[31] In the Galleria Nazionale of Palermo. The image is a necrology of the brotherhood of SS. Simon and Jude near the Martorana church and is dated 1396. The obituary panel is adorned with an image of the Imago Pietatis. Cf. Bresc-Bautier (see note 20, above), 76 and illus. 4, as well as Document VIII. See *idem*, 213f., for the contract for another *tabula mortuorum* which the brotherhood of S. Pietro Martire concluded with the painter Giovanni de Buychello in 1414. On a confraternità panel with images in the Bigallo, see H. Kiel, *Il Museo del Bigallo a Firenze* (1977), no. 5 and illus. 36–37.

[32] See note 27 and Chapter III, note 8.

[33] See Chapter I, note 41.

[34] List of Art Works, no. 12. See Vetter, 179 and 198, and illus. 97–98. On the codex, see A.M. Ciaranfi in *Riv. R. Istituto d'Archeol. e Storia dell'Arte*, 1 (1929), 325ff., and the contribution by A. Neff in Atti des XXIV Congr. Internaz. di Storia dell'Arte in (Bologna, 1979), who argues for a Venetian (indirectly Byzantine) influence on the drawings and miniatures, which, however, appear to me to have some relationship to the Bolognese school (which W. Grape, in *Pantheon*, 32 [1974], 10, accounts for by assuming intense contacts with Venice) and to the Emilian dugento frescoes in the cathedral of Modena and in the baptistery of Parma (images lying chronologically between the original painting of these interiors and the work of the "master of 1302"). On the dating to 1293, or 1293–1300, see Ciaranfi, ibid., 327. The relationship, in content and in spirit, to the milieu of the Poor Clares is evident. While the graphic style of the forty-four full-page drawings is strongly stamped by Byzantine models, the idea of the compendium consisting solely of pictures or of the wholly pictorial supplement (e.g., for psalters) originated in the Gothic North.

[35] See note 14.

[36] On the material in the Veneto, which is best exemplified by the painted crosses of Zadar/Zara (Garrison, nos. 453–55), see G. de Francovich in *Revue de l'Art*, 39 (1935), 185ff. The "miraculous crucified Christ" of San Marco (Garrison, no. 452), now restored to its original condition, has still not been sufficiently examined from the standpoint of art history. For the "prehistory" of the painted cross in Lombardy, the reader is referred to the crucifixes made by sculptors and goldsmiths from the tenth and eleventh centuries. See A. Peroni in *II. Kolloquium über spätantike und frühmittelalterliche Skulptur*, Heidelberg (Mainz, 1970), 75ff.

[37] In 1054 the papal legate Cardinal Umberto di Silva Candida took offense at the "hominis morituri imago." See L.H. Grondijs, *L'iconographie byzantine du crucifié mort sur la croix* (1941), 129ff.

[38] Garrison, nos. 521 and 524. Cf. O. Demus, *Byzantine Art and the West* (New York, 1970), 218.

[39] Garrison, no. 543. Evidence given in H. Belting, *Die Oberkirche von S. Francesco in Assisi* (Berlin, 1977), 25 and 43.

[40] Garrison, no. 459. See also Chapter I, note 51.

[41] See note 13, above.

[42] See the literature on Giotto.

[43] See Chapter IV, note 19.

[44] See Chapter IV, note 19.

[45] Francovich, 18 note 21.

[46] Francovich, illus. 11. See also F. Santi, *Galleria Nazionale dell'Umbria*, Catalogue (Rome, 1969), no. 112. The crucifix (179 x 130 cm) comes from S. Maria di Roncione near Deruta.

[47] Francovich, illus. 1 and 2. The group of Tivoli has often been reproduced (for literature, see Chapter IV, note 19), for example, in color by R. Bossagli et al., *La scultura Italiana* (Milan, n.d.), pl. 40. On the Berlin Madonna figure of presbyter Martinus, cf. the catalogue *Bildwerke der christlichen Epochen von der Spätantike bis zum Klassizismus*,

Skulpturenabteilung der Staatl. Museen Berlin (Munich, 1966), no. 207 and illus. 24. Like the others, the group in Tivoli is essentially life-sized and has even kept its polychromy. Interactions between living persons and such lifelike "dolls" were therefore aesthetically possible.

[48] Pallucchini, illus. 9. I thank the owner, Cavall. Sorlini, Venice, for access to this work and for a photograph of it.

[49] W. Felicetti-Liebenfels, *Geschichte der byzantinischen Ikonenmalerei* (Olten-Lausanne, 1956), illus. 53.

[50] D. Dalla Barbara Brusin and G. Lorenzoni, *L'arte nel Patriarcato di Aquileia del sec. IX al sec. XIII* (Padua, 1968), 79ff. and illus. 187–88.

[51] O. Demus, *Die romanische Wandmalerei* (Munich, 1968), pl. XXVII, and Brusin–Lorenzoni (note 50), 55ff. and illus. 139.

[52] P. Toesca and F. Forlati, *Die Mosaiken von San Marco* (1957), illus. p. 9; and for SS. Apostoli, in the Cappella Orlandini, see Pallucchini, illus. 257–58 (*idem*, illus. 7, the Deposition in S. Benedetto Vecchio in Padua, thirteenth century).

[53] For a detailed treatment of this topic, see Corbin, esp. 114ff. See also Chapter IV, note 3.

[54] See Chapter IV, note 55.

[55] Francovich, illus. 31.

[56] In Francovich, illus. 61, showing the group before its restoration. See the new arrangement, first reproduced in *Burlington Magazine*, 89 (1947), frontispiece next to p. 55. The account of the miracle-working crucifix in A. Ansaldi, *Descrizione delle sculture, pitture ed architetture della città . . . di Pescia* (Pescia, 1816), 18ff., probably refers to this work.

[57] Francovich, illus. 60.

[58] See Chapter IV, note 55.

[59] See Chapter IV, notes 3 and 6 (especially Corbin, and Parker, passim). On the *depositio* of a crucified Christ mentioned in a text from Aquileia, see Bartholomaeis, 461. Cf. also Young, *Drama*, I, 164; Parker, 93ff.; and Corbin, 114 (on the burial in Florence of a crucified Christ that had been removed from the cross).

[60] Corbin, 114 and 120.

[61] Corbin, 114ff., 188ff., and 212f. Entirely different texts played a role in Italy, where the development into a procession outside the church with stations and living images begins at once, promoted by the role of the brotherhoods and the climate. "The mixture of liturgy and of texts paraphrasing the Bible" was inspired by popular performances with lauds (op. cit., 114). The "genuine tendency toward the idea of a play" begins only in Italy (op. cit., 188).

[62] Corbin, 207ff. on the *planctus*, which finds its "adoptive home" in Italy where, contrary to what Young, in his *Drama*, believed, it is not part of the liturgy (Corbin, p. 212); also see Corbin, 213f., on the role in this context played by the laud in transmitting and altering the *planctus* (see also d'Ancona, I, 123f.). On the *planctus*, the song of Mary's lamentation, there is, just as for the laud (see note 70), an extensive literature: see, for example, Young, *Drama*, I, 493ff.; W. Lipphardt, *Studien zu den Marienklagen und*

der *germanischen Totenklage* (1934); B.M. Lépicier, *Mater Dolorosa* (1948); and esp. Meier, passim. See also Chapter IV, notes 54, 55, and Chapter V, note 21.

63 See note 57 and Chapter IV, note 20.

64 Young, *Drama*, I, 503 note 6 (on a missal from Friaul) and 505.

65 See Chapter IV, note 22.

66 Meier, 153ff.

67 Meier, 156ff. and 160, as well as Corbin, 213ff. On Ephraim, see the edition, *Sancti Patri nostri Ephraim Syri opera omnia* (Rome, 1746), III, 574f.; and A. Luis in *Marianum*, 5 (1943), 266ff. On the *Gesta Pilati*, see C. von Tischendorf, *Evangelia apocrypha* (Leipzig, 1853).

68 *PL* 182, 1133ff., apparently declared to be a revelation of Mary to Augustine. Cf. H. Barré in *Revue d'ascetique et de mystique*, 28 (1952), 243ff. Cf. also Meier, 160f. On the so-called text of Anselm, see *PL* 159, 284ff. On Jacopone's borrowing from Pseudo-Bernard (the quarrel among the heavenly virtues), see d'Ancona, 124ff.

69 Meier, 167.

70 F. Testi, *La musica italiana nel medioevo e nel Rinascimento* (Milan, 1969), 109ff. On the early laud, see d'Ancona, I, 106ff., 119ff., and 134ff. (the dramatic laud with recitations in dialogue form can be traced back to readings from the Bible, in contrast to the lyrical or monodic laud inspired by hymns, which it integrates); Bartholomaeis, 216ff. (gives a classification of the lauds into monologues and dialogues, into those intended for performance and those which were not, and into dramas involving relatively large groups of people), and 206ff. and passim (on the development of the lauds and the lay play in the various regions of Italy); P. Toschi, *L'antico dramma sacro italiano* (Florence, 1926), 129ff.; Liuzzi (see note 21), passim; and Corbin, 213f. On the Laudesi, see Meersseman, 954ff. On the relation of the monodic laud to the hymnographic tradition and that of the sequences, and on the matutinal songs (Ps. 148–50) of the clergy, see Testi, op. cit., 109ff.

71 A.M. Rossi, *Manuale di storia dell'ordine dei Servi di Maria* (Rome, 1956), and *idem, I 700 anni dei Servi di Maria* (Florence, 1933).

72 See note 22, above. On the place of Jacopone's lauds in the contemporary anthologies of lauds, see R. Bettarini, *Jacopone e il laudario Urbinate* (Florence, 1969).

73 Bartholomaeis, 328f. (MS from the Abruzzi). See also note 11.

74 For the literature, see note 40.

75 See note 22. These are verses 96, 97. Mary rejects Jesus' request that she remain behind on earth: "Son, don't say that! I want to die with You."

76 Verses 116–119: "Son, so white and red / Son, unequaled / Son, on whom should I lean? / Son, why have You abandoned me?"

77 Bartholomaeis, 274ff. and 277ff.

78 Bartholomaeis, 274f. See also note 11. The statutes of the brotherhood of S. Stefano (1327) are supplemented by a volume containing sixteen lauds, including lamentations of Mary for Holy Thursday (a *lamentatio* of the Virgin, with the invitation "Venete a pianger con Maria") and Good Friday ("Levate gl'occhi e resguardate," or "Udie, gente," with Mary as she looks for her Son in the city).

[79] Bartholomaeis, 277ff. on Gubbio (here we hear of angel wings "da fare la Devotione," wigs, beards, masks, and doves); and d'Ancona, I, 164, on Perugia (where there is mention of "una croce e colonna de la Devotione..., tre chiuove torte dai crocefixo, uno crocefixo grande acto a fare la Devotione, uno storpiccio acto a la Devotione dei morte, doie ladrone," among other objects, such as a "sopreponte," i.e., an elevated walkway, for the centurion and for Longinus).

[80] See note 79. The name appears to suggest that the performed laud developed from the compulsory religious practices of the brotherhoods (on these, see Meersseman, 454, 504ff., and 600); on this hypothesis, see d'Ancona, 163ff. and 184ff. *Devozione* becomes the name for a dramatic laud. But it is still bound, temporally and with regard to location, to the liturgy (without mingling with it), which it "illustrates," just as it brings the sermon to life. It is therefore an "act of piety" (*idem*, 185) and not yet an independent literary genre. Nevertheless, it is the most important form of popular, vernacular theater.

[81] D'Ancona, I, 165 and passim. See also, A. d'Ancona, *Sacre rappresentazioni dei sec. XIV, XV e XVI* (Florence, 1872); P. Toschi, *Del dramma liturgico alla rappresentazione sacra* (Florence, 1940); M. Apollonio, *Storia del teatro italiano*, I (Florence, 1938); E. Faccioli, *op. cit.* (see note 22), 131ff. We possess many accounts of the *rappresentazioni*, for example, of the Gonfalone brotherhood in the colosseum of Rome (M. Vatasso, *Per la storia del dramma sacro in Italia*, 2, Studi e Testi 10 [1903], 71ff.), as well as of the similar performances on feast days in Florence (e.g., the magnificent performance of 1438 in SS. Annunziata, the plan for which was included in Brunelleschi's construction of the stage). The tendency was to enliven the material through topical interludes and to lengthen it to such a degree that several performances became possible.

[82] See note 79, above.

[83] See note 79, above.

[84] D'Ancona, 90.

[85] See Chapter IV, note 54. On the change of gestures between the liturgical drama and the vernacular play (with integration of the public into the play), see A. Roeder, *Die Gebärde im Drama des Mittelalters* (Munich, 1974), esp. 95ff., 107ff., and 143ff.

[86] On the crucifix of Cividale (250 x 233 cm), see G. Marchetti and G. Nicoletti, *La scultura lignea del Friuli* (Milan, 1956), 25ff., and recently, M. Semff, "Die Triumphkreuzgruppe im Dom zu Seckau," *Wiener Jahrbuch für Kunstgeschichte*, 30/31 (1977–1978), 47ff. and 71ff. (dating: second quarter thirteenth century).

[87] See Chapter IV, note 55. On the function of the display gesture and the gesture of the regard, which are "never spontaneous 'expressive motion,' but signals, demonstrative signs," and which imply in the old terms for them: *designare* and *repraesentare*, a separation between the actor and his role, see Roeder (note 85, above), 97f.

[88] On the connection between theater and sermon, see d'Ancona, I, 185ff.; and Bartholomaeis, 328ff.

[89] See Meersseman, 937ff. and 1121ff., on compulsory sermons in the Marian brotherhoods and others under Dominican control.

[90] Baxandall, 49ff.

[91] "Nos predicamus Christum crucifixum." This Crucifixion fresco is attributed to Cavallini and dated to 1308–1309. It is in the Capella L. Brancaccio in S. Domenico Maggiore in Naples. Cf. F. Bologna, *I pittori alla corte angioina di Napoli, 1266–1414* (Rome, 1969), 115ff. and pl. III.6.

[92] See note 90, above.

[93] See Chapter I, note 52.

[94] An early example is Pacino da Bonaguida's large panel in the Accademia in Florence. For this transformation of the sermon tract into an image distinguished by the fact that it maintained and "quoted" the structure of the text, the preferred sites were chapter halls, sacristies, and choir chapels.

[95] See H. Belting, *Die Oberkirche von S. Francesco in Assisi* (Berlin, 1977), 80ff.

[96] Bartholomaeis, 328ff., and V. de Bartholomaeis, *Il teatro abruzzese del Medio Evo* (Bologna, 1924).

[97] Bartholomaeis, 325ff.

[98] See note 22, above.

[99] Bartholomaeis, 328ff.

[100] Bartholomaeis, 329. Each station of the Passion is sung about and contemplated by one or more persons from the story of the Passion. This form still persists, *mutatis mutandis*, in the arias of Bach's Passion cantatas.

[101] Bartholomaeis, 329ff., and *idem, Il teatro abruzzese* (note 96), 317ff.

[102] D'Ancona, I, 185f.

[103] *Ibid.*, I, 189ff.

[104] *Ibid.*, I, 191f. One should not assume that the performance took place on a flat stage having only a single space for the action, and in such a way that actors and audience confronted each other. This kind of stage was developed only in the Renaissance. Nonetheless, there was certainly a temporarily erected stage that was viewed from several sides, and that could be enclosed with curtains. On the medieval stage, see the important contributions of A.H. Nelson, among others, in J. Taylor and A.H. Nelso, *Medieval English Drama* (Chicago, 1972); A.M. Nagler, *The Medieval Religious Stage* (New Haven, 1976); and M. Radke-Stegh, *Der Theatervorhang* (Meisenheim a. G., 1978), 105ff. and 120ff. (gives an analysis of the Annunciation play of SS. Annunziata in 1438).

[105] Examples of this begin with the paintings of the "Isaac Master" in Assisi and reach an early culmination in Giotto's frescoes in the Arena Chapel in Padua.

[106] Meier, 168ff.

[107] *Ibid.* See also d'Ancona, I, 128ff., on the lyrical interludes and the requests to contemplate the biblical events with the "inner eyes" (*occhi della mente*) and to reproduce them within oneself. The edition of the text in English translation prepared by Ragusa and Green is the easiest to use. See Chapter III, note 13.

[108] See Chapter III, note 20.

[109] List of Art Works, nos. 33 and 6.

[110] List of Art Works, no. 10. Vetter, illus. 99.

[111] List of Art Works, no. 37. Vetter, illus. 100.

[112] List of Art Works, no. 36. This is a peculiar manuscript, a pocket book in the

form of a small pad of folded parchment folios (ca. 15.5 x 4 cm, and ca. 15.5 x 16 cm opened), bound on one of the narrow sides and furnished there with a handle. The folios are marked on their backs with Roman numerals (I–XXXXI) and for the most part are inscribed only on the inner side of the folded sheet of parchment in a number of columns. On folio I there is a monogram referring to the owner of the MS, who is evidently depicted on folio II, apparently at the feet of Peter. Contents: prayers for the canonical hours and similar material. On folio XXXIII there appears the Imago Pietatis between two angels. This image is placed between the Easter tables (beginning with 1291) and John 1:1, perhaps in order to designate the feast of Easter and the Passion preceding it. Only two other books of this type, including one equally old owned by an Italian notary (1283–1284), are known (see M. Garand in *Scriptorium*, 25 [1971], 18ff.).

[113] List of Art Works, no. 12. See note 34.

[114] See note 3.

[115] For example, in the former panel of Arezzo; see E.B. Garrison in *Burlington Magazine* (1947), 211.

[116] I am obliged to Mr. D. Blume for a photograph. M. Hunold's dissertation for the University of Bonn deals with this interesting fresco cycle.

[117] See Chapter II, note 4.

[118] Meiss, *op. cit.* (Chapter IV, note 15), 61ff. and 122ff.

[119] Vetter, illus. 102.

[120] Regarding this description, see Chapter I, note 45. On the leaf from the book of chants, see List of Art Works, no. 21.

[121] Cf. List of Art Works, no. 37 (Vienna), as well as G. Leidinger, *Meisterwerke der Buchmalerei* (Munich, 1920), pl. 21; W. Mersmann, *Der Schmerzensmann* (Düsseldorf, 1952), XXXIII; and illus. 5, on the Clm. 23094 in Munich.

[122] See note 112, and Vetter, 370, illus. 103, on Cod. IQ 233, fol. 145v of the library of the University of Breslau (from the Poor Clares' convent there, from around 1280).

[123] On the codex, see note 34. On the image and prayer on fol. 183v, see Vetter, *Iconographia*, 212ff., and Vetter, 197ff. On the legend of Bernard's embrace, see Chapter IV, note 21.

[124] List of Art Works, no. 2; Bacci, 105ff. (for a detailed discussion of the reconstruction); Schrade, 176f. (on the sacrificial symbolism); Braunfels, 321ff.; and Jászai, 22ff. and 29ff. (iconography). The Berlin lectern (inv. 32), like the eagle lectern in the Metropolitan Museum of Art (used as a lectern for reading epistles), appears to be descended from Giovanni Pisano's pulpit in S. Andrea in Pistoia. It was acquired in Pisa in 1881.

[125] Roeder, *op. cit.* (note 85), 45ff.

[126] List of Art Works, no. 29. See especially R. Papini, *Pisa. Catalogo delle cose d'arte*, ser. I, fasc. II (Pisa), II, 148f., no. 278; P. Bacci, *La ricostruzione del pergamo di G. Pisano nel duomo di Pisa* (Milan, 1926), 105ff.; and E. Carli, *Il pergamo del duomo di Pisa* (Pisa, 1975), 32 and pl. 101. It has the same dimensions as the Pisan eagle lectern.

[127] Cf. the lectern of the pulpit from S. Giovanni Fuorcivitas in Pistoia and a fragment in the Camposanto in Pisa (Papini, *op. cit.* [note 126], II, no. 277).

128 Bernard, *De pretioso unguento pietatis* (*PL* 183, 831).

129 Bernard, *Liber ad milites templi cap. XI: De sepulcro* (*PL* 182, 932).

130 On these statutes, see Chapter III, note 8. The pertinent material is in fol. 38 of MS 52 (Fondo Osped. 3) of the Archiginnasio, Bologna.

131 *PL* 182 (see note 129), 932f. See also *PL* 183, 621, where the topic is God's *caritas* and at the same time his *pietas*, which nothing manifests so clearly as does the mystery of his Incarnation, according to this passage.

132 *PL* 182 (see note 129), 936.

133 *PL* 182 (see note 129), 934: "Sed quae, inquis, iustitia est, ut innocens moriatur pro impio? Non est iustitia sed misericordia."

134 Jacopo Passavanti, *Lo specchio della vera penitenza* (Florence, 1725), 52f.: With hands crossed in front of her breast, the Mother of God threw herself down before the Judge and begged him "pietosamente che dovesse il rigore della sua giustizia temperare colla benignità della sua misericordia." Passavanti, 42ff. (Chap. 4), discusses at length the definition of the *misericordia* of God (he also gives, p. 45f., a graphic description of the Imago Pietatis: "il sangue suo grida e proferra misericordia e pietade: il lato aperto vi mostra amore di cuore . . . le braccia aperte, il capo chino vi trae a pace ... "). The tension between justice and clemency (on this subject, see H. Friedrich, *Die Rechtsmetaphysik in Dantes Göttlicher Komödie* [Frankfurt, 1942], 145ff.) greatly occupied thirteenth-and fourteenth-century thought. Cf. also a sermon of Jacopone da Todi (d'Ancona, I, 124ff.), which is said to have taken over the image of the dispute of the heavenly virtues Misericordia and Pax with Veritas and Justitia from the Pseudo-Bernardine *planctus* (on this point, see note 68).

135 *PL* 182 (see note 129, above), 937.

136 *Tractatus de corpore Domini* (*PL* 182, 1149ff.). See also Chapter IV, notes 6 and 10.

137 See Chapter I, p. 12, for the first discussion of this point.

138 See p. 133 and note 8.

139 List of Art Works, no. 14.

140 See Chapter II.

141 List of Art Works, no. 6. On its original function as half of a diptych (there are hinge marks on the left moulding of the frame), see Kermer, no. 76.

142 Cf. a work in the Tretjakov Gallery of Moscow: V.N. Antonova and N.E. Mneva, *Katalog drevnerusskoj zhivopisi Gos. Tretjakovsk Gal.*, I (Moscow, 1963), no. 337, illus. 256. This fourteenth-century Serbian specimen represents the type of the model.

143 Garrison, no. 462 (at the time still in the Stoclet collection). The legible part of the inscription reads: "Ecce hic est Christus Jesus Rex Judaeorum . . . Serv . . . salus nostre . . . pro nobis pendevit in ligno."

144 List of Art Works, no. 33.

145 Garrison, no. 461.

146 Pallucchini, illus. 193.

147 E.H. Gombrich, *Art and Illusion* (Princeton, 1960; 3rd ed. 1969), 79f. Cf. 60f. for the role of expectation and verifying observation in the viewer's experience of art, and

70f. for the "principle of the adapted stereotype," which *mutatis mutandis* is also applicable in our case.

[148] See Chapter VI, Section "The Cross and the Descent from the Cross. . . . " and note 39 above.

[149] Hager, illus. 163; and van Os, pl. 14c.

[150] List of Art Works, no. 34.

[151] List of Art Works, no. 23; the church of S. Andrea in Mosciano. Within a series of full-length figures, an area is demarcated with moulding; in it the torsos of Mary and Christ from the triad can still be seen. The wall beneath these half-length figures is covered with a simulated curtain.

[152] Van Os, 71 and pl. 14a; in the Barber Institute, Birmingham.

[153] J.H. Stubblebine, "Segna di Buonaventura and the Image of the Man of Sorrows," *Gesta*, 8/2 (1969), 3ff.

[154] List of Art Works, no. 16.

[155] The singular association—unusual even for the Veneto-Adriatic artistic milieu—of Byzantine painting technique and stylistic forms and motifs that are partially western is perplexing. The inner and outer sides are contemporary. Unfortunately, the colors have for the most part turned brown. For a description, see van Os, passim. I would like to thank van Os and the collector in The Hague for the opportunity to see this work.

[156] See Pallucchini, illus. 207, 210, and 226; as well as M. Muraro, *Paolo da Venezia* (1969), illus. 11 and 13.

[157] List of Art Works, no. 35. See esp. Pallucchini, illus. 99–101.

[158] List of Art Works, no. 31; and Chapter I, note 43.

[159] See Chapter III, note 8.

Appendix A
Pietas and Imago Pietatis
The Image in Historical Accounts and Inscriptions

[1] See Chapter III, note 8.

[2] See Chapter IV, note 30: "et in facie ipsius tume [*sic*] in medio sit pietas cum uno angelo a quolibet latere."

[3] P. Debongnie, ed., *Ste. Catherine de Gênes 1447–1510: Vie et Doctrine, et Traité de Purgatoire* (Bruges-Paris, 1960), 7.

[4] On this passage in the inventories of the Duke of Berry, see I.M.I. Guiffrey, *Inventaires de Jean Duc de Berry (1401–16)* (Paris, 1894), I, 290.

[5] See A. Campana, in *Scritti di storia dell'arte in on. M. Salmi* (Rome, 1962), II, 405ff. See also H. Belting, *Giovanni Bellini. Pietà* (Frankfurt, 1985).

[6] See Chapter I, note 45. But cf. the possible correction of this statement in Appendix B, note 21.

⁷ *Mélanges G. Hulin de Loo* (Brussels-Paris, 1931), 17.

⁸ See Chapter I, note 43, and List of Art Works, no. 31.

⁹ See Vetter, 215ff., where additional literature is cited, and List of Art Works, no. 31, for bibliography.

¹⁰ R. Besozzi, *La storia della Basilica di S. Croce in Gerusalemme* (Rome, 1755), 155.

¹¹ Vetter, 215.

¹² In the Wallraf-Richartz Museum of Cologne, inv. 744 (Umbrian, last quarter fifteenth century). This indulgence panel measures 81.5 x 50.3 cm (see B. Klesse, *Katalog der ital., französ. und span. Gemälde bis 1800 im Wallr.-Rich.-Museum*, Katalog VI [Cologne, 1973], no. 744 and pl. 21).

¹³ E. Mâle, *L'art religieux de la fin du moyen âge en France*, 5th ed. (Paris, 1949), illus. 53.

¹⁴ Cf. Chapter IV, note 57.

¹⁵ V. de Bartholomaeis, *Laude drammatiche e rappresentazioni sacri* (Florence, 1943), I, 7.

¹⁶ A. d'Ancona, *Sacre Rappresentazioni* (Chapter VI, note 81), I, 303ff., and esp. 311. In the same source (p. 324), the nail which is driven through Jesus's body is referred to as pitiless or unfeeling (*dispietato*).

¹⁷ Cf. Chapter III, note 45.

¹⁸ List of Art Works, no. 18, and p. 29. See also the account of the image on a tabernacle in Bopfingen (1408) for which Hans Böblinger is said to have made "a figure of mercy with two angels" (G.v.d. Osten, "Engelpietà" in *Reallexikon der deutschen Kunstgeschichte*, V [1967], 601).

¹⁹ The mimetic relation between the two kinds of *pietas* which is reflected in the image–viewer (and God–man) relationship is important. Both kinds of *pietas* (the act of divine *pietas*, to which the transformation of the Host in St. Gregory's Mass was also attributed, and the response of human *pietas*, which is actually a product of the Creator's influencing of his creature through his grace), are summarized best in an early fifteenth-century English psalter with the formula: "Pietas Tua, Domine, operetur in me" (Vetter, 222 and 227).

²⁰ See Chapter VI, note 134.

²¹ On the panel, the donor holds a scroll on which is mentioned the *promissione* of life, "que nunc est et future," through *pietas*.

²² In the National Gallery in Prague. The inscription reads: "Passus sum pro te; dum peccas, desine pro me. Ego sum panis vivus qui de celo descendi. Si quis manducavit ex hoc pane, vivet. Aspice mortalis, pro te datur hostia talis." On this panel, see *Narodni Galerie v Praze: Ceské Umení Gotické* (Prague, 1964), no. 103 and pl. 21. The Christ of this Angel Pietà holds the eucharistic chalice in front of him and points to his wounds.

²³ In the National Museum in Warsaw. See Dobrzeniecki, 214f. and illus. 145.

²⁴ List of Art Works, no. 28.

Appendix B
Lament and Accusation
The Verse from Jeremiah in the Rhetoric of the Middle Ages

[1] Meiss, *Black Death*, 123f. On exegetical and doctrinal inscriptions on images which define the degree of reality, for example , of the image of the crucified Christ, see the important study by R. Bugge, "Effigiem Christi qui transis, semper honora. Verses Condemning the Cult of Sacred Images in Art and Literature," *Acta ad Archaeol. et artium historiam pertinentia* (Norwegian Institute, Rome), 6 (1975), 127ff.

[2] Meiss, *Black Death*, illus. 121.

[3] Ibid., illus. 124 (from the school of Niccolò di Buonaccorso). The verses "Cur homo miraris..." are added to the Lamentation of Mary of Good Friday in Cod. Plut. XXV.3 of the Laurenziana, fol. 141 (see List of Art Works, no. 12; and Chapter VI, note 34) and there also associated with an image that, however, is not reproduced.

[4] In the National Library in Prague: Cod. UK XIV.A.17, fol. 11a–13a. See also E. Urbánková and K. Stejkal, *Pasionál Premyslovny Kunhuty—Passionale Abbatissae Cunegundis* (Prague, 1975), pls. 11a–13a.

[5] See Chapter VI, section "The Cross and the Descent from the Cross . . . "

[6] See Introduction, note 15.

[7] List of Art Works; no. 28, and Appendix A, p. 196.

[8] See the literature on Claus Sluter.

[9] C. Sterling and H. Adhémar, *Ecole Française des siècles XIV, XV et XVI*, Catal. Louvre (Paris, 1963), no. 32.

[10] Meiss, *Black Death*, illus. 123.

[11] See Chapter IV, note 50.

[12] M. Lehr, *Geschichte und krit. Katal. der deutschen, niederländischen und französischen Kupferstiche im 15. Jh.*, no. 677, pl. 281.

[13] *S. Gregorii Magni Liber Responsalis* (*PL* 78, 767).

[14] See Chapter VI, p. 196.

[15] Transmitted from the *Liber Sacerdotalis* in the edition of C. Castelloni (Venice, 1523); see also Young, *Drama*, I, 128.

[16] Young, *Drama*, I, 511. See also Chapter IV, note 55, and Chapter VI, section "The Cross and the Descent from the Cross...."

[17] For detailed discussion of this point, see Chapter VI, section "The Cross and the Descent from the Cross...."

[18] See Chapter IV, note 57.

[19] Matthaeus de Aquasparta, "Sermo I in Assumptionem b. Mariae Virginis," ed. C. Piana, *Bibl. Francesc. Ascetica Medii Aevi* IX (1962), 170f.

[20] Engerrand de Monstrelet, *Chronique*, ed. L. Douet d'Arcq (Paris, 1857), I, 269ff.

[21] Thus we should perhaps consider whether a speaking figure of the dead Christ that arises from the grave (see Chapter I, note 45 and Appendix A) was, despite its irrational elements, a possible visualization of the Imago Pietatis, at least in the popular imagination.

[22] R. Kalidova and A. Kolensky, *Das hussitische Denken im Lichte seiner Quellen* (Berlin, 1969), 127.

Appendix C
Western Art after 1204
The Importation of Relics and Icons

[1] Anonymus Halberstadensis, *De peregrinatione in Greciam et adventu reliquiarum de Grecia*, Monumenta Germaniae Historica, Scriptores, XXIII, 118ff. Cf. C. de Riant, *Des dépouilles religieuses enlevées à Constantinople par les Latins*, Mémoires de la Société nationale des Antiquaires de France, vol. 36 (Paris, 1875), 42 and 100ff., and also *idem*, *Exuviae sacra Constantinopolitanae*, I (Geneva, 1877), 19ff. The interpretive essay (*Des dépouilles*) and the Comte de Riant's edition of the texts (*Exuviae sacrae*), together with F. de Mély, *Exuviae sacrae Constantinopolitanae: la croix des premiers croisés. La sainte lance. La sainte couronne* (Paris, 1904), remain the standard works on the "theme". On the Crusades in general and on the Fourth Crusade in particular, see S. Runciman, *A History of the Crusades*, III (Cambridge, England, 1954); K.M. Setton, *A History of the Crusades*, II (Philadelphia, 1962); H.E. Mayer, *The Crusades* (Oxford, 1972); J. Dufournet, *La conquête de Constantinople* (Paris, 1969); R.L. Wolff, *Studies in the Latin Empire of Constantinople* (London, 1976).

[2] Also see A. Laiou, "Venice as a Centre of Trade...," *Atti XXIV. Congr. Internaz. Storia dell'Arte*, Bologna, 1979 (Milan, 1980), II, 11ff. Other literature: F. Braudel, *The Mediterranean and the Mediterranean World in the Age of Philip II*, 2 vols. (New York, 1976); R.L. Wolff, *Studies* (see note 1, above); F.C. Lane, *Venice. A Maritime Republic* (Baltimore, 1973); S. Borsari, *Studi sulle colonie veneziane in Romania nel XIII secolo* (Naples, 1966); G. Luzzatto, *Studi di storia economica veneziana* (Padua, 1954); A. Pertusi, ed., *Venezia e il Levante fino al secolo XV*, 3 vols. (Florence, 1973–1974).

[3] Caesarius of Heisterbach, *Annales Cistercienses*, ed. Manrique, 1206, III, 6. E.A.R. Brown, "The Cistercians in the Latin Empire of Constantinople," *Traditio*, 14 (1958), 63ff., and B.M. Bolton, "The Cistercians in Romania" in D. Baker, ed., *The Orthodox Churches and the West* (Oxford, 1976), 169ff.

[4] G. Millet, *Le monastère de Daphni* (Paris, 1899), 25ff. The buildings to the west of the church attest to the presence of the Latin order in the Attic monastery. However, the Cistercians' alleged destruction of the mosaic of the Pantocrator in the dome is mere legend.

[5] C. de Riant, *Des dépouilles*, 27.

[6] *Ibid.* 32ff., 40, 80. Cf. G. Constable, "Troyes, Constantinople and the Relics of St. Helen in the Thirteenth Century" in *Mélanges offerts à R. Crozet* (Poitiers, 1966), 1035ff., and P.J. Geary, "St. Helen of Athyra and the Cathedral of Troyes in the Thirteenth Century," *Journal of Medieval and Renaissance Studies*, 7 (1977), 149ff.

[7] Geary, *op. cit.*, 165 and pl. VI. This image is located in the left course of window K in the high choir of Troyes.

[8] E. Assman, ed., *Gunther von Paris. Die Geschichte der Eroberung von Konstantinopel*, Geschichtsschreiber der deutschen Vorzeit, ed. K. Langosch, vol. 101 (Weimar, 1956), 63f.

[9] Geary, *op. cit.*, 152ff., and C. de Riant, *Des dépouilles*, 4f. On the relation between the possession of relics, church construction, and "fund-raising tours," see P. Heliot–M.L. Chastang, "Quêtes et voyages de reliques au profit des églises françaises du Moyen Age,"

Revue d'Histoire Ecclésiastique, 59 (1964), 789ff., and 60 (1965), 5ff.

[10] C. de Riant, *Des dépouilles*, 4.

[11] On this argument, see the literature in note 6 above, especially Geary, *op. cit.*, 166, pl. VI.

[12] F. de Mély, *Le Trésor de Chartres, 1310–1793* (Paris, 1886), xix, 69f. Immediately after its arrival a feast-office was instituted for the new saint whose relic was displayed in a bust reliquary "de vermeil doré" and with a painted face. On the trumeau figure of Saint Anne on the central north portal of Chartres, see W. Sauerländer–M. Hirmer, *Gotische Skulptur in Frankenreich 1140–1270* (Munich, 1970), pl. 87.

[13] Sauerländer–Hirmer, *op. cit.*, pls. 59 and 62.

[14] C. de Riant, *Des dépouilles*, 13.

[15] The well-known passage (*Apologia ad Guillelmum S. Theodorici abbatem*, PL 182, col. 914–16), composed ca. 1124 against extravagance in religious architecture, is often cited and has frequently been translated (e.g., by F.G. Grimme, *Goldschmiedekunst im Mittelalter* [Cologne, 1972], 173f.). Shortly before, in the 1119 tract *De pignoribus sanctorum*, Guibert of Nogent criticized no less sharply the excesses of relic cults. On this and the cult and criticism of relics in general, see K. Guth, *Guibert von Nogent und die hochmittelalterliche Kritik an der Reliquienverehrung* (Ottobeuren, 1970), esp. 72ff. and 153ff. on Bernard's treatise. See also N. Herrmann-Mascard, *Les reliques des Saints* (Paris, 1975), *passim*, on the forms of relic cults.

[16] H.E. Kubach–A. Verbeek, *Romanische Baukunst an Rhein und Maas. Katalog der vorromanischen und romanischen Denkmäler* (Berlin, 1976), I, 477ff. and III, 182–184.2.

[17] Recently, W. Sauerländer, "Die Sainte-Chapelle du Palais Ludwigs des Heiligen," *Jahrbuch der Bayerischen Akademie der Wissenschaften* (1977), 1–24. On the history and symbolism of the building, see also S.J. Morand, *Histoire de la Ste. Chapelle Royale du Palais* (Paris, 1790); L. Grodecki, *Sainte-Chapelle* (Paris, n.d.); *idem*, "La Sainte-Chapelle, un édifice exemplaire," *Archaeologia* (1969), 43ff.; R. Branner, "The Ste-Chapelle and the Capella Regis in the Thirteenth Century," *Gesta*, 10 (1971), 19ff. On the treasure and the reliquary of Ste Chapelle, see A. Vidier, *Le Trésor de la Ste-Chapelle*, Mémoires de la Société de l'Histoire de Paris et de l'Ile de France, 34 (1907), 37 (1910); R. Branner, "The Grande Chasse of the Ste-Chapelle," *Gazette des Beaux-Arts*, 77 (1971), 5ff. The appearance of the Grance Chasse on the altar platform is conveyed through drawings in the Gaignières Collection.

[18] Gualterius Cornutus, *Historiae susceptionis Corone spinee*, in De Riant, *Exuviae sacrae*, I, 45ff. and esp. 51, where we read, "Gaudebat...[Louis] quod, ad exhibendum honorem huiusmodi, suam Deus praeelegerat Galliam, in qua...salutis nostrae mysteria celebrantur," and on page 47 it is stated directly: "Sicut...Christus ad suae redemptionis exhibenda mysteria Terram promissionis elegit [i.e., the Holy Land], sic ad passionis suae triumphum devotius venerandum nostram Galliam [i.e., France] videtur...elegisse." On the history of the donation (or sale) of the Crown of Thorns, see C. de Riant, *Des dépouilles*, 50ff. and 72ff., as well as F. de Mély, (see note 1, above), passim. On the Byzantine hyperpyron, see A.M. Watson, "Back to Gold and Silver," *The Economic History Review*, 20 (1967), 1ff.

[19] M.M. Gauthier, "Le couvertures precieuses des manuscrits à l'usage de la Ste-Chapelle" in *VII. Centenaire de la mort de St. Louis*, Actes des Colloques de Royaumont et de Paris, 1970 (Paris, 1976), 141ff.

[20] Robert de Clari, *La conquête de Constantinople*, ed. Ph. Lauer (Paris, 1924), 82 (English trans. by E.H. McNeal. *The Conquest of Constantinople* [New York, 1936], 103). On Robert de Clari, A.M. Nada Patrone, *Roberto de Clari. La conquista di Constantinopoli (1198–1216). Studio critico, traduzione e note* (Genoa, 1972), and J. Dufournet, *Les écrivains de la IVe croisade: Villehardouin et Clari* (Paris, 1973), II, 341ff. On the Greek side, the keeper of the palace chapel wrote a supplementary and corroborating description only a few years before Robert of Clari: see A. Heisenberg, *Nikolaos Mesarites. Die Palastrevolution des Johannes Komnenos* (Würzburg, 1906), with an edition of the Greek text, pp. 28ff., and F. Grabler, *Die Kreuzfahrer erobern Konstantinopel*, Byzantinische Geschichtsschreiber, IX (Graz, 1958), 285ff., with a German translation.

[21] Cf. M.M. Gauthier, "Reliquaires du XIIIe siècle..." *Atti XXIV. Congr. Internaz. Storia dell'Arte*, Bologna, 1979 (Milan, 1980), II, 55ff.

[22] Cf. the bibliography in note 17, above.

[23] Vienna, National-Bibl. Cod. 1921, fol. 218: H. Hermann, *Beschreibendes Verzeichnis der illumin. Handschriften in Osterreich*, VIII, Bd. V, Teil 3 (Vienna, 1930), 244 and pl. CI.1. Cf. also the MS Morgan 67, fol. 1 in New York, a ca. 1470 Psalter from Rouen. One of the early ensembles from the relic treasure of Ste Chapelle is the libretto reliquary in Florence that Charles V gave to his brother Louis of Anjou: see Th. Müller–E. Steingräber in *Münchner Jahrbuch der Bildenden Kunst* (1954), 31 and Figs. 1 and 2.

[24] B. de Montesquiou-Fézensac, *Le Trésor de St. Denis* (Paris, 1975), I, 10, and 22, as well as pl. 6. On the *oratorium, ibid.,* 4. Of course the name of the Boukoleon palace has an entirely different derivation.

[25] For bibliography, see P. Volkelt, *Die Bauskulptur und Ausstattungsbildnerei des frühen und hohen Mittelalters im Saarland* (Saarbrücken, 1969), and the catalogue, *Die Zeit de Staufer. Geschichte-Kunst-Kultur* (Stuttgart, 1977), no. 565–66 and figs. 367–69. Cf. also R. Rückert, "Zur Form der byzantinischen Reliquiare," *Münchner Jahrbuch der Bildenden Kunst*, 3d F., 8 (1957), 20ff.; A. Frolow, *La relique de la Vraie Croix* (Paris, 1961), nos. 135, 503, and 504; idem, *Les reliquaires de la Vraie Croix* (Paris, 1965), passim, and C.W. Solt, *The Cult of Saints and Relics in the Romanesque Art of South-Western France and the Impact of Imported Byzantine Relics and Reliquaries on Early Gothic Reliquary Sculpture* (Dissertation, Catholic University of America, Washington, D.C., 1977).

[26] The 1208 act of donation by which the *sancturarium s. crucis* was bequeathed to the monastery has been preserved. The Limburg staurotheke was produced in 963–68 in Constantinople at the order of the courtier Basilios: J. Rauch, "Die Limburger Staurothek," *Das Münster*, 8 (1955), 16ff., and H. Belting–G. Cavallo, *Die Bibel des Niketas. Ein Werk der höfischen Buchkunst in Byzanz und sein antikes Vorbild* (Wiesbaden, 1979), 26.

[27] Catalogue, *Die Zeit der Staufer* (see note 24, above), no. 565.

[28] Described by Gunther von Pairis, ed. Assmann (note 8 above), 109f. The donation resulted in the king's confirmation of all the monastery's possessions (including the newly acquired relics).

[29] P. Toesca, "Un capolavoro dell'oreficeria veneziana della fine del dugento," *Arte Veneta* (1951–1952), 15ff.; H.R. Hahnloser, "Das Venezianer Kristallkreuz im Bern. Histor. Museum," *Jahrbuch des Bern. Historischen Museum*, 34 (1954), 35ff.; F. Maurer, *Die Kunstdenkmäler des Kantons Aargau*, III. *Das Kloster Königsfelden* (Basel, 1954), 255ff.; P. Huber, Bild und Botschaft (Zurich, 1973), 146ff. with illustrations.

[30] On the diptych in Chilandar, see Sv. Radojcic, "Miniature d'Origine Veneziana nel Monastero di Hilandar" in *Atti XVIII Congr. Internaz. storia dell'arte* (Venice, 1956), 166ff., and Huber, (see note 29, above), 137ff.

[31] H. Belting, "Zwischen Gotik und Byzanz," *Zeitschrift für Kunstgeschichte*, 41 (1978), 256. Illustration in P. Huber, *Athos* (Zurich, 1959), Fig. 158.

[32] Catalogue, (see note 27 above).

[33] Laiou, "Venice" (see note 2 above).

[34] Frolow, *Relique* (see note 24 above), no. 435 and *idem, Reliquaires* (see note 24), 106 and Fig. 56.

[35] Paris, Louvre. Lit.: Frolow, *Relique*, no. 454, and *idem, Reliquaires*, Figs. 18–20; *L'art et la cour. France et Angleterre 1259–1328* (Ottowa, 1972), no. 39, and M.M. Gauthier in *Monuments et Mémoires F. Piot,* 59 (1974), 203ff.

[36] Gualterius Cornutus, *Historia* (note 18 above), 55, reports that an *eminens pulpitum* was erected in 1239 before the walls of Paris for the arrival of the Passion relics and the newly arrived *loculus* was displayed from it. On cult exhibitions in the Middle Ages, see G.F. Koch, *Die Kunstausstellung* (Berlin, 1967), 32ff. and 125ff.

[37] "Haec cruz quae luxit [?] nobis, bis sanguine fluxit. Quam scio quod tinxit Christi cruor ac benedixit."

[38] Gauthier, "Reliquaires" (see note 21, above).

[39] J. Braun, *Die Reliquaire des christl. Kults und ihre Entwicklung* (Freiburg i. Br., 1940), 301ff. and 380ff., as well as E. Meyer, "Reliquie und Reliquiar im Mittelalter" in *Festschrift C.G. Heise* (Berlin, 1950), 58ff. on the "speaking" reliquaries, and Braun, *loc. cit.*, 55ff. and Meyer, *loc. cit.*, 61ff. on the display vessels which since the fourteenth century have been known by the name *monstrantia*.

[40] Les Billanges, Haute Vienne. See the catalogue, *Les Trésors des Eglises de France* (Paris, 1965), no. 357, pl. 69. See also the statuette of Saint Stephen from the Maas region in the Metropolitan Museum, The Cloisters (catalogue: *The Year 1200* [New York, 1970], no. 106), and a statuette of Stephen from the Vasilevski collection in the Hermitage (F.A. Lapkovskaja, *Prikladnoe Iskusstvo srednikh vekov v. Gos. Ermitaze* [Moscow, 1971], pl. 56).

[41] O. Demus, *Die Mosaiken von San Marco in Venedig* (Baden, 1935), 44, and *idem,* "Bisanzio e la pittura a mosaico del Duecento a Venezia" in *Civiltà Europ. e Civiltà Veneziana 4, Venezia e l'Oriente fra tardo medioevo e rinascimento* (1966), 125ff., as well as idem, *The Church of San Marco in Venice* (Washington, 1960), 18.

[42] C. de Riant, *Des dépouilles* (see note 1, above), 64f.

[43] Montesquiou-Fézensac, (see note 24, above), 10.

[44] See Gauthier, "Reliquaires" (see note 21, above).

[45] Catalogue: *Bildwerke der christlichen Epochen...aus den Beständen der Skulpturenabteilung der Staatlichen Museen* (Berlin) (Munich, 1966), no. 301 and pl. 39.

[46] On the expression *vernacles*, see H.C. Lea, *A History of Auricular Confessions and Indulgences in the Latin Church*, III (Philadelphia, 1896), 501ff. On the Veronica, see note 47, below.

[47] The Veronica was venerated in a relic ciborium dated to 1197 in St. Peter's and was endowed with an indulgence in 1216 by Innocent III. S.K. Pearson, *Die Fronica* (Strassburg, 1887); Dobschütz, 218ff.; Ringbom, 23, 29, 70; A. Chastel, "La Véronique," *Revue de l'Art* (1978), 71ff.

[48] Catalogue: *Venezia e Bisanzio* (Venice, 1974), no. 81.

[49] Dobschütz, passim.

[50] Robert de Clari, *op. cit.* (see note 20), 66f. Villehardouin's chronicle reports the same thing.

[51] R. Gallo, *Il Tesoro di S. Marco e la sua storia* (Venice, 1967), 133ff. Cf. esp. the oldest extant treatise on this image: Giov. Thiepolo, *Trattato dell'Imagine della Gloriosa Vergine dipinta da S. Luca* (Venice, 1618), passim. Unfortunately there are no old literary accounts.

[52] Robert de Clari, "La conquête" (note 20 above), 107.

[53] See note 52. On these events, see R.L. Wolff, "Footnote to an Incident of the Latin Occupation of Constantinople: The Church and the Icon of the Hodegetria," *Traditio*, 6 (1948), 319ff.

[54] W. Krönig, *The Cathedral of Monreale* (Palermo, 1965), pl. VI (*La Madonna Bruna*). See also *loc. cit.*, Fig. 63, for the related mosaic in the cathedral.

[55] New York, Metropolitan Museum of Art. Cf. Garrison, no. 96, and Hager, 81f. and Fig. 102.

[56] Cf. note 55. They are classified under type (e.g., diptychs) at various places in Garrison's index.

[57] On the following, C. Belting-Ihm, *Sub matris tutela. Untersuchungen zur Vorgeschichte der Schutzmantelmadonna*, Akad. Wiss. Abhandl. (Heidelberg, 1976).

[58] On this theme, H. Belting, "An Image and Its Function in the Liturgy: The Man of Sorrows at Byzantium," *Dumbarton Oaks Papers*, 34–35 (1982), 1ff.

[59] R. Pallucchini, *La pittura veneziana del Trecento* (Venice, 1964), Figs. 205–206, as well as the catalogue: *Museo di Torcello* (Venice, 1978), no. 56.

[60] C. Bertelli, "The Image of Pity in S. Croce in Gerusalemme," in *Essays in the History of Art Presented to R. Wittkower* (1967), 40ff.

[61] Hager, 134ff., and J. White, *Duccio. Tuscan Art and the Medieval Workshop* (London, 1979), 95ff. and 119ff.

[62] Bologna, Archiginnasio MS Fondo Ospedale I (Fondo Battuti 42), fol. 1r: A. Gaudenzi, *Statuti della Soc. del Popolo di Bologna*, II, Fonti per la storia d'Italia 4 (1896), xlviii and 421ff.; catalogue: *Mostra storica nazionale della miniatura* (Rome, Florence, 1954), no. 169; M. Fanti, "Fondo Ospedale della B.C. dell'Archiginnasio," *L'Archiginnasio*, 58 (1963), 7.

[63] R. Haussherr, *Der tote Christus am Kreuz. Zur Ikonographie des Gerokreuzes* (Bonn, 1963). The Italian material is supplied by Garrison, and by E. Sandberg Vavalà, *La croce dipinta italiana e l'Iconographica della passione* (Verona, 1929). On our aspect, Hager, 75ff., and O. Demus, *Byzantine Art and the West* (New York, 1970), 218.

[64] Theodoricus, *Libellus de Locis Sanctis* (1164–1174), ed. M.L. and W. Bulst, Editiones Heidelbergenses XVIII (Heidelberg, 1976), 18. Cf. also M.L. Bulst, "Die Mosaiken der 'Aufstehungskirche' in Jerusalem und die Bauten der 'Franken' im 12. Jh.," *Frühmittelalterliche Studien*, 13 (1979), 442ff. and esp. 461f.

[65] Cf. A. Berger-Fix, "Das Wimpassinger Kreuz und seine Einordnung in die Kunst des 13. Jahrhunderts," *Wiener Jahrbuch für Kunstgeschichte* 33 (1980), 31ff.

[66] A. Schneider et al., *Die Cistercienser* (Cologne, 1974), 29, and W. Braunfels, *Abendländische Klosterbaukunst* (Cologne, 1969), 300f.

[67] O. Demus–M. Hirmer, *Romanische Wandmalerei* (Munich, 1968), 132.

[68] On the icon in Aachen-Burtscheid, see R. Kroos, "Byzanz und Barsinghausen," *Niederdeutsche Beiträge zur Kunstgeschichte*, 6 (1967), 103ff., and F. Schmitz-Cliever, "Repertorium medicohistoricum Aquense," *Aachener Kunstblätter*, 34 (1967), 245ff. On the icon in Freising, C. Wolters, "Beobachtungen am Freisinger Lukasbild," *Kunstchronik*, 17 (1964), 85ff.

[69] A. Stange, "Deutsche romanische Tafelmalerei," *Münchner Jahrbuch der Bildenden Kunst*, 7 (1930), 136ff. Cf. also the catalogue: *Die Zeit der Staufer* (see note 24, above), nos. 430–35.

[70] For general bibliography, see note 47. On the Mandylion in particular, see Dobschütz, 102ff., 158ff., 29ff.; A. Grabar, *La Sainte Face de Laon, le Mandylion dans l'Art orthodoxe* (Prague, 1931); K. Weitzmann, "The Mandylion and Constantine Porphyrogennetos," *Cahiers Archéologiques*, 11 (1960), 163ff.; C. Bertelli, "Storia e vicende dell'Immagine Edissena di S. Silvestro in Capite a Roma," *Paragone*, 217 (1968), 3ff., and K. Gould, *The Psalter and Hours of Yolande of Soissons*, Speculum Anniversary Monographs IV (Cambridge, Mass., 1978), 81ff.

[71] Robert de Clari, *La conquête* (see note 20, above), 82f. Cf. also Nikolaos Mesarites, ed. Heisenberg (see note 20, above), 31, and ed. Grabler (see note 20, above), 285ff.

[72] Riant, *Exuviae sacrae* (see note 1, above), II, 134f.

[73] Bertelli (see note 70, above), passim.

[74] C. Dufour Bozzo, *Il 'Sacro Volto' di Genova* (Rome, 1974).

[75] Vincent of Beauvais, *Speculum Historiale*, VIII, 29.

[76] According to Mariano of Florence (for 1517): Bertelli (see note 70, above).

[77] He speaks of an "effiges Christi a pectore superius" (*Otia imperialia* 3.25): cf. Dobschütz, 292*f.

[78] Matthew Paris, *Chronica* (Corpus Christi College, Cambridge, MS 16, fol. 49v): cf. also Dobschütz, 294*, 297* on the text, and M.R. James, *The Drawings of Matthew Paris*, The Walpole Society 14 (1925–1926), 6f., 25f. and pls. IV, XXIX, as well as Gould (see note 70, above), 86f.

[79] Constantine Porphyrogenitus, *De cerimoniis*, I, 1, 1, ed. I. Reiske (Bonn, 1829), 15f. Cf. Pallas, 69f. ad 74f.

[80] Florence, Bibl. Laurenziana, MS Plut. XXV.3, fol. 15v: "Haec linea bis sexties ducta mensuram dominici corporis monstrat. Sumpta est autem de Constantinopoli ex aurea cruce facta ad formam corporis Christi." On the MS, see A. Neff, "A new interpretation of the supplicationes variae miniatures," *Atti XXIV. Congr. Internaz. Storia dell'Arte*, Bologna, 1979 (Milan, 1980), II, 173ff.

[81] Grabar (see note 70, above), 7ff.

[82] Gould (see note 70, above), 81ff. and pl. 7.

Bibliography

Bibliography on the Imago Pietatis
General and on the Image of S. Croce

Bauerreiss, R. *Pie Jesu. Das Schmerzensmannbild und sein Einfluss auf die mittelalterliche Frömmigkeit.* Munich, 1931.

Berliner (see Literature Cited in Abbreviated Form).

Berliner, "Arma" (see Literature Cited in Abbreviated Form).

Bertelli, C. "The Image of Pity in S. Croce in Gerusalemme." *Essays in the History of Art Presented to R. Wittkower.* 1967, 40ff.

Breitenbach, E. "Israhel van Meckenem's Man of Sorrows." *Quarterly Journal of the Library of Congress,* Washington, D.C., 1974, 21ff.

Bulst, W. *Das Grabtuch von Turin.* Frankfurt, 1952.

Dobrzeniecki (see Literature Cited in Abbreviated Form).

Endres, J.A. "Die Darstellung der Gregormesse im Mittelalter." *Zeitschrift für Christliche Kunst,* 30 (1917), 150ff.

Mayer, A.L. "Das Grabtuch von Turin als typisches Beispiel spätmittelalterlicher Schaudevotion." *Archiv für Liturgiewissenschaft,* 4.2 (1956), 348ff.

Mersman, G. *Der Schmerzensmann.* Düsseldorf, 1952.

Osten, G.v.d. *Der Schmerzensmann. Typengeschichte eines deutschen Andachtsbilds von 1300–1600.* Berlin, 1935.

———. "Job and Christ. The Development of the Devotional Image." *Journal of the Warburg and Courtauld Institutes,* 16 (1953), 153ff.

Panofsky (see Literature Cited in Abbreviated Form).

Ringbom (see Literature Cited in Abbreviated Form).

Schrade, H. "Beiträge zur Erklärung des Schmerzensmannsbildes." In *Deutschkundliches, F. Panzer zum 60. Geburtstag.* Heidelberg, 1930, 164ff.

Stubblebine, J. "Segna di Buonaventura and the Image of the Man of Sorrows." *Gesta,* 8.2 (1969), 3ff.

Suckale (see Literature Cited in Abbreviated Form).

Thomas, A. "Das Urbild der Gregoriusmesse." *Rivista di Archeologia Cristiana,* 10 (1933), 51ff.

Van Os (see Literature Cited in Abbreviated Form).

Vetter (see Literature Cited in Abbreviated Form).

Vetter, "Iconografia" (see Literature Cited in Abbreviated Form).

Wentzel, H. "Das Turiner Leichentuch Christi und das Kreuzigungsbild des Landgrafenpsalters." *Neue Beiträge z. Archäologie und Kunstgeschichte Schwabens.* Stuttgart, 1952.

Byzantium and the East

Bauerreis, R. "Basileus tes Doxes. Ein frühes eucharistisches Bild und seine

Auswirkung." *Pro Mundi Vita. Festschrift zum Eucharistischen Weltkongress.* Munich, 1960, 49ff.

Dobrzeniecki (see Literature Cited in Abbreviated Form).

Dufrenne, S. "Images du décor de la Prothèse." *Revue des Études Byzantines*, 26 (1968), 297ff.

Gamber, K. "Misericordia Domini. Vom Prothesisbild der Ostkirche zum mittelalterlichen Erbärmdechristus." *Deutsche Gaue*, 46 (1954), 46ff.

Grigoriadou-Cabagnols, H. "Le décor de l'église de Samari." *Cahiers Archéologiques*, 20 (1970), 182ff.

Hamann-MacLean, R. *Grundlegung zu einer Geschichte der mittelalterlichen Monumentalmalerei in Serbien und Makedonien.* Giessen, 1976, 62ff.

Millet, G. *Recherches sur l'iconographie de l'évangile.* Paris, 1916, 483ff.

Pallas (see Literature Cited in Abbreviated Form).

Van Os (see Literature Cited in Abbreviated Form).

Xyngopoulos, A. "Byzantinai eikones en Meteorois." *Archaiologikon Deltion*, 10 (1926), 37ff.

Italy

Bertelli (see under "General and on the Image of S. Croce," above).

Campana, A. "Notizie sulla 'pietà' riminese di Giov. Bellini." In *Scritti di storia dell'arte in onore di M. Salmi.* II, 405ff. Rome, 1962.

Dvorak, J. "Eine Studie eines römischen Reliefs von Giambellino." *Umeni*, 16 (1968), 348ff.

Eisler, C. "The Golden Christ of Cortona and the Man of Sorrows in Italy." *Art Bulletin*, 51 (1969), 107ff. and 233ff.

Horster, M. "Mantuae Sanguis Preciosus." *Wallraf-Richartz-Jahrbuch*, 25 (1963), 151ff.

Meiss, M. *Painting in Florence and Siena after the Black Death.* Princeton, 1951.

———. "An Early Altarpiece from the Cathedral of Florence." *Metropolitan Museum of Art Bulletin*, 12 (1954), 302ff.

———. *French Painting in the Time of Jean de Berry. The Late Fourteenth Century and the Patronage of the Duke.* 1967.

Panofsky (see Literature Cited in Abbreviated Form).

Spencer, J.R. "The Lament at the Tomb by Filippino Lippi." *Allen Memorial Art Museum*, 24 (1966), 24ff.

Stubblebine (see under "General and on the Image of S. Croce," above).

Vayer, L. "L'imago pietatis di Lorenzo Ghiberti." *Acta Historiae Artium*, 8 (1962), 45ff.

Central Europe

Bauerreiss (see under "General and on the Image of S. Croce" and "Byzantium and the East," above).

Berliner (see Literature Cited in Abbreviated Form).

Dijon: le Christ de pitié en Brabant-Bourgogne autour de 1500. Dijon, 1971.

Miodonska, B. "The Optovice Breviary. An Unknown Czech Manuscript of the Fourteenth Century." *Umeni*, 16 (1968), 213ff.

————. "Der Schmerzensmann aus Gressau." *Festschrift T. Müller.* 1965, 101ff.
Sterling, C. "Jean Hey le Maître de Moulin." *Revue de l'Art,* 1 (1928), 27ff
Suckale (see Literature Cited in Abbreviated Form).
Troescher, G. "Die 'Pitié-de-Nostre-Seigneur' oder 'Notgottes'." *Wallraf-Richartz-Jahrbuch,* 9 (1936), 148ff.
Vetter (see Literature Cited in Abbreviated Form).

Bibliography on the Devotional Image

Aurenhammer, H. *Die Mariengnadenbilder Wiens und Niederösterreichs in der Barockzeit.*
Baron, F. In *Bull. Monum.,* 126 (1968), 141ff. On the late Gothic votive statues in France.
Baxandall (see Literature Cited in Abbreviated Form).
Berliner (see Literature Cited in Abbreviated Form).
Berliner, "Arma" (see Literature Cited in Abbreviated Form).
Il dolore e la morte nella spiritualità dei sec. XII e XIII. Centro Studi Spiritualità Medievale in Todi, Convegno V. 1967.
Dürig, W. *Imago. Ein Beitrag zur Terminologie und Theologie der römischen Liturgie.* Munich, 1952.
Fritz, R. "Das Halbfigurenbild in der westdeutschen Tafelmalerei um 1400." *Zeitschrift für Kunstwissenschaft,* 5 (1951), 161ff.
Garrison, E.B. "A New Devotional Panel in Fourteenth Century Italy." *Marsyas,* 3 (1946), 15ff.
Guardini, R. *Kultbild und Andachtsbild. Brief an einen Kunsthistoriker.* Würzburg, 1939.
Haussherr, R. "Über die Christus-Johannes-Gruppen. Zum Problem 'Andachtsbilder' und deutsche Mystik." *Beiträge zur Kunst des Mittelalters (Festschrift H. Wentzel).* Berlin, 1975, 79ff.
Füglister, R.L. *Das lebende Kreuz.* 1964.
Kantorowicz, E. "Ivories and Litanies." *Journal of the Warburg and Courtauld Institutes,* 5 (1942), 56ff.
Kermer (see Literature Cited in Abbreviated Form).
Klein, D. *Reallexikon der deutschen Kunstgeschichte,* I, 681.
Kluckert, E. *Die Erzählform des spätmittelalterlichen Simultanbildes.* Tübingen, 1974.
Krönig, W. "Rheinische Vesperbilder aus Leder und ihr Umkreis." *Wallraf-Richartz-Jahrbuch,* 24 (1962), 97ff.
Labrot, G. "Un type de message figuratif: l'image pieuse." *Mélanges d'archéologie et d'histoire* (École française de Rome), 78 (1966), 595ff.
Lachner, E. "Devotionsbild." *Reallexikon der deutschen Kunstgeschichte,* III, 1367ff.
Mayer, A.L. "Die Liturgie und der Geist der Gotik." *Jahrbuch für Liturgiewissenschaft,* 6 (1926), 68ff.
Meiss (see Literature Cited in Abbreviated Form).
Meiss, M. "The Madonna of Humility." *Art Bulletin,* 18 (1936), 435ff.
————. "An Early Altarpiece from the Cathedral of Florence." *Metropolitan Museum of Art Bulletin,* 12 (1954), 302ff.
Osten, G.v.d. *Der Schmerzensmann.* Berlin, 1935.

Pächt, O. "Die Gotik der Zeit um 1400 als gesamteuropäische Kunstsprache." *Europäische Kunst um 1400* (catalogue). Vienna, 1962.

Panofsky (see Literature Cited in Abbreviated Form).

Paulus, H. "Andachtsbild." *Religion in Geschichte und Gegenwart*, I (1957), 363ff.

Pfaff, R.W. *New Liturgical Feasts in Later Medieval England*. Oxford, 1970.

Pinder, W. "Die dichterische Wurzel der Pieta." *Repertorium für Kunstwissenschaft*, 42 (1920), 145ff.

Post, R.R. *De moderne Devotie*. Amsterdam, 1950.

Previtali, G. "Il 'Bambino Gesù' come 'imagine devozionale' nella scultura italiana del Trecento." *Paragone. Arte*, 249 (1970), 31ff.

Rapp, U. *Das Mysterienbild*. Würzburg, 1952.

Ringbom (see Literature Cited in Abbreviated Form).

Ringbom, S. "Devotional Images and Imaginative Devotions." *Gazette des Beaux-Arts* 73 (1969), 159ff.

Röhrig, F. "Pietà." *Lexikon für Theologie und Kirche*. VIII, 497f.

Rosenberg, A. *Die christliche Bildmeditation*. 1955.

Scharfe, M. *Evangelische Andachtsbilder*. Stuttgart, 1968.

Schlegel, U. "A Christ-Child by A. Lorenzetti." *Art Bulletin*, 52 (1970), 1ff.

Schmidt (see Literature Cited in Abbreviated Form).

Schuck, J. *Das religiöse Erlebnis bei Bernhard von Clairvaux*. Würzburg, 1922.

Schorr, D.C. "The Mourning Virgin and St. John." *Art Bulletin*, 22 (1940), 61ff.

―――. *The Christ Child in Devotional Images in Italy during the Fourteenth Century*. New York, 1954.

von Simson (see Literature Cited in Abbreviated Form).

Smith, M.T. "The Use of Grisaille as a Lenten Observance." *Marsyas*, 8 (1959), 43ff.

Spanner, A. *Das kleine Andachtsbild*. 1930.

Stadlhuber, J. "Das Laienstundengebet vom Leiden Christi in seinem mittelalterlichen Fortleben." *Zeitschrift für katholische Theologie*, 72 (1950), 282ff.

Stuebe, I.C. "The Johannisschüssel: From Narrative to Reliquary to Andachtsbild." *Marsyas*, 14 (1969), 1ff.

Suckale (see Literature Cited in Abbreviated Form).

Swarzenski, H. "Quellen zum deutschen Andachtsbild." *Zeitschrift für Kunstwissenschaft*, 4 (1935), 141ff.

Teuber-Weckersdorff, C. *Das Diptychon als kunsthistorisches Problem*. Dissertation, Innsbruck, 1956.

Thomas, A. "Vesperbild." *Lexikon für Theologie und Kirche*. X, 755.

Ulbert-Schede, U. *Das Andachtsbild des kreuztragenden Christus in der deutschen Kunst*. Munich, 1968.

Vetter (see Literature Cited in Abbreviated Form).

Wentzel, H. "Christkind." *Reallexikon für deutsche Kunstgeschichte*. III, 590ff.

―――. "Eine Wiener Christkindwiege in München und das Jesuskind der Margaretha Ebner." *Pantheon* 18 (1960), 276ff.

―――. "Ein Elfenbeinbüchlein zur Passionsandacht." *Wallraf-Richartz-Jahrbuch*, 24 (1962), 193ff.

Wiegand, E. *Die böhmischen Gnadenbilder*. Würzburg, 1936.

List of Art Works
Especially Mentioned in the Text

No. 1

Altenburg, Staatliches Lindenau Museum, inv. 47, 48.

Diptych by P. Lorenzetti, 1330 (each panel 29.2 x 19.9 cm). Left panel shows the Virgin and Child; the right shows the Imago Pietatis in a tomb with hands crossed downward.

R. Oertel, *Frühe italienische Malerei in Altenburg* (Berlin, 1961), 68f.

No. 2 (fig. 31)

Berlin, Staatliche Museen, Skulpturenabteilung, inv. 32.

Epistle lectern by Giovanni Pisano (34 x 46 cm, Carrara marble) from the pulpit in Pistoia. An Imago Pietatis held in the shroud by two full-length angels. Acquired in Pisa in 1881.

Bildwerke der christlichen Epochen (catalogue) (Munich, 1966), no. 301, with further literature; H. Schrade, "Beiträge zur Erklärung des Schmerzensmannsbildes," in *Deutschkundliches, F. Panzer zum 60. Geburtstag* (Heidelberg, 1930), 176f.; P. Bacci, *La ricostruzione del pergamo di G. Pisano nel duomo di Pisa* (Pisa, 1926), 105; W. Braunfels, "Zur Gestalt-Ikonographie der Kanzeln des N. und G. Pisano," *Das Münster*, 2 (1949), 321ff.; W. Mersman, *Das Schmerzensmann* (Düsseldorf, 1952), XIIIf.; M. Seidel, *G. Pisano: Il pulpito di Pistoia* (Florence, 1965); H. Kloter, "Ein Bildwerk aus der Hütte des G. Pisano," *Jahrbuch der Berliner Museen*, N.F. 7 (1965), 157ff.; G. Jászai, *Die Pisaner Domkanzel*, Dissertation, Munich, 1968; Vetter, 219; C. Gomez-Moreno, in *Metropolitan Museum Journal*, 5 (1972), 71.

No. 3 (fig. 23)

Berlin, Staatliche Museen, Gemäldegalerie, inv. 4.

Panel (68 x 86 cm) by G. Bellini, in profile. Frame (ca. 1500). Three-figured Lamentation, with the Virgin and St. John.

F. Heinemann, *Giovanni Bellini e i Belliniani* (1962), cat. 168, pl. 85; Ringbom, 82, 108f.; G. Robertson, *Giovanni Bellini* (Oxford, 1968), 98; and N. Huse, *Studien zu Giovanni Bellini* (Berlin, 1972), 81.

No. 4 (fig. 18)

Bologna, Bibl. Comm. dell'Archiginnasio. Fondo Osped. 3, MS 52, fol. 1. Invent. Soc. delle Laudi di Noxadella (1329).

The Virgin of Mercy. In the illuminated capital letter "I," the Imago Pietatis with horizontal arms in the sarcophagus.

M. Salmi, "La miniatura," in D. Fava, ed., *Tesori Bibl. d'Italia: Emilia e Romangna* (1932), 300; C. Mesini, "La Compagnia di S. M. d. Laudi e di S. Francesco di Bologna,"·*Archivum Franciscan. Historicum,* 52 (1959), 361 ff.; M. Fanti, "Il 'Fondo Ospedle' n. Bibl. Com. dell'Archiginnasio," *L'Archiginnasio,* 58 (1963), 1ff.; and C. Belting-Ihm, *Sub matris tutela. Untersuchungen zur Vorgeschichte der Schutzmantelmadonna,* Heidelberger Akademie der Wissenschaften, Abhandlungen (1976), illus. 1.

No. 5

Bologna, Pinacoteca Nazionale.

Polyptych (167 x 218 cm) by Giotto (signed) from S. Maria degli Angeli (ca. 1330). In the center of the predella, a tondo with the Imago Pietatis between the tondi of the Virgin and the evangelist John (inside), and of John the Baptist and Magdalene (outside). Christ on a blue field, with a deathlike pallor, glazed eyes, and open mouth.

A. Emiliani, *La Pinacoteca Nazionale di Bologna* (Bologna, 1967), nos. 62–64, with bibliography.

No. 6 (fig. 101)

Brussels, Stoclet Collection

Venetian panel (32 x 22.5 cm) from around 1300. An Imago Pietatis with arms crossed over the breast, in front of a cross with a red inscription plaque and two lamenting angels on a golden field. Tempera on wood. Hinge marks from the other half of the diptych visible on the molding of the frame to the left.

R. von Marle, "Italian Paintings of the Thirteenth Century in the Collection M.A. Stoclet in Brussels," *Pantheon,* 4 (1931), 316ff.; Garrison, no. 267; D. Lion-Goldschmidt, *La Collection A. Stoclet* (Brussels, 1956), 7 and colorplate on p. 5; Pallucchini, 63 and illus. 206; Kermer, no. 76 and illus. 95.

No. 7 (fig. 80)

Cambridge, Corpus Christi College, MS 26, fol. VII.

Matthew Paris, *Historia maior* (St. Albans, mid-thirteenth century). Drawing at the end of the text showing the Imago Pietatis in bust, together with a Virgin with her

Child and a veronica, both half-length. See also Chapter VI, note 3.

M.R. James, *The Drawings of Matthew Paris*, The Walpole Society, vol. 14 (Oxford, 1926), no. 25, pl. IV; R. Vaughan, *Matthew Paris* (Cambridge, 1958); Ringbom, 66 note 57, and 70; Dobschütz, 294*, 297*; and K. Gould, *The Psalter and Hours of Yolande of Soissons* (Medieval Academy of America, 1978), 81ff.

No. 8 (fig. 25)

Cambridge, Mass., Fogg Art Museum, inv. 1927.306.

The so-called *Fogg Pietà* (second quarter of fourteenth century) (43 x 50 cm), Florentine. Multi-figured Lamentation beneath the cross with a five-figured main group in which the Virgin and Christ are emphasized as an independent motif. Chromatic richness of muted, pale colors.

R. Fremantle, *Florentine Gothic Painters from Giotto to Masaccio* (London, 1975), 105ff. with bibliography, and illus. 211.

No. 9 (fig. 29)

Cambridge, Mass., Fogg Art Museum, inv. 1937.49.

Formerly of the Winthrop Collection, New York. Panel (ca. 62 x 38 cm, frame detached) attributed to Roberto di Oderisio (ca. 1355). Tempera on wood. An Imago Pietatis wearing the Crown of Thorns and pointing to the wound in his side, in a sarcophagus between the Virgin and John, amid the *arma* on a dark blue field.

A. Quintavalle, "Un dipinto giovanile di R. d'Oderisio," *Boll. d'Arte*, 26 (1932–33), 232ff.; and F. Bologna, *I pittori alla Corte Angioina di Napoli 1266–1414* (Rome, 1969), 301ff., pl. VII, 30, 31.

No. 10

Cividale, Museo Archeol. Nazionale, MS 86, fol. 167 (39 x 25.6 cm).

Roman missal (ca. 1254) for a church in the patriarchate of Aquileia, probably the cathedral in Cividale. In the illuminated "T," the Imago Pietatis with crossed arms.

A. Santangelo, *Catal. delle cose d'arte e di antichità d'Italia: Cividale* (1936), 139ff.; A. Ebner, *Quellen und Forschungen zur Geschichte und Kunstgeschichte des Missale Rom im Mittelalter* (1896), 23: Vetter, 199; G.C. Menis, *La miniatura in Friuli: Catal. Udine* (Milan, 1972), no. 12 and illus. p. 86; P. Tosca, *Il medioevo* (1927), 1092.

No. 11 (fig. 15)

Empoli, Collegiata, inv. 95.

Fresco by Masolino. The Imago Pietatis in a sarcophagus between the Virgin and

John, who grasp the outspread arms. In the background, the cross on which scourges hang. In the pediment, the Vera Icon.

R. Fremantle, *Florentine Gothic Painters from Giotto to Masaccio* (London, 1975), 492, illus. 1027.

No. 12 (fig. 38)

Florence, Bibl. Med. Laur., MS Plut. XXV.3, fol. 183v, 376v (26.8 x 18.8 cm).

Supplicationes variae for a Minorite circle in Genoa, produced ca. 1293–1300 in Emilia (?). Fol. 183v: Imago Pietatis with crossed arms before the cross, in a border of interlaced foliage in the lower margin. Fol. 376v: An Imago Pietatis with horizontally folded arms (full-page wash drawing).

A.M. Ciaranfi, in *Riv. R. Istituto d'Archeol. e Storia dell'Arte*, 1 (1929), 325ff.; B. Degenhart and A. Schmitt, *Corpus der italienischen Zeichnungen 1300–1450: Teil I* (Berlin, 1968), no. 3, p. 7ff.; Dobrzeniecki, 17; Vetter, 179, 198; A. Neff, "A New Interpretation of the Supplicationes Variae Miniatures," in *Atti XXIV. Congr. internaz. Storia dell'Arte*, 1979 (Milan, 1980), II, 173ff.

No. 13 (fig. 5)

Florence, Accademia, inv. 8467.

Panel (122 x 58 cm) by Giovanni da Milano (1365). On the lower frame between the coats of arms of the Strozzi and the Rinieri, the inscription: "Io govani da melano depinsi questa tavola i MCCCLXV." Four-figured Lamentation with the Virgin, the evangelist John, and Magdalene. Dark and muted colors. Golden ground.

G.L. Calvi, *Notizie dei principali...pittori...in Milano* (Milan, 1859), 37ff.; A. Marabottini, *Giovanni da Milano* (Florence, 1950), 53ff.; L. Marcucci, *Dipinta toscani del sec. XIV* (Florence, 1965), 86ff. and illus. 49; M. Boskovits, "Giovanni da Milano," *I diamanti dell'arte* 13 (1966), 26f.; R. Longhi, *Giudizio sul Duecento e ricerche sul Trecento nell'Italia centrale*, Opere complete VII (1974), 178f.

No. 14 (fig. 10)

Florence, Museo Horne, inv. 55/56.

Diptych (each panel 28 x 25 cm) from Castiglione Fiorentino. Originated in circle of painters around Barna (previously attributed to Simone Martini). Contemporary inscription on the exterior: "tavoletta di misser Giogio di Tommaso." An Imago Pietatis with bleeding wounds in a sarcophagus on a golden ground.

F. Rossi, *Il Museo Horne a Firenze* (Milan, 1967), 137 and illus. 26; Kermer, no. 23 and illus. 34.

No. 15 (fig. 74)

Gradac (Serbia), monastery church

Fresco in the right side-apse (diakonikon), ca. 1271. An Imago Pietatis before the cross on a golden ground, counterpart of a figure of the Virgin in the prothesis.

G. Millet and A. Frolow, *La peinture serbe au moyen âge*, II (Paris, 1957), pls. 50.2 and 51.4; Pallas, 208, 219ff., and 262ff.; R. Hamann-MacLean, *Grundlegung zu einer Geschichte der mittelalterlichen Monumentalmalerei in Serbien und Makedonien* (Giessen, 1976), 64f., 340, 342, and pl. 46b.

No. 16 (fig. 12)

The Hague, private collection, on temporary loan to the S. v. Gijn Mus., Dordrecht.

Venetian triptych (20.1 x 49 cm), second quarter of fourteenth century. Imago Pietatis between the Virgin and the evangelist John (both half-length) on a golden ground. On the exterior sides, a donor scene with St. Dominic (?).

H.W. van Os, "The Discovery of an Early Man of Sorrows on a Dominican Triptych," *Journal of the Warburg and Courtauld Institutes*, 41 (1978), 65ff.

No. 17 (fig. 70)

Jerusalem, Greek Patriarchate.

Gold and enamel icon mounting (39 x 32 cm), Byzantine, beginning of twelfth century. Bust of the Imago Pietatis before the cross and between two lamenting angels. Inscription: "Basileus tes doxes." Frame with enamels of later date. Sent to Jerusalem in 1777 as a gift by a Georgian prince (holding the same painting as now).

W. Mersmann, *Der Schmerzensmann* (Düsseldorf, 1952), VII, XXXIII; M. C. Ross, in *Byzantine Art—A European Art* (catalogue) (Athens, 1964), no. 475; Pallas, 204ff., 244ff.; K. Wessel, *Die Byzantinsiche Emailkunst* (1967), 170ff., no. 53.

No. 18 (fig. 8)

Karlsruhe, Staatliche Kunsthalle, inv. 2431 a/b.

Bohemian diptych (each panel 25 x 18.5 cm), ca. 1360. On the left panel, the Virgin with her Child; on the other, the Imago Pietatis with horizontally crossed arms on a golden ground.

J. Lauts, *Kunsthalle Karlsruhe: Katalog Alte Gemälde bis 1800* (1966), I, 55ff. with bibliography, and II, illus. p. 23.

No. 19 (figs. 49–50)

Kastoria

Two-sided icon, Byzantine, twelfth century. On the obverse side, an Imago Pietatis with horizontally crossed arms before the beams of a cross. On the reverse side, the Virgin and Child. In each spandrel, the bust of an angel.

M. Chatzidakis, in *Actes du XV Congrès international d'études byzantines*, Rapport III. 1. B (Athens, 1976), 184f., pl. XXXVII a/b.

No. 20 (fig. 24)

Milan, Brera, inv. 214.

Panel (86 x 107 cm) by Giovanni Bellini, ca. 1470. Three-figured Lamentation showing the Virgin and John before a landscape. Inscription: "Haec fere quum gemitus turgentia lumina promant / Bellini poterat flere Joannis opus."

F. Heinemann, *Giovanni Bellini e i Belliniani* (Venice, 1962), cat. 160; A. Campana, in *Scritti di storia dell'Arte M. Salmi* (Rome, 1962), II, 405ff.; Z. Wazbinski, in *Bulletin Musée Nationale de Varsovie*, 5.2 (1964), 39ff.; Ringbom, 82, 108ff.; G. Robertson, *Giovanni Bellini* (Oxford, 1968), see index; and N. Huse, *Studien zu Giovanni Bellini* (Berlin, 1972), 14ff.

No. 21 (fig. 99)

Milan, U. Hoepli Collection.

Folio from a book of Gregorian chants (50 x 36.5 cm) with the Easter antiphon. From central Italy, mid-thirteenth century. A Imago Pietatis with horizontally crossed arms is shown in an illuminated "R" ("Resurrexi et adhuc...").

P. Toesca, *Monumenti e studi per la storia d. miniatura: la coll. U. Hoepli* (Milan, 1930), 24, no. XVI, pl. XI.

No. 22 (fig. 59–60)

Meteora, Greece. Monastery of the Transfiguration.

Diptych icon (27 x 21 and 22 x 19 cm), Byzantine, end of 14th c. An Imago Pietatis before the cross; on the other panel, the lamenting Virgin.

A. Xyngopoulos, in *Archaiologikon Deltion*, 10 (1926 [1929]), 37ff. (fundamental); *Byzantine Art—A European Art* (catalogue) (Athens, 1964), no. 210; Pallas, 198ff.; M. Chatzidakis, in K. Weitzmann et al., *Frühe Ikonen* (1965), pls. 62–63; Kermer, no. 11, illus. 17.

No. 23 (fig. 106)

Mosciano near Florence, S. Andrea.

Fresco, end of thirteenth century. Above a curtain there appears an Imago Pietatis with horizontally folded arms between the Virgin and John (?).

Photograph: Soprintendenza Firenze, no. 127906.

No. 24 (fig. 62)

Moscow, Tretjakov Gallery, inv. 28834.

Part of a diptych icon (43 x 31 cm), Byzantine, thirteenth to fourteenth century. Shows the lamenting Virgin.

V.I. Antonova and N.E. Mneva, *Katalog drevnerusskoj zhivopisi Gosud. Tretjakovsk. Gall.* (Moscow, 1963), I, no. 326; *Iskusstvo Vizantii v Sobranijach SSR* (catalogue) (Moscow, 1977), no. 952.

No. 25 (fig. 102)

Moscow, Tretjakov Gallery, inv. 22944

Icon (109.5 x 93 cm), Serbian (?), fourteenth century. Shows an Imago Pietatis with arms crossed on the breast before a cross with a Slavic inscription: "Car Slavie" (Basileus tes doxes).

Antonova and Mneva (see no. 24), I, no. 337; and the catalogue *Iskusstvo* (see no. 24), no. 975.

No. 26 (fig. 41)

New York, Metropolitan Museum, inv. 06.180.

Panel by Michele Giambono (54.9 x 38.8 cm), Venice, ca. 1425–30. An Imago Pietatis in a marble sarcophagus with a corporal. Outstretched arms. Cross with three nails on a golden ground. At the left St. Francis is shown receiving the stigmata. Plastically applied drops of blood.

N.E. Land, *Michele Giambono: A catalogue raisonnée,* Dissertation, University of Virginia, 1974, 151, cat. 6, with bibliography.

No. 27

Nicosia (Cyprus), Patriarchate (Phaneromeni).

Icon (259 x 43 cm) of Hagia Paraskeve with a medallion showing the Imago Pietatis.

D.T. Rice, *The Icons of Cyprus* (London, 1937), no. 8; A. Papageorgiou, *Icons of Cyprus* (Geneva, 1969), 92, pl. p. 38; Pallas, 200f.

No. 28 (fig. 109)

Parma, baptistery.

Fresco in the northwest apse. Two-figured Lamentation with a tomb (early fourteenth century). Banderole in front of the Imago Pietatis with inscription: "Hic semper, dum transis, recolle Tui vulnera regis qui te degegtum [*sic*] vocat ad hectera letum." Two prophets holding scrolls with verses from Zachariah 13:6 and Isaiah

53:5. Under the image the inscription: "MCCCL...Boni...grisma."

L. Test, *Le Baptistère de Parme, son histoire, son architecture, ses sculptures, ses peintures* (Florence, 1916), 256ff., illus. 212; and M. Meiss, "The Problem of F. Traini," *Art Bulletin*, 15 (1933), 144f.

No. 29 (fig. 100)

Pisa, cathedral.

Epistle lectern (height 51 cm) by Giovanni Pisano, from the cathedral pulpit. Shows an Imago Pietatis held in the shroud by angels; below are depicted people who are being resurrected.

R. Papini, *Pisa. Catal. d. cose d'arte*, ser. I, fasc. II.2, 148f., no. 278.; P. Bacci, *La ricostruzione del pergamo di G. Pisano nel Duomo di Pisa* (Milan, 1926), 105; and E. Carli, *Il pergamo del duomo di Pisa* (Pisa, 1975), 32 and pl. 101. See also the bibliography for No. 2 above.

No. 30

Pisa, Museo Nazionale.

Polyptych by Simone Martini from S. Caterina (1320). An Imago Pietatis is shown between the Virgin and St. Mark, in the tomb with a burial shroud, in the center of the predella (35 x 64 cm).

Hager, 114; E. Carli, *Il museo di Pisa* (Pisa, 1974), 51ff., illus. 58, pl. X, with bibliography; G. Contini, *L'opera completa di Simone Martini*, Classici dell'Arte Rizzoli (1970), no. 3.

No. 31 (fig. 14)

Rome, San Croce in Gerusalemme.

Mosaic icon (19 x 13 cm; 28 x 23 cm with frame) of the Imago Pietatis with folded arms (before a cross with the inscription: "Basileus tes doxes"), Byzantine, ca. 1300. On the reverse side, St. Catherine in full-figure.

C. Bertelli, "The 'Image of Pity' in San Croce in Gerusalemme," in *Essays in the History of Art Presented to R. Wittkower* (London, 1967), 40ff., with bibliography (fundamental); Pallas, 209f.; Ringbom, 29, 66, 126; E. Breitenbach, "I. von Meckenem's Man of Sorrows," *Quarterly Journal of the Library of Congress* (1974), 21ff.

No. 32 (fig. 73)

Tatarna (Tripotamon, Greece). Church of the Birth of the Virgin.

Mosaic icon (17.5 x 12 cm) of the Imago Pietatis (before a cross with the inscription: "Basileus tes doxes"), Byzantine, ca. 1300.

A. Xyngopoulos, in *Byzantine Art—A European Art* (catalogue) (Athens, 1964), no. 167; M. Chatzidakis, in K. Weitzmann et al., *Frühe Ikonen* (1965), XXVIII, and pl. 48; Pallas; Bertelli (see no. 31 above), 41f.

No. 33 (fig. 103)

Torcello, Museum.

Venetian panel (41 x 43 cm) with the Imago Pietatis before the cross. Two lamenting angels above, the Virgin and John below, on a vermillion ground. Black, profiled frame.

Garrison, no. 152; Pallucchini, 63 and illus. 205; *Venezia e Bisanzio* (catalogue) (Venice, 1974), no. 82; *Museo di Torcello* (catalogue) (1978), no. 56 with colorplate.

No. 34 (fig. 13)

Trieste, Museo Civico.

Triptych from the atelier of Paolo Veneziano (ca. 1328–30). On the upper register of the right wing, the Imago Pietatis in a sarcophagus before the cross.

Garrison, no. 388; M. Walcher Casotti, *Il trittico di S. Chiara di Trieste e l'orientamento paleologo nell'arte di P. Veneziano* (Trieste, 1961); Pallucchini, 25f., illus., 36, 39; L.R. Loseri, ed., *Pittura su tavola dalle collez. dei Mus. Civici ed Arte di Trieste* (Milan, 1975), sec. II, cat. 1, pl. 1c.

No. 35 (fig. 11)

Venice, San Marco

Pala Feriale (119 x 322 cm; individual panels 56 x 42.4 cm) by Paolo Veneziano and his sons, 1343–1345. In the center of the upper register, the Imago Pietatis is shown between the Mater Dolorosa and the evangelist John (depicted as the Byzantine apostle type).

H.R. Hahnloser, ed., *Il Tesoro di S. Marco, I: La Pala d'Oro* (Florence, 1965), 115ff. and pl.; *Venezia e Bisanzio* (catalogue) (Venice, 1974), no. 89 with bibliography.

No. 36 (fig. 97)

Venice, Museo Correr.

Breviary from Spalato. Pocketbook made of folded folios (opened 15.5 x 16.5 cm; folded together 15.5 x 4 cm) in the form of a small pad (1291). On fol. XXXIII (between the Easter tables beginning in 1291 and the evangelist John), the Imago Pietatis appears between two angels on a golden ground.

Pallucchini, illus. 12.

List of Art Works 283

No. 37

Vienna, Österreichische Staatsbibliothek, cod. 1898, fol. 14v.

Psalter (19.2 x 14 cm), Paduan (?), ca. 1270. In the illuminated "Beatus Vir" the Imago Pietatis appears, with a loincloth clumsily elongated downwards.

Vetter, 199, illus. 3; I. Hänsel, "Die Miniaturmalerei einer Paduaner Malerschule im Ducento," *Jahrbuch der österreichischen byzantinischen Gesellschaft,* 2 (1952), 111f., illus. 15.

Index

*Page numbers in roman refer to text, in italic to illustrations.

Ghirlandaio, Domenico
Birmingham, *183*
Blickaustausch. *See* Neumeyer, A.
Blue Cross Master. *See under* Cross, painted
Bohemia, 29–32, 38, 168
   diptych (Karlsruhe), 2, 29, *30–31*, 32, 168,
     176, 194, 279
Bologna, *13*, 34, *45*, *85*, *89*, *138*, 276
Book illumination
   Book of Hours of Johanna of Naples
     (Vienna), *206*
   Book of Hours of Yolande of Soissons
     (New York), *63–64*
   breviary from Spalato (Venice), *166–167*,
     170, 283
   choir book (Milan), *169*, 280
   devotion and forms of, 14, 56
   Franciscan devotional book (Florence),
     35, 142–143, 166, 170, 179
   gospel manuscript from Karahissar
     (Leningrad), *104–105*, 108, 120
   miniatures, 35
   Octoechos miniature (Messina), *112*,
     115–116
   Roman missal (Cividale), 277
   statutes from a brotherhood, frontispiece
     (Bologna), 58, *138*–141
   The Virgin of Mercy (Bologna), 43, *45*,
     276
   Trinity miniature (Vienna), 3, 6
Boston, 77
Bourges, *81*
Bread, the living, 194
Brigitta of Sweden, 165
Brotherhoods, lay, 7, 18, 22, 24–25, 58, 78,
    133, *138*–142
   image symbolism and, 217–218
   Laudesi, *38*, 139
   Passion plays and, 75, 156–160
   sermons and, 162
   See also Orders, religious
Brugge diptych (London), 56, *57*
Brussels, *175*
Budapest, *11*
Byzantine art
   impact in Italy, 41–43, 215–217
   impact in Northern Europe, 33, 156,
     167–168, 218
Byzantine mosaic icon San Croce in
    Gerusalemme (Rome), 23, *39*, 60,

106, 109–110, 122–123, 131, 184,
   191–192, 216, 282
Byzantine Patriarchs, 101–103

Cambridge (Mass.), 54, *134–135*
Canons. *See* Music
Case study form and function relationship,
   43–52
Case study. *See* Research
Cavallini, school of fresco (Naples), *161*–162
Charles IV of Bohemia, 29–32, 168
Charles V, 78
Chartres, 204
Christ and Mary. *See* Mary
Christmas liturgy, 113
Christus patiens, 144–145, 170
Christus, Petrus triptych with donor portrait
   (Washington), 23, *55–56*
Cividale, *155*, 166, 169
   Planctus of, 86, 152, 155, 159–160,
    199–200
Clerical plays. *See* Drama, religious
Close-up views
   in literature, 165
   See also Portrait forms
Cloth-borne images. *See* Epitaphios
Cologne, *193*
Color variations, 180
Communion. *See* Liturgy, Western
Compasio. See Pity
Comte De Riant, 205
Confraternities. *See* Brotherhoods
Constantinople, 101, 105
   1204 conquest and pillaging of, 120–121,
    132, 203, 211
   relics traffic from, 132–133, 203–205
Contexts of images, Eastern. *See* Easter
    Passion, Byzantine; Liturgy, Eastern
Contexts of images, Western
   corporate sphere, 133–138, 141–142
   family devotions, 22–23
   Italian panel painting development and
    the, 1–2, 216–217
   lay brotherhoods, 7, 18, 22, 24–25, 58, 75,
    78, 133, 138–142, 156–160, 162, 217
   liturgical, 132–138, 141–142
   mendicant orders, 7, 58, 133–138
   political, 18, 22, 25, 205
   private sphere, 22, 56–57, 138–143
   See also Cult image functions

The Image and Its Public

The Image and Its Public

soteriological aspects, 65ff., 118–119,
187–188
structural change stages of, 177, 181
Threnos symbolism and, 98–100, 114
universal formula and variable context,
197
Veronica images and, 132–133
as visible expression of ritual functions,
107–108, 187–188
See also Research, art historical
Passion portraits (*Imago Pietatis*)
breviary, 166–*167*, 170, 283
illuminated "R" (Milan), *169*, 280
Meteora diptych icon, *107*, 109, 111, 280
Passion relics. *See* Relics
Passion, stations of. *See* Stations of the
Passion
Passion story applied to assassination,
200–201
Patriarchs, Byzantine, 101–103
Patronage, private, 26–27, *55*, *67*
donor inscriptions, 24, 127, 178
Pec, *108*
Pelagonitissa. *See* Mary
Perspective, single point, 16, 54
Perugia, 139
Pescia Descent from the Cross, S. Antonio,
73–75, 153–154
Petit tableau devotional practice and, 56
Philip von Schwaben, King, 208
Philippe Auguste of France, king, 206
Philosophical views
mysticism, 18, 56–57
Nominalism, 18
See also Cult image functions
Pictorial rhetoric. *See* Realism and pictorial
rhetoric; Viewers, roles of
Pietà
altar sculpture by Tommaso Piseno (Pisa),
60, *71*, 74, 181
angel (Paris), *70*, 74, 83, 168
with angels fresco (Rome), 84, *88*
panel by Giovanni da Milano (Paris), 84,
87
polyptych by Jacopino di Francesco,
85–87, *89*, 199
Pietà form, 52–53, *54*, 79–80, 84–86,
191–194, 199
with angels, *70–71*, 74
See also Mary, Mother and Son icons

Pietà, Master of the Fogg Lamentation
(Cambridge), 41, 45, 52–53, *54*, 277
Pietas concept, the, 3, 84–85, 191–194
Piety
lay, 24–25, 140
liturgical, 140, 143–144
Passion portrait painting and, 131,
184–185
pietas and, 172–174
popular, 133
See also Brotherhoods, lay
private, 24, 57–58
burial and, 110
icon use and, 26–27, 109–110, 181
official liturgy and, 23, 56, 91
public, 24, 143–144
mass-movement, 139
sermons and, 143–144, 161–164
See also Devotional image functions;
Orders, religious
Pilgrimage, 23, 82
economics and, 204
See also Crusaders
Pilz, W., 225
Pisa, 141
Tomb of Archbishop Scarlatti, *79–80*
Pisano, Giovanni
Pisa cathedral pulpit lectern, 170,
171–172, 282
Pistoia pulpit epistle lectern (Berlin), 35,
43, 60, 65–68, 78, 170–172, 213, 275
realism and pictorial rhetoric of, 65–68,
66, 84–85
Pisano, Giunta
Christus patiens painted cross (Bologna),
6, 12, *13*, 26, 144–145
painted cross (Assisi), 144–*145*, 168, 180
Piseno, Tommaso marble altar (Pisa), 60,
71, 74, 181
Pity, invitation to (*compasio*), 46, 58, 145,
162, 172–173, 191–194, 200
Plague of, 7, 1348
Plastanica, 99, 102, 124–128
Pocketbook, *167*, 283
Poetry. *See* Literature
Political aspects, 24, 139, 141
Popes. *See Names of individuals*
Portrait form, 38, 138

close-up, 5, 40, 50–51, 62, 91, *94*, 105,
169, 178

diachronic aspects, 4, 46, 128, 188
functional form identification, 40,
    54–55, 58–59, 60, 62, 64, 128,
    131–132, 141–143, 169
    scope of, 3–4
    summary, 187–189
Panofsky and, 41–56(*passim*), 131, 224
Ringbom and, 1–2, 45, 49–50, 56, 225
See also Bibliography; names of individual
    scholars
Rhetoric, religious
    Jeremiah 1:12 and, 197–201
    See also Realism and pictorial rhetoric
Ringbom, Sixten, 1–2, 225
    on devotional images and *Andachtsbild*,
    45, 49–50, 56
Rivalry of images. *See* Authenticity questions
Robert de Clari, 206, 215, 218.
Roberto di Oderisio Christ with *arma*
    (Fogg), 61–63, 85, 87, 277
Roeder, A., 171–172
Romania, 203
Rome, 95, 218
    Fresco from St. Paul Outside the Walls,
    84, 88
    S. Croce in Gerusalemme mosaic, 23, 39,
    60, 106, 109–110, 122–123, 131, 184,
    191–192, 216, 282
Royal gifts of relics, 205–206, 208

Sacramental images, 68–74, 72–73, 76–80,
    89, 99
Sainte Face panel (Laon), 220
Samari, 123
Sarcophagus pictorial motif, 34, 108, 123,
    169, 193
Saturday, Holy. *See* Easter Passion
Schmidt, G., 225
Schrade H., 170
Scourging, Christ's. *See* Stations of the
    Passion
Sculpture
    cult, 20
    Deposition groups (*Depositio Christi*),
    74–75, 143–144, 149–155, 168
    examples, 73, 148, 149, 151, 152, 153
    functions of, 1, 75–80, 155–156,
    159–161
    Epitaphios (Bourges), 80–81
    Imago Pietatis by Giovanni Pisano, 65–68,

66, 84–85, 170–172
    Imago Pietatis panel by Michele
    Giambono, 77–79, 146, 281
    Pietà by Tommaso Piseno (Pisa), 60, 71,
    74, 181
    tomb of Archbishop Scarlatti (Pisa),
    79–80
    trumeau figure relic symbols, 204–205
Sculpture, Italian by Giovanni Pisano,
    171–172
Segna da Buonaventura, 182
Sens, 204
Serbia, 125, 176
Sermons Passion images in, 103
Sermons, Passion, 143, 161–164
Seuse, Heinrich, 57
Shroud of Christ, 35, 65, 66–67, 171–172
    Amnos Aer, 127
    Eucharistic, 99
    Pisano's pulpit (Pisa), 170, 171–172, 282
    the Shroud of Turin, 105–106, 126
    See also Epitaphios
Sicard of Cremona, 6
Siena, 25
Sienese diptych
    Circle of Barna da Siena, *Imago Pietatis*
    diptych (Florence), 14, 32, 33, 41, 60,
    176, 278
    the crucified Christ (Budapest), 11, 12,
    33, 138, 174
    the Virgin (London), 10, 12, 33, 138, 174,
    176
Sienese master (Guido?), S. Bernardino
    Madonna, 24
Simeon's prophecy, 101, 114, 118, 140
Simson, O. von, 225
Sinai, 118
Sittow, lost work of, 78
Sixtus IV, Pope reliquary of, 69, 73–74, 168
Sixtus V, Pope, 73
Slavic Passion ritual, 102–103
Sleep, metaphor of Christ's, 103–104, 118
Sleeping figures (*anapeson*), 104, 118, 120
Sluter, Claus, 198
Social functions of images, 16–27(*passim*),
    22, 59–60, 62, 64, 216–217
    See also Contexts of images; Viewers
Soteriological aspects, 103, 114
Sotiriou, G. and M., 225
"Speaking image" functions, 3, 6–7